Intertextual Encounters in American Fiction, Film, and Popular Culture

Intertextual Encounters in American Fiction, Film, and Popular Culture

by

Michael Dunne

Bowling Green State University Popular Press
Bowling Green, OH 43403

Library of Congress Cataloging-in-Publication Data

Dunne, Michael, 1941-
    Intertextual encounters in American fiction, film, and popular culture /
by Michael Dunne.
        p.   cm.
    Includes bibliographical references and index.
    ISBN 0-87972-847-7 -- ISBN 0-87972-848-5 (paper)
    1. Popular culture--United States. 2. United States--Intellectual life.
3. Motion pictures--United States--History. 4. American fiction--History
and criticism. 5. Intertextuality. I. Title.

    E169.1.D87 2001
    306'.0973--dc21

                                                                    2001035018

Cover design by Dumm Art

ACKNOWLEDGMENTS

Many people assisted me in many ways while I worked on this project. I am deeply grateful to them for the better parts of this book. Bill Connelly provided me with some valuable information about medieval matters. Kevin Donovan kindly directed me to *Henry V*. David Lavery helped me by providing information about several movies, including *The Player* and *Barton Fink*. My wife, Sara Lewis Dunne, did the same regarding *Seinfeld*. Dennis Hall supplied some useful information about Dennis Miller. Bob Holtzclaw allowed me to borrow his *Rocky and Bullwinkle* tapes for several months. Larry Mintz and Jim Welsh edited and published early versions of some of this material in *Humor: International Journal for Humor Research* and *Literature/Film Quarterly* and then graciously granted approval to revise and republish it.

Bruce Nemerov, Mayo Taylor, and the rest of the staff at the MTSU Center for Popular Music were unfailingly helpful and supportive. The MTSU English department aided me with a released time grant, as did the University Faculty Research Committee. I was assisted most of all by a Non-Instructional Assignment grant during the 1999-2000 academic year. My sincere thanks go to all of these academic agencies.

My acute colleague, Will Brantley, read an entire early draft of this book and kindly made many useful suggestions for revision. Fawning thanks, Will! Russell Reising performed a similar favor with acuteness and kindness on behalf of Popular Press.

As always, my wife, Sara, has been unfailingly patient and supportive throughout the research and writing of this book. My obligations to her go way beyond anything dreamed of on *Seinfeld*.

CONTENTS

INTRODUCTION

Surely when William Faulkner gave his 1936 novel the title *Absalom, Absalom!*, he intended that his readers should bring their knowledge of the Biblical King David and his children Absalom, Amnon, and Tamar into play while reading this new narrative about Thomas Sutpen and his children Henry, Charles, and Judith.[1] Through a similar decision, Rembrandt deliberately called up another store of literary knowledge in the composition and the title of his painting, *Aristotle Contemplating the Bust of Homer* (1653). In both cases, we would say today, these artists were practicing intertextuality—even though Rembrandt and Faulkner had never heard of the term. When Rembrandt's painting was parodied in the 1970s pop poster version, in which a gorilla contemplates a skull in the manner of Hamlet, the intertextual possibilities merely increased.

Approaching intertexuality from the direction of the audience rather than the artist, we may note the list of improving "resolves" that the youthful James Gatz entered into the back of his Hopalong Cassidy adventure book in F. Scott Fitzgerald's novel *The Great Gatsby* (1925). Few American readers will fail to note parallels among the fictional boy's plan of improvement and the similar plans adopted by countless real and fictional adherents of the approach to life that we usually call the American Dream. What happens when we encounter this list in Fitzgerald's novel, then, can be understood not only in the diegetic sense that it helps to explain how the poor boy, James Gatz, became the rich criminal, Jay Gatsby, but also extradiegetically as exemplifying a form of intertextuality in which the incidents and characters of Fitzgerald's novel interact with ideas and stories already constituting part of most readers' experience. By the same token, most movie-goers watching Joel and Ethan Coen's Hollywood film *Barton Fink* (1991) for the first time will probably feel that much of what they are seeing is somehow familiar. This shock of recognition occurs because the makers of the film and the members of the film's prospective audience have seen many other movies about Hollywood. Therefore, the Coens can deliberately allude to, imitate, and parody these films in their own original work. The Coen brothers know, for example, that when we see a "serious" New York playwright heading out to Hollywood to write for the movies, we can expect to see art encountering, and being trivialized by, commercialism. When *Barton Fink* rings surprising changes on this familiar story, the similarities and differences between this film and the others that constitute part of our past cinematic experience create some sort of intertextuality. A similar sort of cultural experience comes unavoidably into play when we see Bugs Bunny and Elmer Fudd enacting a Wagnerian scene in *What's Opera, Doc?* (1957) or when we see an animated Bugs repeatedly meeting an animated Humphrey Bogart in *Eight Ball Bunny* (1950). In all of these cases, intertextual encounters take place—between artists, between texts, and between texts and their audiences.

Today intertextuality is one of the most controversial and productive critical modes used to study literature. While the electronic Modern Language Association *International Bibliography* for 1963-1980 lists only ten items related to intertextuality, 2241 items were published during the years 1981-1999. Most of these scholarly works focus on the printed word, as the very term *intertextuality* would suggest. However, as we have already seen, film and other popularly mediated texts are equally available to such analysis because producers and viewers of films and television shows are—like authors and readers—unavoidably familiar with sources, influences, and generic similarities evident in the (visual) texts immediately present. The same may be assumed about the producers and consumers of popular music. In fact, the discourse of contemporary American popular culture is increasingly coming to accept certain postmodern assumptions about the textuality of *all* experience. As Thaïs Morgan representatively observes in her essay, "Is There an Intertext in this Text?: Literary and Interdisciplinary Approaches to Intertextuality" (1985), "With the view that any event—whether in verbal, visual, aural, or kinesic 'discourse'—can be analyzed as a text, or a hierarchy of relations among codes and their constituent elements, the gateway is open to applying the concept of 'intertextuality,' defined generally as the structural relations among two or more texts, to any of the disciplines in the humanities and the social sciences" (8). Or, as Robert Stam explains in his *Subversive Pleasures: Bakhtin, Cultural Criticism, and Film* (1989), "In the broadest sense, intertextual dialogism refers to the infinite and open-ended possibilities generated by all the discursive practices of a culture, the entire matrix of communicative utterances within which the artistic text is situated and which reach the text not only through recognizable influences but also through a subtle process of dissemination" (15). Given these critical assumptions—not to mention the testimony of our own experience, even if this experience has not been consciously articulated—our exposure to and awareness of intertextuality is likely to increase exponentially, whether or not we read any of the critical works indexed by the MLA. It is therefore only prudent to think about what these intertextual encounters amount to, how they work, and why we might want to follow the example of the many others who have been willing to lavish so much attention on intertextuality.

The first question should naturally be: just what is intertextuality anyway? Beginning with a negative premise, I will say that intertextual encounters should be distinguished from the customary rhetorical situation in which texts are considered by artists and audience alike to be mimetic analogs or representations of real-life people, places, and things. Aristotle gives the first positive account of the customary process in Chapter 25 of his *Poetics* (circa 335-322 BCE) when he writes, "The poet being an imitator, like a painter or any other artist, must imitate one of three objects—things as they were or are, things as they are said or thought to be, or things as they ought to be" (Bate 36). Toward the end of the Nineteenth Century Henry James reveals in "The Art of Fiction" (1884) that, although artists' understanding of representation has surely changed since the times of the Greeks, a similar set of assumptions about imitation is still operating: "The only reason for the existence of a novel is that it does attempt to imitate life" (Kaplan & Anderson 388-89). According to the critical premises articulated by Aristotle and James, we can postulate that when Nathaniel Hawthorne wrote *The Scarlet Letter,* he intended his book to be an imitation or representation of the life of a woman named Hester Prynne who had not actually lived in seventeenth-century Boston but who behaves in Hawthorne's book as she would have done had she actually lived there and then—at least according to mid-nineteenth-century views of these matters. This is what we mean by a mimetic text. From the point of view of an audience sharing these textual assumptions, Aristotle also maintains, in Chapter 3, that "Objects which in themselves we view with pain, we delight to contemplate when reproduced with minute fidelity: such as the forms of the most ignoble animals and of dead bodies. The cause of this again is, that to learn gives the liveliest pleasure, not only to philosophers but to men in general" (Bate 21). And James writes about the audience for mimetic texts similarly: "One can speak best from one's own taste, and I may therefore venture to say that the air of reality (solidity of specification) seems to me the supreme virtue of a novel . . ." (Kaplan & Anderson 394). Reading Hawthorne's book about Hester is, in this sense, analogous to knowing her in life. Something along these Aristotelian/Jamesian lines is what most of us usually assume when confronted with any sort of text: a song, a novel, a film, a soap opera, or an animated cartoon.

When considering texts from an intertextual perspective, however, we must postulate an intermediate state between the real-life situation and its (inter)textual form. For example, Hawthorne may have intended to base his mid-nineteenth-century novel on an imaginary but lifelike

Puritan named Hester Prynne, but Roland Joffé based his 1995 film—to some degree, at least—on Hawthorne's text. Hawthorne's *The Scarlet Letter* is thus mimetic, while Joffé's is intertextual. By the same token, historians and other political writers confronting certain actual persons—Julius and Ethel Rosenberg and their government accusers—in the late-1940s and afterwards, created liberal and conservative interpretive texts of various sorts based on the real-life activities of these persons. E. L. Doctorow and Robert Coover, on the other hand, based their much later, intertextual, novels, *The Book of Daniel* and *The Public Burning,* to a large degree on these very interpretive texts rather than simply on the Rosenbergs themselves. In the same way, some songwriter might conceivably have based a love song mimetically on the real-life attributes of his or her lover, but Cole Porter and Lorenz Hart were almost certainly basing "You're the Top" and "My Funny Valentine" intertextually on the countless other love songs with which they and their listeners might naturally be assumed to be familiar.

Most attempts to define intertextuality begin by noting that the first usage of the term is usually traced to Julia Kristeva's *Semeiotike: recherches pour une semanalse* (1969). While trying to explain the extraordinary appeal of the newly discovered critical works of Mikhail M. Bakhtin (1895-1975), Kristeva typically writes that, within Bakhtin's system, "any text is the absorption and transformation of another. The notion of *intertextuality* replaces that of intersubjectivity, and poetic language is read as at least *double.*"[2] While some critics have suggested that Kristeva tends to inflect Bahktin's ideas somewhat to suit her own critical project,[3] the influence of Kristeva's ideas has nevertheless been widespread and highly significant. In Morgan's formulation, for example, " 'Intertextuality' has been touted since the late 1960s as the panacea for many of the critical pitfalls involved in historically oriented approaches to literature and in the New Criticism" (1). Some explanation for this critical revolution may lie, as Morgan implies, in the intrinsic appeal of any sophisticated alternative to hermetic theories of organic interpretation, especially since, as Morgan shows, there is some indefiniteness attaching to the general use of the concept *intertextuality.*

In relation to the first part of Morgan's explanation, readers of a certain age may recall a sense of restrictedness characterizing the organic hermeneutics promulgated by critics like Cleanth Brooks and Robert Penn Warren, as in this passage from their *Understanding Fiction*: "A good writer . . . knows that characterization, setting and atmosphere, plot, style, tone, symbolism, theme, and various other elements must be functionally related to each other to create a real unity—a unity in which every part bears an expressive relation to other parts"

(645). In the wake of deconstructive doubts about the "actual" existence of the text and its "author," confidently following the path of organic close analysis became impossible for many—or most—critical readers, especially those concerned with the cultural contexts of these texts. Intertextuality, at the very least, might offer some breathing room to such readers.[4]

The problem of "indefiniteness" may also be viewed as a paradoxical advantage.[5] Intertextual critics primarily focused on authors and others focused more on texts have complained equally about the difficulties involved in precisely defining intertextuality. Jay Clayton and Eric Rothstein, for example, write in their *Influence and Intertextuality in Literary History* (1991): "Since both terms have too many operative definitions for us to fix on one for each, we will start with the generalization that influence has to do with agency, whereas intertextuality has to do with a much more impersonal field of crossed texts" (4). Glenn A. Meeter writes in a similar vein about William Faulkner's intertextual strategies: "The impossibility of a complete disentangling of intertextuality's web . . . should not keep us from attempting a partial one—though in the face of [Roland] Barthes's definition of intertextuality as almost infinite we may prefer to use the word 'allusion,' implying as it does an intention of the author that is at least partially a conscious one" (495). After dutifully complaining, however, these critics have gone on about their business with what certainly looks like a high heart. Like the characters in the Tom Lehrer song who "had to make do with gin" when "the water tasted bad for a week,"[6] the critics cited above, as well as the thousands of other authors listed in the *MLA International Bibliography,* have been inspired and invigorated by the prospects of intertextuality, however loosely defined. I suspect that much of the appeal for these writers—as for me—lies in trying to account for the richness of their/ our own experiences as readers, viewers, and consumers of hieratic and demotic cultural products. Whatever else may be said for or against intertextuality, there is an unmistakable and pleasurable sense of community attached to the process, a community actually or potentially embracing artists and members of their rhetorical audiences. And both this pleasure and this sense of community are surely worth talking about.

At one time Stanley Fish gladdened many hearts with his critical proposition that interpretation is a function of what he called "interpretive communities." As Fish writes in "Interpreting the *Variorum*" (1977)[7]: "Interpretive communities are made up of those who share interpretive strategies not for reading (in the conventional sense) but for writing texts, for constituting their properties and assigning their intentions" (171). Although many rejoiced in the sense of collegiality and empowerment offered by the prospect of sharing imaginative experience with readers similarly disposed, other critics condemned Fish for a variety of critical sins, mostly having to do with the possibility of establishing an accurate system of hermeneutics.[8] It seems to me significant that, even when disputing his analysis, Fish's opponents often show an equal attraction to the ideal of community. Steven Mailloux, for example, writes, contra Fish, that "critical interpretations differ, not because critics belong to different interpretive communities of readers, but because they belong to different interpretive communities of *critics*" (184; Mailloux's emphasis). Whether or not Fish can be used as a reliable guide, then, the prospect of rhetorical community is clearly attractive to many. This attraction to the possibility of communion also seems to me largely responsible for the phenomenal recent popularity of Mikhail Bakhtin's critical ideas.[9] As we have seen, it was Julia Kristeva's attraction to Bakhtin's criticism that led to the theorization of intertextuality in the first place. Kristeva's motivation seems perfectly understandable when we read comments such as the following, from Bakhtin's "The Problem of the Text in Linguistics, Philology, and the Human Sciences: An Experiment in Philosophical Analysis": "Two utterances, separated from one another both in time and in space, knowing nothing of one another, when they are compared semantically, reveal dialogic relations if there is any kind of semantic convergence between them (if only a partially shared theme, point of view, and so forth)" (*Speech Genres and Other Late Essays* 124). Or, as Bakhtin says more directly in "Toward a Methodology for the Human Sciences": "Any understanding is a correlation of a given text with other texts" (*Speech Genres* 161). Texts encountering texts, utterances encountering utterances, ideas encountering ideas, human beings encountering human beings—there is a definite sense in thinking like Bakhtin's that, as they used to say in sci-fi movies, "we are not alone." This sense is crucial to the kinds of intertextual encounters that I will discuss in this book.

Proceeding provisionally, I will say that intertextual encounters occur whenever an author or the author's text recognizes, references, alludes to, imitates, parodies, or otherwise elicits a reader's familiarity with, other texts, however defined. Thus, intertextual encounters may be tracked through any component of the famous rhetorical triad—creator, text, recipient. To date, much highly sophisticated critical attention has been bestowed on all three components of the intertextual triangle.

As an example of the focus on authorial intertextuality, we might consider Antony H. Harrison's proposal in his *Victorian Poets and Romantic Poems: Intertextuality and Ideology* (1990): "This study investigates a complex of issues that emerge when authors refer, either explic-

itly or in less immediately visible ways, to the work of earlier writers."
And Harrison helpfully continues: "The fabric of literary relationships
determined in this way has come to be discussed under the rubric of
'intertextuality' by such theorists as Roland Barthes, Julia Kristeva,
Gerard Genette, and Michael Riffaterre" (1). Whether intentional or not,
the artist's activity becomes the focus of such intertextual encounters.
And this is the case even when a writer is reluctant to use the term *intertextuality*, as Denis Donoghue is in the following passage from his 1995
book about Walter Pater:

> To be specific: I do not claim that Pater influenced Ashbery, but I note that on
> one occasion Ashbery's reading of a passage in Pater's *Plato and Platonism* led
> to his writing a poem. For that occasion, Pater was a presence to Ashbery; the
> two writers came into one field of force. I feel shy using the word "intertextual-
> ity," but it is a better word than "influence" because it establishes a field of
> action and leaves readers free to consider many lines of force, affiliations, tra-
> jectories. (8)

It is therefore sometimes helpful to approach intertextuality by watching
one artist encountering another, as when John Ashbery encounters
Walter Pater, or vice versa. With equal pertinence we might watch
Chuck Jones or Jay Ward encountering the cartoonists who were their
predecessors as creators of the classic American animated cartoon.

Intertextualities may also be studied as properties residing within
individual texts or in the imaginary spaces in which texts somehow
interact with other texts.[10] This sort of relationship is described in passing by Frank Stack, in *Pope and Horace: Studies in Imitation* (1985):
"In Charles Cotton's *Scarronides . . . Being the First Book of Virgils
Aeneis in English Burlesque* (1664), a parody of the first book of the
Aeneid, the relevant passages in Latin are at the bottom of the page and
'the reader is desired for the better comparing of the *Latin and English*
together, to read on forward to the ensuing Letter of Direction' before
comparing the two" (20). In doing so, the reader encounters two texts
productively encountering and illuminating each other intertextually. In
more modern times, we may consider the intertextual encounters
involved in *Candy* (1964), the novel by Terry Southern and Mason Hof-
fenberg that ostentatiously echoes Voltaire's well-known *Candide* (1761)
in its plot and characters as well as in its title. In a similar way, films like
Mel Brooks's *Young Frankenstein* (1974) and Carl Reiner's *Dead Men
Don't Wear Plaid* (1982) provide instances of extra-literary intertextual
encounters as these newer films interact deliberately with generically
similar films that would be familiar to most potential viewers. All of

these examples seem to me to demonstrate the condition that Robert Stam refers to as "the interanimation and the interfecundation of texts" (17). According to Bakhtin's most famous English advocate, Michael Holquist, Bakhtin's theory of "dialogism" involves similar assumptions: "Dialogism argues that all meaning is relative in the sense that it comes about only as the result of the relation between two bodies occupying *simultaneous but different space,* where bodies may be thought of as ranging from the immediacy of our physical bodies, to political bodies and to bodies of ideas in general (ideologies)" (20-21; Holquist's emphasis).

Finally—as the cinematic examples above perhaps suggest—intertextualities may be thought of as experiences belonging to a member of a text's rhetorical audience. For a variety of reasons, we all carry around with us enough mediated experience to stimulate intertextuality within our own aesthetic sensibilities. As Roland Barthes writes in his controversial essay, "The Death of the Author" (1977), "a text is made of multiple writings, drawn from many cultures and entering into mutual relations of dialogue, parody, contestation, but there is one place where this multiplicity is focused and that place is the reader, not, as was hitherto said, the author. The reader is the space on which all the quotations that make up a writing are inscribed without any of them being lost; a text's unity lies not in its origin but in its destination" (148). Outside of literature proper, we can see an assumption similar to Barthes's underlying Robynn J. Sitwell's analysis of the audience's response to live performances of Phil Collins's fabulously successful pop song, "In the Air Tonight": "This is not to say that the recording is not in some way present during these [live, acoustic] performances; on the contrary, it is foregrounded in the minds of the audience as they poise on the edge of their seats, waiting for the drum break, a moment they know will not and cannot come" (68). The "minds of the audience," like the consciousness of Barthes's "reader," may therefore be understood to be a site of intertextuality. As a result, the nineteenth-century Mississippi planter at the center of *Absalom, Absalom!* may therefore remind us of Fitzgerald's far better known twentieth-century bootlegger Jay Gatsby. Perhaps Bob Dylan's contemporary, live-concert version of "Like a Rolling Stone" interacts in our heads with the very different version on a scratchy old vinyl album. In these cases, intertextual encounters occur, and communities potentially expand.

Although the opportunity to discuss intertextual encounters may be exciting and new, many of the materials that we might discuss have been around for a very long time. This collusion of the new and the old is hardly unique to the critical issue of intertextuality. Theorists seeking to distinguish postmodernism from modernism often point out that, no matter what textual practice a given critic might assert as the epitome of postmodernism, it probably has some historical antecedent in the works of a canonical modernist such as Luigi Pirandello or Berthold Brecht. In keeping with this cautionary argument, most of those currently writing about intertextuality readily admit that intertextual practices have long characterized creative activities in all of the arts. Gary Taylor, for example, reports extensively on the intertextual conditions under which William Shakespeare introduced his *Henry V* (1598-99). Concerning the author's involvement in intertextuality, Taylor writes, "For his more serious political material Shakespeare undoubtedly drew upon Raphael Holinshed's Chronicles (1587) and Edward Hall's *The Union of Two Noble and Illustre Families of Lancaster and York* (1548)—books he had already turned to for earlier history plays" (28). Concerning Shakespeare's original audience, Taylor explains: "What the play's first audience made of it we can only guess. London had apparently already seen, in the late 1580s and early 1590s, at least three other plays on Henry's reign" (3). One fairly certain guess is that an audience familiar with other plays about Henry could not avoid comparing Shakespeare's version to the others intextextually.

As many adherents of the postmodern position point out, however, historical instances of a textual practice must be distinguished from historical awareness of these practices as parts of a critical movement or habit of mind. Whatever Pirandello or James Joyce did in their texts—however allusive they became or however self-conscious of their stylistic practice—neither writer saw himself as a post-modernist or as a practitioner of intertextuality because these concepts had not been recognized and articulated at that time. In the same sense, contemporaries of Pirandello and Joyce—like the contemporaries of Shakespeare—did not and could not see these artists as practitioners of intertextuality. We, however, can see them in this light, and we can also see other artists as proleptic ancestors of the movement that we have begun to recognize as especially characteristic of our times.

For instance, when the example of the ancient Greeks began to hold sway in Augustan Rome, Publius Vergilius Maro undertook the task of writing an epic for contemporary Roman culture by following the Greek models that he could confidently assume his audience's familiarity with. When the Roman audience layered Virgil's epic work upon the Greek models they had formerly encountered, intertextual encounters occurred. When the next epoch of classical imitation arose in England following the Civil War, John Dryden, took it for granted that Virgil's work should be contextualized by its Greek antecedents. Dryden thus characteristically observes in his "Preface to Fables, Ancient and Modern" (1700): "Homer's invention was more copious, Virgil's more confined; so that if Homer had not led the way, it was not in Virgil to have begun heroic poetry; for nothing can be more evident, than that the Roman poem is but the second part of the *Ilias*; a continuation of the same story, and the persons already formed" (Bate 162). To complete the circle, Dryden and many of his contemporaries translated or "imitated" familiar classical texts in the full expectation that their readers would systematically compare the two texts. Dryden's *Aeneid* (1697), Alexander Pope's *Iliad* (1715) and *Odyssey* (1725-26), Samuel Johnson's aptly subtitled "The Vanity of Human Wishes, In Imitation of the Tenth Satire of Juvenal" (1749)—all ostentatiously invited their readers to call up previous experience of a classical work so that the old and new texts could be mentally (or even physically) placed side by side. As Frank Stack observes, "Johnson printed *London* and *The Vanity of Human Wishes* with just a few words indicating the beginning of the Latin paragraphs, presumably assuming the reader had his own copy of Juvenal to hand if he wished" (21). That the audience was now composed primarily of readers rather than listeners made such intertextual encounters both more likely and more intense.

The twentieth-century experience of what many call High Modernism put a different generation of writers and readers in similar situations. Like Virgil, for example, James Joyce presumed his reader's familiarity with Homer's *Odyssey* while composing his own *Ulysses* (1922). Leopold Bloom's adventures in Dublin must therefore be read in the intertextual context of Odysseus's adventures in the Mediterranean if Joyce's novel is to be fully appreciated. Since the same might be said about the ironic adventures of the characters in Ezra Pound's "Hugh Selwyn Mauberley (Life and Contacts)" (1920) and T. S. Eliot's "The Waste Land" (1922), the intertextual operations of classic texts like the *Odyssey* may be taken as a given in many of the works comprising the High Modern literary canon. The writer's intertextual efforts in this intellectual environment may be characterized by a remark of George Williamson in *A Reader's Guide to T. S. Eliot* (1966): "Informed by history or tradition, [Eliot's] sense of difference cooperates with his sense of likeness, and in his method finds satisfaction in forms that run from contrast to contrariety, or that point difference in likeness as well as likeness in difference, combining them in paradox or the metaphor of incompatibles by discovering a hidden congruity" (18). One of Eliot's poems thus may require that we follow him through the *Odyssey*, or the works of Christian mystics, or the history of English poetry on the way to an epiphany peculiar to Eliot's own poem. As this explanation suggests, moreover, the burdens entailed in such intertextualities fall heavily on Eliot's readers. Hugh Kenner makes a similar point regarding Eliot's *"miglior fabbro,"* Ezra Pound. Writing about one of the *Pisan Cantos* in *The Pound Era* (1971), Kenner says, "This extraordinary homage, a structural X-ray of Whitman's intricate poem, in articulating itself has stirred into life many voices; we can identify Theocritus, Nicolas Este, Aeschylus, Kipling, Mencius who invoked 'two halves of the tally'" (487-88). The challenge of such reading is, of course, one of the identifying qualities of the modernist artistic project. It suggests the humble reader sitting with "The Waste Land" open on one side of the desk and Eliot's notes on the other. But, isn't this the way most people have to read Dante today or Dryden's "Absalom and Achitophel," if they read these writers at all? That is to say, we have probably all learned—like the readers of Johnson's *London* and *The Vanity of Human Wishes* two centuries ago—to function with one eye focused on a primary text and the other focused on one or more intertexts.

Apparently, as Linda Hutcheon writes in *A Poetics of Postmodernism* (1988), "No text is without its intertexts . . ." (vii). And, we have learned that this is also—or perhaps more commonly—true when the texts in question consist of something other than words on a page. Anthony Lane reports on this experience while writing in the 9 February 1998 issue of *The New Yorker*. Lane's principal topic is the relatively recent phenomenon of the "novelization" of successful films into mass-market paperbacks, but his discussion fits my current point about intertextual encounters as well:

If you came to New York, for instance, and saw the new Broadway production of "Ragtime," bought a recording of the Toscanini "Otello" at Tower Records, caught a matinee of "The Wings of the Dove," and passed a tranquil twenty minutes at the Met in front of Rubens's "Venus and Adonis" or David's "The Death of Socrates," you would not only finish your stay feeling very tired; you would have spent it encountering nothing but other people's encounters with other works of art. . . . There are two morals to be drawn from this cautionary tale. The first is that artistic alchemy—operization, musicalization, call it what you will—offers remarkable powers of refreshment, not merely because you can pre-order drinks during the interval but because works with which we presume ourselves to be familiar are made new, often shockingly so, when viewed and reforged through imaginations more skilled than our own. (77-78)

As Lane's witty construction assumes, contemporary Americans are immersed in a mediated maze of intertextualities, some of which they probably are aware of and some of which probably pass them by.

A wide variety of sources provides corroborative testimony. Hutcheon, for example, notes in *A Poetics of Postmodernism* both the "parodic intertextuality" that results when Anton Dvorak's musical compositions mix "popular and high art forms" and the "parodic intertextuality" apparent in the "photographic pirating of Sherrie Levine and Richard Prince" (132, 190). Mimi White shares equally intertextual assumptions when she proposes in a 1986 article in *Cinema Journal* that "it is almost impossible to watch television without being referred to other aspects of the medium in some way" (61). In a newspaper article about musical re-mixes and remakes, the reporter, Thor Christensen, writes, "But history is full of examples of recycling in the arts. Andy Warhol turned old photos and drawings into works of pop art. Woody Allen took an old Japanese spy film, redubbed it with wacky dialogue and—voila!—created 1966's *What's Up, Tiger Lily*" (3D). My own intertextual experience points in the same direction, as when a helpful wall plaque at the Summer 1998 *George Segal, A Retrospective* exhibition at the Jewish Museum in New York City explains to me:

Many of Segal's sculptures allude to sources in earlier art in a manner ranging from great subtlety to overt homage. In *Portrait of Sidney Janis with Mondrian Painting,* Segal portrayed the prominent art dealer looking at one of his favorite works: *Compulsion,* 1933, a classic abstraction by Piet Mondrian. . . . *Picasso's Chair* is a replica in three dimensions of Picasso's etching no. 74 from the "Villard Suite" (1933). Segal used it as "a blueprint from which [to] build a genuine cubist sculpture" that conforms to his own aesthetic, namely an object fabricated from found elements and combined with a direct cast figure.

Segal's titles are, of course, helpful cultural guides, but without the wall plaque, my experience would have been intertextually impoverished, as would the experience of most spectators.

Obviously, many intertextual encounters may be determined primarily by the alertness of the recipients. This is Thaïs Morgan's objection to what she sees as Roland Barthes's overly optimistic assumptions about audience awareness: "We are left with the uncomfortable implication that any set of intertexts will always be only those intertexts noticed by the individual analyst" (19). Morgan's concern recalls Randall Jarrell's objections to Ezra Pound's later *Cantos,* expressed many years before (1956): "[A]ll these fragmentary citations and allusions remind you that if you had read exactly the books Pound has read, known exactly the people Pound has known, and felt about it exactly as Pound had felt, you could understand the *Cantos* pretty well" (265). Michael Riffaterre, on the other hand, finds the issue of audience alertness less problematic. In his essay "Intertextual Representation: On Mimesis as Interpretive Discourse," Riffaterre writes, "Intertextuality is not just a felicitous surplus, the privilege of a good memory or a classical education. The term refers to an operation of the reader's mind, but it is an obligatory one, necessary to any textual decoding. Intertextuality necessarily complements our experience of textuality" (142). Bakhtin also sounds optimistic, as in this passage from *The Dialogic Imagination*: "In the actual life of speech, every concrete act of understanding is active: it assimilates the word to be understood into its own conceptual system filled with specific objects and emotional expressions, and is indissolubly merged with the response, with a motivated agreement or disagreement. To some extent, primacy belongs to the response, as the activating principle; it creates the ground for understanding, it prepares the ground for an active and engaged understanding. Understanding comes to fruition only in the response" (282). Not withstanding concerns expressed by critics like Morgan, therefore, I have been convinced by Riffaterre, Bakhtin, and other proponents of intertextual methods of aesthetic perception that there is sufficient warrant to proceed with an analysis of some intertextual encounters that I believe I have participated in or noticed.

In the first principal section of this book, three chapters test a variety of strategies on a variety of intertextual literary encounters. Chapter 1 investigates two novels about self-made men written by highly esteemed American authors: F. Scott Fitzgerald's *The Great Gatsby* and Nathanael West's *A Cool Million*. These two works invite analysis as they interact intertextually with each other and even more so as they interact with the narrative tradition of what many authorities call the American Dream. Especially as this narrative pattern is developed in the fiction of Horatio Alger, Jr., several conventional expectations about individual moral character and about ultimate happiness develop. When these expectations are forced to interact with their late, ironic developments in the careers of Fitzgerald's Jay Gatsby and West's Lemuel Pitkin, difference results, particularly in the direction that the intertextual literary critic Northrop Frye has called the "theory of modes." Generations of critical interpreters have accorded both novels—particularly *Gatsby*—a staggering number of interpretations. Seeing how these books interact intertextually with a literary tradition opens still another avenue. My focus in Chapter 2 is on another myth of American culture, one underlying narratives produced—at intervals covering more than a century—by Nathaniel Hawthorne, William Faulkner, and Flannery O'Connor. Rather than focusing on how historical change may have affected the three authors' representational styles, as the previous chapter might have indicated, this chapter uses a structural approach to stress similarities, echoes, congruencies, among the visions of these three writers concerning the mythic American encounter of an innocent rustic with the challenges of urban life. Seeing how this narrative intertext dominates over characterization, theme, and even authorial intention in these three works allows us to grasp the power of the myth as well as the subtle intertextual encounters that it engenders. My texts in Chapter 3 are also fictional works that interact with cultural intertexts, although in this case the texts are more literal than mythic. Two novels about the electrocuted "atom" spies, Julius and Ethel Rosenberg, are the primary texts, and the subject is how *The Book of Daniel* (1971), by E. L. Doctorow, and *The Public Burning* (1977), by Robert Coover, react intertextually with what we might call the "matter" of the Rosenbergs. Since most of this material consists of interpretations and analyses of the Rosenbergs' behavior, motivations, guilt or innocence, the "matter" of the Rosenberg case is primarily narratological and so easily susceptible to intertextual encounters with these two works of fiction. Historical narratives of various sorts are thus also texts with which American fiction can productively interact.

In my second principal section, my texts are films. Although films were produced based on *Sanctuary* (1961), *The Great Gatsby* (1926, 1949, 1974), and *The Book of Daniel* (1983), the intertextual relations of these films to the novels do not figure in my earlier discussions. Chapter 4 does address issues of this sort, however, in considering the many filmed adaptations produced between 1904 and 1995 of Nathaniel Hawthorne's most famous work, *The Scarlet Letter.* As is the case with the two novels based on the "matter" of the Rosenbergs, anyone viewing a film based on *The Scarlet Letter* during that near-century of remakes must be aware that a prior textual version already exists. Thus, any film based on *The Scarlet Letter* is always already intertextual—whether or not the individual viewer has actually read the book. Unlike my discussion of the Hawthorne-Faulkner-O'Connor sequence of print narratives, furthermore, this inquiry into the intertextual relations of these films to Hawthorne's romance will stress the ways in which the changing historical circumstances in which the films were made enter into the films themselves. Chapter 5 also presumes the influence of both tradition and contemporary circumstances by examining the intertextual relations between Ridley Scott's 1991 film, *Thelma & Louise,* and the long tradition of films in which male buddies set out on the road to escape the constraints of everyday life. While there is often considerable animated discussion about whether there even *is* such an entity as film genres, I assume in my discussion that there is a film genre composed of male-buddy "road pictures." My focus is on how this genre is inflected by gender when the buddies turn out to be two women. Watching the intertextual dialogue between *Thelma & Louise* and more traditional male buddy pictures like *Butch Cassidy and the Sundance Kid* and *Easy Rider* provides added insight into Scott's film as well as into the genre that it both follows and modifies. Chapter 6, the final chapter in this section, turns even further toward the purely cinematic by examining the intertextual dimensions of two "Hollywood Pictures": Joel and Ethan Coen's *Barton Fink* (1991) and Robert Altman's *The Player* (1992). As with the cinematic version of a literary classic—but for other reasons—a movie about the movie business is always already intertextual. Viewers must begin with their considerable previous experience of other films, and they cannot help applying information and judgments provided within the diegetic narrative to that narrative itself. Furthermore, since most Hollywood pictures—including *Barton Fink* and *The Player*—also contain metadiegetic films (films within films), viewers also cannot avoid comparing the diegetic and the metadiegetic intertextually. Altman complicates all these encounters further by deliberately embedding his film within the surrounding discourse of contemporary American popular culture. His diegetic representation therefore contains references to contemporary social trends, consumer products, and actual films and film stars. Especially in the case of the many celebrity cameos in the film, *The Player* enters into a vigorous intertextual dialogue with American popular culture.

Other dialogues of this sort are the subjects in my third principal section. Chapter 7 focuses on the kind of popular song lyric that exploits allusion, stylistic imitation, and self-referentiality to call forth the listener's familiarity with other forms of popular representation, including other song lyrics. Cole Porter's highly sophisticated lyrics of the 1920s and '30s—such as "You're the Top"—insist that the listener bring references to the hieratic Mona Lisa and Strauss symphonies as well as to the demotic Jimmy Durante and the Kentucky Derby to the immediate situation of a love song. Because the referential dimension in songs of this sort is so much more original and engaging than the romantic representation, intertextuality is highlighted. Porter's lyrics—including "You're the Top"—also invoke other lyrics, as when the loved one is compared to a "Berlin ballad." Lyrics by other highly ingenious writers including Lorenz Hart and Ira Gershwin reveal the same intertextual leanings, especially through their covert and overt textual self-consciousness. In short, intertextuality flourishes in the classic American popular song. Chapter 8 takes up a similar form of intertextuality in popular animation. Since a cartoon allowing Bugs Bunny to meet animated versions of

Humphrey Bogart and Bette Davis might well have been shown in a movie theater prior to the screening of a film starring one of these actors, intertextual encounters between animated and feature films might be assumed. It is clear also that cartoons follow all the popular film genres so that Bugs or Daffy Duck might well appear in an animated Western, gangster picture, or costume epic. As with the song lyrics studied in the previous chapter, moreover, overt and covert textual self-consciousness also characterizes these classic cartoons. In later years, when these cartoons became part of what Raymond Williams called the undifferentiated "flow" of television,[11] the Warner Brothers characters could not avoid interacting extra-textually with Superman, Captain Kangaroo, the stars of colorized classic films, the heroes of sporting events, and other icons of popular culture. The same may be said of the first highly successful cartoon series designed exclusively for television: the animated anthology created by Jay Ward and usually referred to as the *Rocky and Bullwinkle* show. As in the classic Warner Brothers cartoons, Ward's serials, parodies, and recurring features presumed, and intertextually exploited, his audience's deep familiarity with the rich resources of American culture. In Chapter 9, the related assumption that contemporary popular culture has become intertextual almost to the point at which forms and genres disappear prompts my use of the highly contested term *postmodern*. *Seinfeld*, the "show about nothing," is, in this sense, a show about intertextuality. Dennis Miller, "the postmodern comedian," operates always as the same hip, knowing, compulsively allusive persona whether "doing the news" on *Saturday Night Live,* performing stand-up comedy on his own talk-show, acting in films like *Bordello of Blood*, commenting on the action on *Monday Night Football,* or serving as the author of his best-selling books, *The Rants*. Miller embodies and personifies the form of postmodern sensibility that views every aspect of experience as a synchronous text, and so he is a living, breathing manifestation of intertextuality.

My subject in this book, then, is the appearance of some intertextual encounters consisting of allusions, references, generic affiliations, and instances of self-referentiality in some American works of fiction, some films, and some popular cultural forms. It is naturally my hope that these intertextualities will function in a representative sense for the many others that lack of space—as well as my own lack of knowledge—preclude my including. These intertextual readings of highly varied texts yield highly varied results, and yet they all point to the conclusion that intertextualities can easily be discovered whenever we approach a certain kind of text with the appropriate kind of attention. My conclusion proposes this very happy discovery as the stimulus for searching out more intertextualities in the representative examples I have used and in whatever other modes and media potential scholars might choose. Given the barren and acrimonious climate that defines so much contemporary criticism in all the media, such opportunities seem to me cause for great celebration.

PART I

INTERTEXTUAL ENCOUNTERS IN FICTION

The aesthetic-rhetorical textual situation that we now call intertextuality has had a very long literary history. As we have seen already, when Virgil set out to write an epic for his own (Roman) culture (c. 26-19 BCE), he followed the available (Greek) model and clearly assumed that his audience would recognize the parallels. Colin Graham Hardie therefore explains in *The Oxford Classical Dictionary,* "It was a commonplace among ancient critics . . . that the first half of the Aeneid was an *Odyssey,* the second half an *Iliad,* with Turnus as the new Achilles." In fact, according to Hardie, "At first, the extent of Virgil's adaptations of other poets, 'plagiarisms,' filled critics with an almost dismayed amazement" (1126). Eventually, it appears that these "plagiarisms" were reconfigured as intertextualities. Certainly by the time of Dante, Virgil's epic was ready for an intertextual encounter in the *Inferno* (c. 1321).

Dante's willingness to engage in intertextualities was hardly unique during the fourteenth century, according to John Dryden. As Dryden explains in his "Preface to Fables," "In the serious part of poetry, the advantage is wholly on Chaucer's side; for tho' the Englishman has borrowed many tales from the Italian, yet it appears, that those of Bocace were not generally of his own making, but taken from authors of former ages, and by him only modelled; so that what there was of invention, in either of them, may be judged equal" (Bate 169). That is to say that the intertextualities sparked by Chaucer's encounters with Boccaccio were preceded by Boccaccio's intertextual encounters with the works of even earlier writers. Moreover, textual affinities of this sort could function as a form of enrichment for artists and their audiences as well, and no one but the kind of originality police offended by Virgil's intertextualities would object. This is the point decisively made by Northrop Frye in *Anatomy of Criticism* when he applauds the intertextual strategies of "Chaucer, much of whose poetry is translated or paraphrased from others; Shakespeare, whose plays sometimes follow their sources almost verbatim; and Milton, who asked for nothing better than to steal as much as possible out of the Bible" (96).

Shakespeare's history plays obviously provide a crucial example. As we have seen already, the Bard's *Henry V* involves intertextualities pointing equally toward the author, the text, and the audience. Frye maintains in *Anatomy of Criticism*: "Shakespeare's *Henry V* is a successfully completed romantic quest made tragic by its implicit context: everybody knows that King Henry died almost immediately and that sixty years of unbroken disaster followed for England—at least, if anyone in Shakespeare's audience did not know that, his ignorance was certainly no fault of Shakespeare's" (221). Furthermore, as Gary Taylor explains, the play's intertextual encounters also extend forward in time: "*Henry V* has not only been consistently revived in times of national crisis; it has also been, at such times, consistently rewritten. When patriotism wants a play, the play Shakespeare produced—for just such an occasion—is found insufficiently simple and unnecessarily disquieting; the serious scenes, moreover, always suffer the most dramatic surgery. Laurence Olivier's famous 1944 film, dedicated to the commandos and airborne troops of Great Britain—'the spirit of whose ancestors it has been humbly attempted to recapture . . .'—cut almost 1700 lines" (11). Again, it could be only the most literal-minded literary critic who might object to these intertextual historical adaptations.

Samuel Johnson, for one, was perfectly comfortable with Shakespeare's intertextual strategies. As Johnson writes in his "Preface to Shakespeare" (1765): "Our authour's plots are generally borrowed from novels, and it is reasonable to suppose, that he chose the most popular, such as were read by many, and related by more; for his audience could not have followed him through the intricacies of the drama, had they not held the thread of the story in their hands. . . . The stories, which we now find only in remoter authours, were in his time accessible and familiar" (Kaplan & Anderson 213-14). In this respect, Johnson epitomizes the intertextual assumptions of his literary epoch, and he also follows a familiar critical disposition in approaching the intertextual encounters of the past largely in terms of narrative texts.

In his "Essay of Dramatic Poesy" (1668), John Dryden reveals the same dispositions in having his up-to-date character, Eugenius, say about the ancient authors:

Next, for the plot, . . . it has already been judiciously observed by a late writer, that in their tragedies it was only some tale derived from Thebes or Troy, or at least something that happened in those two ages; which was worn so threadbare by the pens of all the epic poets, and even by tradition, itself of the talkative Greeklings (as Ben Jonson calls them), that before it came upon the stage it was already known to all the audience: and the people, so soon as ever they heard the name of Oedipus, knew as well as the poet, that he had killed his father by mistake, and committed incest with his mother, before the play. . . . (Bate 136)

Eugenius's arch description of classical intertextuality is required by Dryden's intention to analyze the then-current literary-critical conflict over whether the "ancients" or the "moderns" were the most suitable objects for imitation. The judicious middle ground between these two extreme positions—usually embraced by Dryden himself—is held in this essay by Neander. Significantly, in making Neander's case, Dryden draws both his specific examples and the structure of his analysis in terms of narrative rather than lyric genres. In this way, the practice of comparing and contrasting later (usually narrative) literary texts with earlier ones is very well-established historically.

Northrop Frye, for one, has recognized the operation of this sort of intertextuality in later times and in narrative forms other than those dominant in the days of Dryden and Johnson. In his *Anatomy of Criticism,* for example, Frye notes that "it is often only in such titles as *For Whom the Bell Tolls, The Grapes of Wrath,* or *The Sound and the Fury,* that we can clearly see how much impersonal dignity and richness of association an author can gain by the communism of convention" (98). More obvious examples of intertextuality in prose fiction might include the resonances of chivalric romance in *The Natural* by Bernard Malamud (1952), the conventions of the neo-classic novel in *The Sot-weed Factor* by John Barth (1960), and the plot and characterizations of Shakespeare's *King Lear* in *A Thousand Acres* by Jane Smiley (1991). Echoes, allusions, imitations, and parodies of earlier narratives appear insistently in a vast array of fictional plots, structures, characters, and themes developed by American prose writers. Some of these intertextual encounters are my subject in the following three chapters.

Narratives recounting the rise and development of the American Dream of success, first of all, carry especially rich resonances for American authors and readers because participants on both sides of these narrative transactions are irresistibly immersed in this national mythic dream. The mutations of American Dream narratives over a specific span of time may therefore be profitably approached as a form of fictional intertextuality. My first chapter focuses on two novels about self-made men: F. Scott Fitzgerald's *The Great Gatsby* and Nathanael West's *A Cool Million,* especially in the light of how these narratives are shaped, positively and negatively, by the earlier success narrative popularized by Horatio Alger, Jr. In Fitzgerald's narrative, his protagonist technically succeeds in his quest for wealth, position, and the love of Daisy, the beautiful woman who has served as his inspiration. Since each dimension of this "success" is qualified by significant imperfections, Gatsby's successful quest must be read ironically. Furthermore, Fitzgerald introduces other aspirants for success into his novel—chiefly his narrator, Nick Carraway—and so the entire narrative of success in Fitzgerald's America must be read ironically against the univocal success narrative that must be presupposed as its originary intertext. This function is served by the fiction of Alger, whose very name can function synechdocally for this narrative, even to those who have never read one of his books. The sincere quest for wealth, social position, and everyday happiness presented without apparent question or ironic shading in Alger's work both epitomizes the American success narrative and provides intertextual resonance for late, ironic developments of this same narrative pattern in the careers of Fitzgerald's Jay Gatsby and Nathanael West's Lemuel Pitkin. Pitkin's devolutionary "progress" functions as a late, bitterly ironic narrative commentary on Alger's text, surpassing even *The Great Gatsby* in its intertextual richness.

In the second chapter in this section a different American myth underlies another series of narratives. Just as the American Dream of success inevitably creeps into the sensibilities of all American writers and readers, so the American prejudice in favor of rural virtue at the expense of urban sophistication seems unavoidable. Since this myth is as likely as the dream of success to be counteracted by experience, it is likely that many American writers will approach the rural-urban conflict ironically. In Nathaniel Hawthorne's story, "My Kinsman, Major Molineux," for example, a naive rube named Robin, who is mistakenly convinced of his own shrewdness, travels from the countryside in which he has grown to be eighteen years of age to the colonial city of Boston in order to take advantage of an offer from his father's cousin to help Robin get an economic start in the world. Once he has arrived in the city, Robin's combination of innocence and arrogance inhibits his search for the Major, leading to a series of fruitless encounters in which Robin is the butt of the laughter of city dwellers including a trollop in a scarlet petticoat and a kindly older gentleman who offers to serve as Robin's mentor. A hundred years later, in his novel *Sanctuary*, William Faulkner sends two equally ignorant rubes to the big city of Memphis to see if they can achieve financial success by attending barber college. Because these two yokels are as deluded as Robin about their own shrewdness, they experience similar frustration and laughing ridicule from city dwellers, including a notorious madam and the venal State Senator, Clarence Snopes, who offers to act as their mentor. Since the two boys' adventures are largely unrelated to the rest of *Sanctuary* in terms of plot and theme, this chapter of the novel stands out as an independent narrative. Its similarity to Hawthorne's tale thus becomes even more apparent, encouraging us to recognize an intertextual encounter between two embodiments of the same narrative structure derived from the same mythic attitudes. Since Flannery O'Connor's short story, "The Artificial Nigger," also shares this structure, the opportunities for intertextual dialogue escalate. O'Connor's Mr. Head and Nelson thus join Hawthorne's Robin and Faulkner's Fonzo Winbush and Virgil Snopes in the same circular quest, meeting along the way their own versions of the scarlet woman and the kindly stranger. Because O'Connor's stated thematic intentions differ so markedly from Faulkner's and Hawthorne's, the points of structural congruence among the three narratives take on increased clarity. It finally seems that the common narrative structure shared by these authors operates with such power that it can obfuscate or frustrate O'Connor's thematic designs, much as it does violence to Faulkner's overall intentions in *Sanctuary*. The critical insights available from a comparison/contrast of these three narratives demonstrate the potentialities of intertextual analysis with especial clarity.

While the discussions in the first two chapters in this section rest on the intertextual influences of American myths, the last chapter in the section derives its principal intertext from literal texts. Thinking about Alger's collective *oeuvre* as a "text" in Chapter 1 makes it easier to move on in Chapter 3 to the intertextual challenges posed by *The Book of Daniel* (1971), by E. L. Doctorow, and *The Public Burning* (1977), by Robert Coover. Since both of these novels propose on one level to represent the historical events surrounding the executions of the famous "atom" spies, Julius and Ethel Rosenberg, they must be presumed to interact intertextually both with each other and with the historical record, still familiar to many readers and readily available to others willing to do minimal research. These readers can also gain easy access to the web of cultural references in which both Coover and Doctorow embed their narratives. Such intertextual inspections reveal the narrative richness of both novels.

Reading these American narratives intertextually in the contexts of their predecessors and successors yields gratifying insights. This process also connects the current project to the long history of intertextual encounters in literature.

INTERTEXTUAL ENCOUNTERS WITH HORATIO ALGER, JR.,
IN *THE GREAT GATSBY* AND *A COOL MILLION*

In "The Archetypes of Literature" (1951), an essay in which he introduces many of the ideas that he later developed in his highly influential *Anatomy of Criticism* (1957), the Canadian intertextual critic Northrop Frye proposes that all imaginative projects probably arise in our human dreams and fears, what we desire and what we dread (18-19). In this light, all narratives depicting the gradual achieving of our dreams can be understood as the forms of romance called quest narratives. The narrative pattern of a romantic quest is, then, a projection of the human desire for achievement and psychological fulfillment. Whereas, in the realm of everyday experience, human beings are victimized by the vicissitudes of chance, inequality, and frustration, in the realm of romance all problems become soluble. The hero of a romantic quest adopts a goal and successfully pursues it despite all barriers and challenges. The vagaries of nature—wind, rain, raging rivers—are overcome, perhaps with difficulty, but overcome even so. The evil deeds of other humans pose challenges no more intimidating than those of nature. The black knight, the evil temptress, the champion of incredible strength can be—and usually are—vanquished by the determined and valiant hero. Even the powers of the underworld—gnomes, dragons, evil sorcerers—yield to the force of the hero. So long as the author of a quest narrative maintains confidence in the powers of this imaginative projection, a social compact allows readers to experience the hero's triumphs vicariously.

In *The Secular Scripture: A Study of the Structure of Romance* (1976), Frye explains that with the passing of time a basic romantic quest narrative eventually mutates into some parodic form. As the quintessential example, Frye cites Miguel de Cervantes' transformation of chivalric romance in *Don Quixote* (1605, 1615), but Frye also points to F. Scott Fitzgerald's *The Great Gatsby* (1925) because it "parodies the 'success story,' the romantic convention contemporary with it" (161). In both cases, Frye argues, the writer's confidence in the transforming power of romantic narrative had weakened in response to what he understood as an alteration in the rhetorical expectations of his readers, and so

Cervantes and Fitzgerald increasingly felt obliged to "displace" the contents and structure of their quest narratives in the direction of ironic verisimilitude. Since Frye's examples of this transformative process are so widely separated historically, we may generalize that sensitive authors will eventually displace most culturally acceptable narrative quest patterns into less and less romantically fulfilling narratives. Tracing such a narrative devolution may thus demonstrate a significant form of intertextuality. Since few concepts have had as much influence on the development of American culture as the powerfully symbolic narrative that we call the American Dream of success, following the course of American Dream narratives through a selected span of literary history should prove especially worthwhile. By focusing on the work of three writers—Horatio Alger, Jr. (1832-1899), F. Scott Fitzgerald (1896-1940), and Nathanael West (1903-1940)—we can see both the persistence of a narrative pattern and its increasingly ironic displacements.

William Coyle writes in an introduction to Alger's *Adrift in New York and The World Before Him* that "Alger's name has outlived his books because it has come to represent a national mythology" (v). Gary Scharnhorst and Jack Bales agree, writing in their standard biography of Alger that with time "[his] name became a shibboleth invoked by the American cult of success" and "the countersign of American Dreamers" (x, xix). This celebrity may seem odd to readers today who have never actually opened a book written by Alger. Even these readers are likely to recognize the name, however, perhaps assuming that it belongs to some otherwise-forgotten fictional character. Ralph D. Gardner plausibly asks in his introduction to Alger's *Silas Snobden's Office Boy,* "[W]ho, upon hearing the phrase, 'a typical Alger Hero,' does not immediately anticipate a report on the uniquely American phenomenon of one who started from scratch and—generally against great odds—reached the top rung of the ladder?" (5). As the critics already cited attest—and as countless others would probably be willing to confirm—Alger's direct influence on the "national mythology" has been enormous. This is S. N. Behrman's point in another introductory essay—to *Strive and Succeed: Two Novels by Horatio Alger.* According to Behrman, Alger "added a concept ['to the American vocabulary'] which has had a large and surviving share in the composition of the American image at home and abroad. The Algerian concept of the infinite possibility in this country for the enterprising, and if you take Alger's word for it, the virtuous, is persistent and inescapable, either for panegyric or disparagement" (v). Behrman's alternative formulation, "either for panegyric or disparagement," points to the varied circumstances in which Alger's novels may later be read. His recognition of the "infinite possibility in this country for the enterprising" makes clear that this later reading should be conducted intertextually in the context of the American Dream of success.

According to Coyle, Alger's narratizing of the dream usually takes a predictable direction: "His favorite [plot] involves a young country boy, usually the son of a widow, who goes to the city or occasionally to the West or to Australia in order to restore the family's fortunes. His native wit and moral rectitude enable him to cope with the strange and hostile environment, and after enduring appropriate vicissitudes, he is able to return home and pay off the mortgage just ahead of foreclosure" (x). Clear—if ironic— anticipations of West's *A Cool Million* (1934) can be heard, as perhaps they can be in Coyle's description of another characteristic of Alger's work: "It was essentially a primer version of the Protestant Ethic: a young man of good character who works hard and saves his money can—indeed, *will*—achieve power and affluence" (vi). Alger's heroes do not smoke, drink, or gamble, avoiding all temptations to the immoral. On the active side of the moral ledger, Alger's positive characters love animals, worship women from afar, and protect the weak and helpless. The moral climate sustaining the heroes is evident in passages like the following, in which the successful businessman Allen Palmer explains to Frank Manton, the title character of *Silas Snobden's Office Boy* (orig. pub. 1889-90), why Palmer is willing to take an interest in the younger man's prospects: "It is the least I can do in return for the prosperity which God has granted me." (128). With due adjustments in tone and diction, this kindly mentoring posture will reappear in Fitzgerald's *The Great Gatsby* and West's *A Cool Million*.

Also clear in these later narratives is another dimension of Alger's habitual narrative style, illustrated by another incident from *Silas Snobden's Office Boy*. When Frank Manton boards a train in pursuit of Luke Gerrish and John Carter, the men who have kidnapped Allen Parker's son, Rob, he little expects that an amazing coincidence is about to occur: "When Frank took his seat on a train bound for Albany, his heart was filled with anxiety, and he did not for some time examine his fellow passengers. When he did so, he was destined to a surprise [sic]. Two seats ahead of him, and sitting alone, was his old employer, Silas Snobden" (229). If Frank had read many novels written by Horatio Alger, Jr., he would have been less surprised by this sort of coincidence, since apparent accident plays such a major role in these narratives. But Alger's characters do not read much fiction, preferring to devote their attention to more immediately practical books. Thus they would probably not be prepared for the sudden reappearances of Shagpoke Whipple in *A Cool Million* or for Jordan Baker's just happening along on Gatsby and Daisy's last afternoon together in Louisville in *The Great Gatsby*. Conditioned by works like *Silas Snobden's Office Boy*, we are more prepared to take such coincidences in stride.

More familiar to Alger's characters—and to most readers too—are the defining (even if unstated) properties of Algerine romance. These are implied by Scharnhorst and Bales when they explain that Alger "introduced in [*Ragged Dick; or, Street Life in New York* (1868)][1] the major contrivances of his juvenile formula—a disadvantaged hero who rises from rags to respectability, a status only partly defined in economic terms; his receipt of a new suit of clothes, a symbolic rite of passage; and his patronage by benevolent adults" (83). The main outlines of Fitgerald's and West's ironic success stories obviously lie here. Some of the complications introduced by these later versions also surface in the idea that success is "only partly defined in economic terms." Money does not, of course, buy happiness, but it figures significantly even so. Despite his acknowledgment of divine benevolence in the process, Allen Parker still describes his success to Frank Manton in largely financial terms: "I am rich, but I was a poor boy. I lived in the country, in a town about thirty miles distant on the Erie road. My father was a farmer, and I a farmer's son" (85). Midway through the narrative, another character, Samuel Graham, tells Frank, "I own a brown stone house up town which lets for three thousand dollars a year, and I have besides some investments in bank stocks" (138). It is only to be expected, therefore, that Frank's own rise in the world should be figured in similar terms. Frank asks Palmer about the $10,000 reward he received for saving young Rob: "And would you keep and invest this money for me?" Palmer replies: "I will do so, and allow you six per cent interest, payable monthly. I will also take you into my banking house at a salary, to begin on, of ten dollars a week" (238). We might, on this basis, expect a bright future for Frank even if his "status [is] only partly defined in economic terms." The last paragraph of *Silas Snobden's Office Boy* therefore tells us: "As for Frank, all goes smoothly with him. He is diligent in business, and is likely to become a rich man" (240). As Frye observes in *The Secular Scripture*, "Bourgeois heroes tend to be on the industrious-apprentice model, shown in its most primitive form in the boys who arrive in the last pages of Horatio Alger working for five dollars a week with a good chance of a raise" (161).

While Alger's characters are not great readers of fiction, other notable American authors were, and so they became familiar with many of Alger's characteristic narrative devices, as Scharnhorst and Bales have demonstrated. Combing the archives in an effort to gauge Alger's influence, these scholars reveal the following about his "Ralph Raymond's Heir" (1869): "Early in this century the story was reissued indiscriminately in a series of cheap Alger reprints, and in 1911, it was read in this format by teen-aged F. Scott Fitzgerald" (106). Intertextual readers of *The Great Gatsby* should therefore be on the lookout for Algerine echoes. Equally arresting is the two critics' discovery about an Alger novel first published in 1877: "Almost a half-century later, at the nadir of the Great Depression, Nathanael West copied whole passages of *Joe's Luck* virtually word-for-word into his Alger parody *A Cool Million*" (114). The textual interactions between each of these later novels and Alger's work should therefore be significant, as well as intertextual encounters between the two later novels, and among works by all three authors and the American narrative of success. In this light, the American Dream of success can itself be seen as the dominant intertext.

Naturally, no later text should be expected to parallel one or more of Alger's narratives exactly. As Scharnhorst and Bales observe, "The metamorphosis of his reputation—from didactic writer for boys, to Progressive moralist, economic mythmaker, and finally political ideologue—seems to have been dictated less by the content of his books than by the context in which the books were read or remembered" (155), a point to which Northrop Frye might well grant assent. As Frye explains in *The Secular Scripture,* from the perspective of cultural history it seems only prudent to take into account the changing conditions of textual reception. But this caution accords well also with Frye's theoretical orientation to narrative history, or with what he calls in *Anatomy of Criticism* his "theory of modes." Beginning in *Anatomy* with the premise that "Fictions . . . may be classified, not morally, but by the hero's powers of action, which may be greater than ours, less, or roughly the same" (33), Frye goes on to construct a five-stage schema in which the hero's powers diminish from the mythic level, through the high- and low-mimetic, and finally to the ironic, in accordance with the audience's diminishing willingness to suspend disbelief (33-34). Since literary attitudes toward the American Dream can be seen to run along the same lines, Frye's theory is of great use in tracking the ways in which later writers establish ironic intertextual relations to earlier works in this mode.

Fitzgerald, for example, clearly intends his character, Jay Gatsby, to follow in the footsteps of Alger's heroes. For one thing, "[Gatsby's] parents were shiftless and unsuccessful farm people" (76) whose unsuitability as models led Gatsby to search for the older mentor who usually plays such an important role in this narrative. For Gatsby, the model is Dan Cody, "a product of the Nevada silver fields, of the Yukon, of every rush for metal since Seventy-five" (77). The immensely rich Cody is as enchanted by the youthful Gatsby as Allen Parker was by Frank Manton, and so Cody soon buys Gatsby new clothes, a step that Scharnhorst and

Bales' discussion of Alger would lead us to expect. Since Gatsby's second mentor, the gambler Meyer Wolfsheim, fixates on the fact that the returned veteran must continue to wear his army uniform in the absence of more appropriate clothing, we must assume that suitable costuming contributes significantly to the development of this success narrative. So does Gatsby's Alger-like abstemiousness. As the narrator, Nick Carraway, reports, "[F]or himself [Gatsby] formed the habit of letting liquor alone" (78), despite the enormous quantities of alcohol consumed at his lavish parties. Echoes of the earlier American Dream narrative can also be heard when Fitzgerald has Nick respond to Gatsby's romanticized, patently false, account of his earlier life by remarking that "The very phrases were worn so threadbare that they evoked no image except that of a turbaned 'character' leaking sawdust at every pore" (52). The chief intertextual point about the passage is not so much that Alger writes like Gatsby's fantasy—although he *does* to some degree!—as that by the time Fitzgerald was writing, the characteristics of this narrative had usually become familiar through reading rather than through immediate experience. It is therefore totally appropriate that he decides to have the young James Gatz preserve his list of practical resolves for self-improvement in "a ragged old copy of a book called 'Hopalong Cassidy'" (134).[2]

Although these parallel episodes link Gatsby univocally with earlier American Dreamers, Fitzgerald intends to have his hero interact more ironically with his predecessors when it comes to women. For one thing, Gatsby does not maintain his virginal status: "He knew women early and since they spoiled him he became contemptuous of them, of young virgins because they were ignorant, of the others because they were hysterical about things which in his overwhelming self-absorption he took for granted" (77). Despite his sexual experience, however, Gatsby falls head-over-heels in love with Daisy Fay. As Gatsby recalls his war-time encounter with Daisy: "Well, there I was, way off my ambitions, getting deeper in love any minute, and all of a sudden I didn't care" (117). In a pure romance, Gatsby's redirection of his energies from socio-economic success to love would be a positive narrative development. Because of Fitzgerald's ironic discounting of romance—evident, for example, in Nick's critique of Gatsby's bogus autobiography—is it unlikely that this development will be presented without criticism. This is clear when Fitzgerald allows Nick to append a more theoretical, and more rhetorically inflated, account of Gatsby's infatuation:

His heart beat faster and faster as Daisy's white face came up to his own. He knew that when he kissed this girl, and forever wed his unutterable visions to her perishable breath, his mind would never romp again like the mind of God. So he waited, listening for a moment longer to the tuning fork that had been struck upon a star. Then he kissed her. At his lips' touch she blossomed for him like a flower and the incarnation was complete. (86-87)

It is also important to add, as many commentators have observed, that Daisy is personally inadequate to bear the spiritual burden of Gatsby's dreams.[3]

That Daisy is destined to fall so far short of Gatsby's ideal suggests the ways in which Americans have shifted their ideological orientation toward the American Dream in the transition from Alger to Fitzgerald. Richard Lehan expresses the world into which Fitzgerald launched Gatsby's quest as follows:

The 1920s seen through the prism of Fitzgerald's novel becomes a strange distillation of unlimited wonder and opportunity foundering on human excess and waste, a heightened and yet insubstantial carnivalesque moment in which personal and national desire give way to resplendent emptiness; indeed the twenties may in many ways be thought of as Gatsby's America. (10)

Working in either direction, from Gatsby's life story back to the culture, or from the milieu of the Roaring Twenties back to the fictional character, we can only expect a sophisticated writer like Fitzgerald to produce a less unequivocal success narrative than the ones produced by Alger.

Significantly, Fitzgerald stresses Jay Gatsby's qualifications to play the leading role in a Twenties version of the American Dream narrative throughout the novel. In the book's fourth paragraph, while Nick is still establishing his own relations to the story, he says that "there was something gorgeous about [Gatsby], some heightened sensitivity to the promises of life" (6). Although Fitzgerald never specifically calls the fulfillment of these promises the American Dream, Nick later dignifies the project of success by calling it Gatsby's "incorruptible dream" (120), an endorsement extended in the novel's concluding paragraphs to embrace all Americans. When the original European explorers first saw "a vivid green breast of the new world," Nick says, "man must have held his breath in the presence of this continent, compelled into an aesthetic contemplation he neither understood nor desired, face to face for the last time in history with something commensurate to his capacity for wonder" (140). It is, of course, significant that the experience is attributed by Nick (and Fitzgerald) to the inclusive "man" rather than merely to Gatsby, but it is equally significant that total fulfillment of the dream is historically fixed in the past. Unlike Alger, that is, Fitzgerald writes about the American Dream as what has been lost "somewhere back in the vast obscurity beyond the city, where the dark fields of the republic rolled on under the night" rather than as what will surely come to the worthy in "the orgiastic future" (141). In this respect, at any rate, the narrative mode in which the American Dream is presented has definitely been mutated by Fitzgerald.

The mutation, as Frye would predict, has been in the direction of irony. Fitzgerald drops many textual hints directing his readers to the skeletal quest narrative behind Gatsby's story.[4] While recounting Gatsby's initial discovery of his love for Daisy, for example, Nick observes that Gatsby suddenly "found that he had committed himself to the following of a grail" (116-17). He also describes Daisy as "High in a white palace the King's daughter, the golden girl" but, significantly, Nick does so only after Gatsby has identified the appeal of Daisy's voice as being "full of money" (94). The skeleton is apparent, that is, but Fitzgerald's coating of irony is unmistakably present as well. Nick's assessment of Gatsby's dream certainly fits this model:

The truth was that Jay Gatsby, of West End, Long Island, sprang from his Platonic conception of himself. He was a son of God—a phrase which, if it means anything, means just that—and he must be about His Father's Business, the service of a vast, vulgar and meretricious beauty. So he invented just the sort of Jay Gatsby that a seventeen year old boy would be likely to invent, and to this conception he was faithful to the end. (77)

Fitzgerald's irony certainly suffuses the apex of Gatsby's achievement. Having established himself as a rich man through criminal means, having secured a vast mansion just across the bay from the estate shared by Daisy and her husband Tom Buchanan, and having finally arranged a happy reunion with Daisy through the agency of Nick and Jordan Baker, Gatsby has in a sense finally achieved everything he set out in search of so many years ago. On the other hand, Gatsby is still a criminal, Daisy is still married to another man, and the happy community established through all this effort embraces only the embarrassed Nick and a piano-playing sponger named Klipspringer. It is therefore appropriate that Fitzgerald has Nick conclude about the incident merely that Gatsby's "count of enchanted objects had diminished by one" (73).

Even in much smaller matters, Fitzgerald diminishes the dignity of this quest narrative through ironic touches. Nick's own desire to achieve worldly success is significantly like Gatsby's—and like that of the typical Alger hero—but Fitzgerald presents Nick's quest in much more jaundiced terms: "I bought a dozen volumes on banking and credit and investment securities and they stood on my shelf in red and gold like new money from the mint, promising to unfold the shining secrets that only Midas and Morgan and Maecenas knew" (7). Fitzgerald seems to be asking, isn't this really what the often-described, much-admired acquisition of money is all about? This questioning is addressed even to sex, as Nick discovers on a very hot summer's day: "That anyone should care in this heat whose flushed lips he kissed, whose head made damp the pajama pocket over his heart!" (89). The ingredients of a quest narrative—especially love and ambition—are surely present in these incidents, and in another time and place they could be structured so as to present an exemplary narrative of success, certainly of a successful quest for the American Dream. Because of the displacements required in Scott Fitzgerald's America, however, an ironic quest is the only version authorized.

This irony is clear when it has become obvious to the reader that Daisy has selfishly chosen security with Tom over love with Gatsby. Nick conjectures that even Gatsby may have figured this out and goes on to reflect:

If that was true he must have felt that he had lost the old warm world, paid a high price for living too long with a single dream. He must have looked up at an unfamiliar sky through frightening leaves and shivered as he found what a grotesque thing a rose is and how raw the sunlight was upon the scarcely created grass. A new world, material without being real. (126)

Fitzgerald is careful to establish that Nick is not sure whether Gatsby has finally come to understand Daisy's shortcomings. If Gatsby has not done so, even at this late point, he is the only one still unenlightened, and so he is definitely inferior to other men as well as to his natural circumstances,[5] including an armed and dangerous Tom Wilson intent on avenging his wife's death.

Even if Gatsby has finally attained a more mature understanding of his lover, he has been quite slow to arrive at the point, and he has done so—as Nick explains—only at the expense of a devastating disillusionment. In this case too, readers may be forgiven if they look down somewhat on Gatsby. As Roger Lewis writes, "[T]he book fosters our appreciation of Gatsby's corrupt dream. Yet such participation can never be wholehearted and can never be complete" (52). The reason for this incomplete identification, as Lewis explains, is Gatsby's "naiveté": "[H]e is completely innocent of the limits of what money can do, a man who, we feel, would believe every word of an advertisement" (51). Because we (and most readers in 1925) presumably *do* know the limits of money, we are in a position superior to Gatsby's, a position dictated by the more complex attitudes toward money and success required in Fitzgerald's America. Under such circumstances, the most appropriate narrative mode available for Fitzgerald to recount the American Dream narrative increasingly becomes the ironic.

Following the Stock Market Crash of 1929 and the arrival of the Great Depression, the cultural suitability (perhaps the necessity) of the ironic mode is even more apparent. As Alan Ross explains, Nathanael West was like most politically aware American writers in the 1930s in the sense that "Their pessimism was not the reverse side of politico-literary idealism, it was a despair born from being witnesses of a suffering enormously outside their control" (ix).[6] Thus, West's version of the American Dream narrative in *A Cool Million* drips with irony from first page to last. As in *The Great Gatsby*, the author's irony touches on matters great and small in *A Cool Million*. Thus, the first sentence begins: "The home of Mrs. Sarah Pitkin, a widow well on in years, was situated on an eminence overlooking the Rat River . . ." (143), signaling through the semantic discrepancy between "eminence" and "Rat" that the reader should expect irony to follow. Surely this is also the purpose of the sentence in the next brief chapter in which former U. S. President Shagpoke Whipple apostrophizes the American flag in his back yard:

All hail Old Glory! May you be the joy and pride of the American heart, alike when your gorgeous folds shall wanton in the summer air and your tattered fragments be dimly seen through clouds of war! May you ever wave in honor, hope and profit, in unsullied glory and patriotic fervor, on the dome of the Capitol, on the tented plain, on the wave-rocked topmast and on the roof of this garage! (147-48)

Whipple's overly elevated vocabulary—*wanton, unsullied, tented*—points toward a restricted linguistic irony, as does West's anachronistic use of apostrophe, but the very deliberate descent in tone from the dome of the Capitol to the roof of the garage captures the larger structural ironies of West's version of the American Dream narrative.

This structural pattern is clear in the final chapter when Whipple summarizes the trajectory of the deceased hero's life for the audience at a political rally of American Fascists:

First we see him as a small boy, light of foot, fishing for bullheads in the Rat River of Vermont. Later, he attends the Ottsville High School, where he is captain of the nine and an excellent outfielder. Then, he leaves for the big city to make his fortune. All this is in the honorable tradition of his country and its people, and he has the right to expect certain rewards.

Jail is his first reward. Poverty his second. Violence is his third. Death is his last. (154)

As in the earlier quotations, West's linguistic irony is apparent, but here the content of Whipple's speech makes clear that West goes beyond even Fitzgerald in displacing the quest-for-success narrative. Like Gatsby—and unlike Alger's heroes—West's hero, Lemuel Pitkin, dies at the end of his quest, but Lem is also a failure all along the way. Whipple clearly identifies the final stage of Lem's quest as his death, but he omits specific mention of Lem's loss of teeth, eye, thumb, leg, and scalp, the incidents that justify the novel's subtitle: "The Dismantling of Lemuel Pitkin."

In order to highlight the ironic quality of his version of the narrative, West deliberately reminds his readers of earlier, univocal versions. As Scharnhorst and Bales explain, portions of West's novel sounds as though directly copied out of Alger's work. The narrator thus says about Lem, "Due to his strong physique, however, and a constitution that had never been undermined by the use of either tobacco or alcohol, Lem succeeded in passing the crisis of the dread pulmonary disease" (171). Lem is also Alger-like in his attitude toward fiction: "I'm not a great one for reading novels. . . . My Aunt Nancy gave my ma one once, but I didn't find much in it. I like facts and I like to study, though" (158). In this last respect, Lem also sounds like the young James Gatz. Lem resembles Fitzgerald's and Alger's heroes further when he meets a potential mentor, Elmer Haney, and Haney says, "Get yourself a haircut, bath and a big meal, then go to my tailors, Ephraim Pierce and Sons, and they will fit you out with clothes" (192). However, despite these clear echoes, Lem is unlike his predecessors in that his strong physique is useful only in keeping him from succumbing to pneumonia in prison, his study yields no practical results, and his mentor is grooming him only to take part in a confidence swindle.

West also follows Alger in outrageously relying on coincidence as a plot device. After Lem leaves the hospital following the loss of his eye, he has no idea what to do next. The narrator then reports: "The poor lad was standing on a windy corner, not knowing which way to turn, when he saw a man in a coonskin hat. This remarkable headgear made Lem stare, and the more he looked the more the man seemed to resemble Shagpoke Whipple" (185). Shagpoke turns up in this opportune fashion throughout the narrative, as does Lem's childhood sweetheart, Betty Prail. However, it is characteristic of West's version of the American Dream narrative that Shagpoke is flat broke when Lem meets him on the windy corner and that, a few pages later, Betty is a street-walker who solicits Lem by asking, "Why so blue, duckie? How about a little fun?" (213). Alger would rather die than write such a scene! Alger might just conceivably have a pick-pocket coincidentally drop a diamond ring into his hero's pocket, as West does (162), but Alger would not then send his hero to prison on a false robbery charge in order to have all his teeth extracted. Coincidence thus plays its predictable structural part in West's version, but the consequences are less predictable. Typically, Lem rescues the rich banker, Levi Underdown, and his beautiful daughter from a carriage accident because he is coincidentally in the right place at the right time (180-81). By an equal coincidence, however, the banker's deafness and Lem's ill-fitting false teeth result in Lem's being blamed for the danger instead of being rewarded for the brave deliverance. In this way, West simultaneously invokes and criticizes the familiar narrative devices.[7]

There is a double-voiced quality present also when West imitates Alger's tendency to report highly specific monetary calculations. As in an Alger novel, Wellington Mape tells Lem that "I pay three dollars a day for my board, and the incidentals carry my expenses up to as high as forty dollars a week" (160). Later Samuel Perkins similarly brags: "I get thirty-five without keep, but it's too little for me. A man can't live on that kind of money, what with the opera once a week and decent clothes. Why, my carfare alone comes to over a dollar, not counting taxicabs" (198). The speeches certainly do sound as if they were copied right out of one of Alger's books! At first, we might think the same about a speech given by the prison warden who has ordered that all of Lem's teeth be extracted to prevent future criminal activities:

Suppose you had obtained a job in New York City that paid fifteen dollars a week. You were here with us in all twenty weeks, so you lost the use of three hundred dollars. However, you paid no board while you were here, which was a saving for you of about seven dollars a week or one hundred and forty dollars. This leaves you the loser by one hundred and sixty dollars. But it would have cost you at least two hundred dollars to have all your teeth extracted, so you're really ahead of the game forty dollars. Also, the new set of false teeth I gave you cost twenty dollars new and is worth at least fifteen dollars in its present condition. This makes your profit about fifty-five dollars. Not at all a bad sum for a lad your age to save in twenty weeks. (175)

Whether or not this is the sort of financial calculation that Nick Carraway might have learned from the books he bought, it is the sort of figuring that often goes on in Alger's novels. Reduced to this level of absurdity, however, the incident advances West's devolutionary narrative and at the same time comments intertextually on the kind of financial calculation often imbedded in the grander American Dream narrative.

Another kind of financial calculation points toward West's principal divergence from the more traditional narrative. In the novel's first chapter, we learn that the mortgage on the widow Pitkin's home carries a twelve per cent annual interest rate (145). When Lem determines to go out into the world to earn enough money to prevent foreclosure, Whipple lends him "thirty dollars minus twelve per cent interest in advance" (158) as seed money. These exorbitant interest rates are presented without comment, except perhaps for connecting them with the lenders' positions in the community. The mortgage is held by a leading citizen, Squire Bird, and the loan is made by a former President of the United States and current president of the Rat River National Bank. Socio-economic class is apparently a factor questioned in West's version of this narrative to a degree unfamiliar from earlier versions.[8] This is especially evident in one of the novel's weaker scenes. After Lem and Shagpoke have been reduced to joining the traveling carnival attached to the Chamber of American Horrors, the narrative recounts a tableau that is part of the show. In this tableau, a widowed grandmother is cheated of her small fortune by dishonest stock manipulators who have sold her some worthless South American bonds. After the woman and her grandchildren have starved to death, two millionaires step over the bodies laughing at their own ingenuity in having pulled off the fraud. This is probably poor theater, and certainly poor fiction, but the episode clearly points to West's searching critique of the basic ideas underlying the American Dream narrative of success.

Many of West's most troubling questions derive from the novel's setting during the Great American Depression. Shagpoke Whipple speaks for the traditional view when he tells Lem after negotiating his high-interest loan that he should ignore "a certain few scoffers"

[who] will tell you that John D. Rockefeller was a thief and that Henry Ford and other great men are also thieves. Do not believe them. The story of Rockefeller and Ford is the story of every great American, and you should strive to make it your story. Like them, you were born poor and on a farm. Like them, by honesty and industry, you cannot fail to succeed. (15)

Whipple's sentiments echo those of Horatio Alger, Jr.—and probably of the young James Gatz—even if the surrounding context tends to ironize some of his vocabulary. More damaging to the traditional view are the many reminders of the actual economic Depression that West scatters throughout the book. Lem is available to participate in Elmer Haney's confidence game because he cannot find honest labor despite persistent attempts to find a job (193). While Betty Prail works at Wu Fong's house of all-American prostitutes, the narrator explains that in 1928 it would have been impossible to find honest American girls willing to engage in such a low trade, but "by 1934 things were different." "Many respectable families of genuine native stock had been reduced to extreme poverty," the narrator adds, "and had thrown their female children on the open market" (202). Lem and Shagpoke join the Chamber of American Horrors tour because they have been unable to support themselves by selling tickets to see Lem's scalped head. The narrator explains that "Although Mr. Whipple was an excellent salesman, the people they encountered had very little money to spend and could not afford to gratify their curiosity no matter how it was aroused" (236). Not much later Lem finds himself once again "submerge[d] in the great army of unemployed." Refusing "to grow bitter and become a carping critic of things as they are," Lem continues to bathe daily in Central Park lake and to make the dispiriting rounds of the employment agencies (247). Apparently as a reward for these stellar habits, the team of Riley and Robbins hire Lem to be their stooge in a vaudeville act in which they alternately tell stale jokes and beat Lem with rolled-up newspapers until one of his artificial parts falls off. Lem is reasonably content with his job: "After all, he reasoned, with millions out of work he had no cause to complain" (250). West wants us to hear the sounds of the traditional American Dream narrative with one ear and the competing message of the proletarian novel of the Depression with the other.[9]

A partial explanation for this devolutionary intertextuality probably lies in Nathanael West's personal disposition. As West candidly said about his own work, all his novels offer readers "nothing to root for" (qtd. in Martin 334). In the case of *A Cool Million,* according to T. R. Steiner, this general pessimism naturally produced an ironic inflection of the traditional narrative: "So, the Alger material becomes very sophisticated and the skeleton for, as well as merging with, a whole series of American motifs, fictions, and myths; American Dreams certainly, but also American Nightmares" (100). In a sense, of course, any pessimistically inclined American writer might have produced such a book at any time since Benjamin Franklin began recording his daily progress toward attaining the American Dream.[10] On the other—and more probable—hand, the circumstances of West's America are likely to be even more influential, as Frye's theory of modes would lead us to expect. The socio-economic development of the culture between the optimistic times of Horatio Alger, Jr., and the America depicted in grim, socially-conscious books like *The Disinherited* by Jack Conroy (1933) and *In Dubious Battle* by John Steinbeck (1936) must have produced striking changes as well as continuities in popular attitudes toward economic opportunity, definitions of success, and the American Dream. Despite Shagpoke Whipple's assurances that America "'takes care of the honest and industrious and never fails them," fewer thoughtful Americans than in earlier times could maintain univocal faith in the American Dream of success. And, as Whipple also maintains, "On the day that Americans stop believing in the American Dream, on that day will America be lost" in terms of its guiding vision (150). For West, this day had arrived both personally and ideologically, and so his approach to the American Dream narrative could be structured only in ironic terms.

All of this discussion goes to show that even if West and Fitzgerald were more acutely aware of the ambiguities attending on the American Dream than were most of their countrymen, they were inescapably part of the national community of American Dreamers. It is therefore no surprise that both writers sought intertextual encounters with their predecessors on this ground, especially with Horatio Alger, Jr. While both of these twentieth-century novelists stand higher today in the esteem of amateur and professional readers of American fiction than Alger does, the common pursuit of all three is still intertextually significant. West's and Fitzgerald's intentions, their achievements, and even their failures in these books can therefore be profitably discussed in terms of their encounters with their largely ignored literary ancestor, and the books of all three in terms of their intertextual encounters with the American myth of success.

2

"ROBIN'S COUNTRY COUSINS":
INTERTEXTUAL ENCOUNTERS IN HAWTHORNE,
FAULKNER, AND O'CONNOR

In the previous chapter I focused on the ways in which an influential myth of American culture—that individual "success" is inevitable, given the correct combination of "luck and pluck"—controls a series of narratives in which, as the twentieth century progresses, the myth is increasingly inflected in the direction of irony. In this chapter, a similarly popular American myth—based on the virtues of rural living, the vices of the city, and the expected interactions between these factors—controls another series of narratives. In the case of the success myth, intertextual encounters result when the univocal narrative, as articulated most notably by Horatio Alger, Jr., mutates while passing through the creative irony of F. Scott Fitzgerald and Nathanael West. In the second case, the primary text examining the myth is the work of an ironic author, Nathaniel Hawthorne, and so the ensuing intertextual encounters turn out to be among three ironic examinations of the same myth—narratized by Hawthorne, William Faulker, and Flannery O'Connor—rather than between a univocal narrative and its later, ironic permutations. Consequently, the most striking illustrations of intertextual encounters among these three ironic narratives occur in terms of their similarities, especially those similarities entailing narrative structure.

Thomas Jefferson definitely articulates the American myth of rural virtue in his *Notes on the State of Virginia* (1787) when he writes, "Those who labour in the earth are the chosen people of God, if ever he had a chosen people, whose breasts he has made his peculiar deposit for substantial and genuine virtue," and he establishes the superiority of agrarian life to urban sophistication by adding that "The mobs of great cities add just so much to the support of pure government, as sores do to the strength of the human body" (164-65). A sentiment similar to Jefferson's is expressed in *The Pioneers* (1823), the first novel of James Fenimore Cooper's Leatherstocking saga, when nature's nobleman, Natty Bumppo, explains his departure from the primitive civilization of Templeton, New York, to go off into the wilderness by saying, "I'm weary of living in clearings, and where the hammer is sounding in my ears from sunrise to sundown" (421). This mythological case is stated again in the theme song of *Greenacres* (1965-1971), the incredibly popular TV show in which a wealthy attorney moves from Manhattan to the sticks: "Green Acres is the place for me./Farm living is the life for me./Land spreading out so far and wide. . . ." All of these related ideas can perhaps be summarized in the somewhat less-famous second stanza of the beloved folk song "A Home on the Range": "I would not exchange my home on the range/For all of the cities so bright" (831). Here in a nutshell is a clear statement of one of the most powerful mythological influences in American culture: a strong belief in the moral superiority of rural living as against the alleged advantages of urbanized civilization. It is surely a short leap to the assumption that Jefferson's agrarian laborer, the Leatherstocking-like outdoorsman, and the all-American rustic figure often called Brother Jonathan could prove equal or superior to any challenges—practical or moral—posed by the city. Constance Rourke summarizes this mythic extension by citing the opinion of nineteenth-century American humorist, Seba Smith, concerning this rural character's supposed armory of virtues: "So far from being a talking boor . . . he is on the contrary singularly wise, penetrating, and observant" (27), or at least that is the way he thinks about himself.

One interesting narrative version of this mythic role can be seen in the highly imaginative autobiographical account published in various versions beginning in 1832 under the name of Davy Crockett (1786-1836). According to Joseph Arpad, editor of one modern version of this work, "Crockett's autobiography reveals [the] innocent mentality and viewpoint [of] a green, unsophisticated backwoodsman who accidentally blunders into the complex world of politics" (30). Although colored by some self-mockery and a contrived air of false modesty, Crockett's autobiography testifies both to the beneficial effects of rustic living and to the moral superiority that such a mode of life supposedly enables the rustic to bring to the challenges posed by urban civilization. In Arpad's words, "The mysterious something [that the autobiographical Crockett brought to all of life's challenges] was his pose as the American Adam, whose affinity with nature allowed him to conquer the dangers of the wilderness and whose innocence and naïve ingenuity allowed him to master the machinations of a corrupt society" (36). This Brother Jonathan in a coonskin cap embodies the myth in a straight-forward fashion rhetorically calculated to represent the mythologized Crockett as a viable Whig political alternative to the equally mythic Democrat, Andrew Jackson. Of course, history took a hand at the Alamo, and so we can only conjecture how the contending myths of rural virtue might have worked themselves out had Crockett survived to participate in future national elections. It is enough for our purposes that, in written form, he embodies this myth so clearly.

As we might expect on the basis of our investigation of the American myth of success, however, many commentators have been moved to develop ironic inflections on rural-urban mythic encounters. After all, even the *Greenacres* song goes on to say, "New York is where I'd rather stay./I get allergic smelling hay." One version of the ironic demurral appears in a work written in the same year in which Jefferson's *Notes on the State of Virginia* was published. In what is probably the first successful American play, Royall Tyler's *The Contrast,* the character Jonathan —later famous in popular versions as Brother Jonathan—fulfills the dramatic function conventionally allotted to comic servants in English plays of the time. Because Jonathan is an American, however, the country-bred lad insists that he is a "waiter" rather than a servant: "I am a true blue son of liberty for all that. Father said I should come as Colonel Manly's waiter, to see the world, and all that; but no man shall master me: my father has as good a farm as the colonel" (2.2, 474). Because of his probably misplaced confidence in himself, Jonathan continually fails to understand what is going on in early Federalist New York City. Politics, for example, are a mystery to Jonathan: "Oh! I have seen a power of fine sights. I went to see two marble-stone men and a leaden horse that stands out in doors in all weathers; and when I came where they was, one had got no head, and t'other weren't there. They said as how the leaden man was a damn'd tory, and that he took wit in his anger and rode off in the time of troubles" (2.2, 475). Jonathan is no more acute when dealing with sex, as he naively reports: "I went to a place they call Holy Ground. Now I counted this was a place where folks go to meeting; so I put my hymn-book in my pocket, and walked softly and grave as a minister. . . . At last I spied a young gentlewoman standing by one of the seats which they have there at the doors—I took her to be the deacon's daughter, and she looked so kind, and so obliging, that I would go and ask her the way to the lecture, and would you think it?—she called me dear, and sweeting, and honey, just as if we were married: by the living jingo, I had a month's mind to bus her" (2.2, 475). When a more experienced servant, Jessamy, explains to him that this woman was probably a strumpet, Jonathan replies, "Mercy on my soul! Was that young woman a harlot! Well! If this is New York Holy Ground, what must the Holiday Ground be!" (2.2, 475). No wonder Jessamy later reports that Jonathan "really has a most prodigious effect upon my risibility" (3.1, 479)! A rural innocent who overvalues his own acuteness is very likely—despite Jefferson's beliefs to the contrary—to fall into laughable mistakes when confronted with the challenges of urban life.

This sort of laughter often resonates throughout the highly contended area in which humor and satire approach each other. In *Beneath the American Renaissance: The Subversive Imagination in the Age of Emerson and Melville* (1988), for example, David S. Reynolds proposes Nathaniel Hawthorne as one of the American writers who chose to treat the national myth of rustic virtue in the humorous direction suggested by Jessamy: "Indeed, [Hawthorne] structured much of his fiction in such a way that it vented the wildest impulses of popular humor but at the same time asserted control over these impulses by regulating them through various controlling devices" (533). The chief device in the case of Hawthorne's tale "My Kinsman, Major Molineux" is a fictional structure that stretches this potentially humorous mythic matter over a series of narrative nodes that will appeal also to later, similarly disposed, American writers, including William Faulkner and Flannery O'Connor. In consequence, Hawthorne's "My Kinsman, Major Molineux" (1832), Chapter 21 of Faulkner's novel *Sanctuary* (1931), and O'Connor's short story "The Artificial Nigger" (1955) all can be understood as highly innovative displacements of a single narrative structure based on the same mythic materials. In each case, fictional characters fitting Louis Rubin's description as "hayseeds, rubes, red-necks, crackers" (120-21) come to the big city convinced that their native shrewdness will allow them to prosper in this unfamiliar, complex environment. As Daniel G. Hoffman writes about Hawthorne's rustic hero, Robin Molineux, "Like his antecedent bumpkins in popular tradition—Brother Jonathan, the peddlers of folk anecdote, Jack Downing, Sam Slick—he is nothing if not shrewd. But Robin is shrewd only by his own report" (119). Like Robin and Brother Jonathan, then, the principal characters in all these narratives are revealed to be woefully mistaken about their abilities. In consequence, their experiences end up following common structural patterns, and intertextual encounters ensue even though the three authors compose their narratives from highly varied thematic intentions.

Hawthorne's handling of this literary material is probably the most familiar of the three and so may be briefly summarized. In his tale, an eighteen-year-old country lad named Robin arrives in the seventeenth-century colonial metropolis of Boston in search of his cousin, Major Molineux, a political functionary of the crown, who has offered to help the young man get an economic start in the world.[1] Robin certainly resembles Brother Jonathan in the narrator's initial description: "He was a youth of barely eighteen years, evidently country-bred, and now, as it should seem, upon his first visit to town" (209). Like Jonathan also, Robin is amazed by all the new sights, and so he walks around town "with as eager an eye, as if he were entering London city, instead of the little metropolis of a New England colony" (210). Because Robin has failed to ask directions from the ferryman in the second paragraph of the tale, he must wander the streets randomly in search of the Major's house, with highly unsatisfactory results: "He now became entangled in a succession of crooked and narrow streets, which crossed each other, and meandered at no great distance from the water-side" (211). Adopting as he goes along increasingly less promising methods of investigation, Robin decides to search for his wealthy relative in the streets in the poorest part of town and eventually "to walk slowly and silently up the street, thrusting his face close to that of every elderly gentleman, in search of the Major's lineaments" (215). All the while Robin is searching ineffectually for his kinsman, "Hunger . . . pleaded loudly within him" (216), but he refuses to abandon his quest.

Both his determination and his ineffectual strategies arise from Robin's most prominent character trait. As the tale asserts eight times, Robin suffers from the delusion that he is a very "shrewd" youth and therefore equal to whatever challenges this unfamiliar environment might pose. This shrewdness also leads Robin to misinterpret the unwillingness of a series of townspeople to aid him in his search. When a respectable elderly man answers Robin's request for directions by threatening to turn him over to the authorities, Robin concludes, "This is some country representative . . . who has never seen the inside of my kinsman's door, and lacks the breeding to answer a stranger civilly" (211). When the patrons of a tavern react with hostility and laughter to a similar request, Robin thinks, "[Is] it not strange, that the confession of an empty pocket, should outweigh the name of my kinsman, Major Molineux?" (215). If Robin were truly shrewd, he would not fall into these predicaments in the first place. If he were simply innocent, he could not fabricate such bizarre rationalizations. In either case, he would probably find his kinsman's house without much difficulty, and thus he would not be subjected to the mocking laughter that follows him through most of the tale.[2]

The rich irony of Robin's imagined shrewdness forces him to prolong his unproductive quest long after a less deluded character would have either succeeded or given up. As he wanders the streets without food or drink, Robin encounters a strumpet in a scarlet petticoat who lives in "a street of mean appearance, on either side of which, a row of ill-built houses was straggling towards the harbor" (216). Like the supposed Deacon's daughter who lived in Brother Jonathan's Holy Ground, this young woman almost seduces Robin, partly on the basis of her incredible claim to be the Major's house-keeper but mostly on the basis of Robin's unacknowledged lust. As the narrator observes in amusement:

"[T]hough the touch was light, and the force was gentleness, and though Robin read in her eyes what he did not hear in her words, yet the slender waisted woman, in the scarlet petticoat, proved stronger than the athletic youth" (218). Another significant character in this narrative is "a gentleman in his prime, of open, intelligent, cheerful, and altogether prepossessing countenance" (224), who offers to help Robin await the Major's arrival. After the Major eventually passes by, tarred, feathered, and humiliated by colonial revolutionaries, this man offers to help Robin get a financial start in the world after all. Though Robin confesses that he has "grow[n] weary of town life" and wishes to return home (231), the tale ends ambiguously, with Robin agreeing to remain in town as the kind stranger's guest for a few more days.

This structurally straightforward tale has been subjected to a dazzling array of historical, New Critical, and Freudian interpretations, as Lea B. Newman demonstrates in her invaluable *A Reader's Guide to the Short Stories of Nathaniel Hawthorne*.[3] Probably the first interpreter to propose that the tale be construed in terms of some literary tradition—rather than autotelically—was Daniel G. Hoffman in *Form and Fable in American Fiction* (1961). Hoffman's summary characterization of the tale seems to anticipate many critics I shall mention subsequently: "Robin, the shrewd youth from the backwoods, proves to be the Great American Boob, the naif whose odyssey leads him, all uncomprehendingly, into the dark center of experience" (121). This interpretation of the tale underlies Hoffman's plausible suggestion that the key to the work might lie in the sorts of mythic and folkloric motifs analyzed in studies such as J. G. Frazer's *The Golden Bough*. Even more productive—and certainly more apt for my current purpose—is an intertextual consideration of the tale in terms of the properties it shares with the analogous narratives written by Faulkner and O'Connor which are based on the same myth. Such a reading obviously must be indebted to the structural approach pioneered by Vladimir Propp and Roland Barthes and refined in texts such as Peter Brooks's *Reading for the Plot*. Both Hoffman's archetypal approach and the structuralist project concur in arguing that major clarifications may be achieved by considering fictional intertexuality primarily in terms of the individual text's affiliations with its predecessors and successors. This is Wallace Martin's point in his *Recent Theories of Narrative*: "Structural analysis of narrative would ideally be able to show how a single surface structure (sequence of events) could be related to as many deep structures as there are interpretations of the tale. Narrative analysts have tended to overlook surface ambiguities and to assign one structural description to stories that have more than one meaning" (103-04).[4]

These invitations to pursue an intertextual strategy based on what Michel Gresset calls "inter-structurality"[5] are seconded by Faulkner's use of the narrative pattern underlying Hawthorne's tale. In his highly controversial novel *Sanctuary*, Faulkner tells the stories of Temple Drake, a college girl who comes to enjoy the vice that she is accidentally dragged into; Horace Benbow, an idealistic lawyer in ineffectual pursuit of justice; a group of bootleggers and criminals; and a southern society composed largely of hypocrites and racists. In response to the question, What is this novel actually *about?* a number of plausible answers might be—and have been—given. In 1939, not long after the novel's original publication, George Marion O'Donnell identified the novel's thematic center as the corruption of Temple Drake. In 1946, Malcolm Cowley proposed the ruination of the South by finance capitalism as the novel's theme. Hyatt H. Waggoner focused thematically on the inadequacy of Horace Benbow's idealism in 1959. As this interpretive succession has taken on a more postmodern cast in recent years, critics are disposed to adopt formulas such as the one used by Gregory Fortner in 1996: "The novel spits out as contentual stuff the confrontation between eye and world enacted in the mode of its telling just as—conversely—the book is 'about' the ruin of vision performed by a mode whose dementing commitment to seeing-in-between is cast by the content as vomitory" (548).[6] One or a combination of these premises will surely account for most of the elements in Faulkner's powerful novel. And yet, when all is said and done, there still remains Chapter 21, in which Virgil Snopes and Fonzo Winbush go to Memphis for no reason directly connected to any of these themes.[7] Although Cleanth Brooks has argued in *William Faulkner: The Yoknapatawpha Country* (1963) that this episode is merely another figure in Faulkner's tapestry of the South's corruption (135-36), his reasoning is more ingenious than persuasive. Nearly three decades later, Joseph R. Urgo tries as ingeniously, and ineffectively, in *Novel Frames: Literature as Guide to Race, Sex, and History in American Culture* (1991), to connect Chapter 21 to the rest of Faulkner's novel by stressing the common thread of "commodified sexuality" (106). The problem for Urgo, Cleanth Brooks, and other thematic interpreters is that this chapter derives much of its significance not from other aspects of *Sanctuary*, but from its own structure as a narrative, that is, as an account of the simple rustic's mythic encounter with the complexities of urban life.[8]

Once more, a summary can be illuminating. In Chapter 21 of *Sanctuary*, Virgil Snopes and Fonzo Winbush, two characters who do not appear elsewhere in the novel, travel by train from rural Yoknapatawpha County, Mississippi, to Memphis, the city that, according to Susan Willis, functions in Faulkner's fiction "as the locus of all that is unwholesome; gamblers, criminals, loose women, and prostitutes." At the same time, Willis explains, "the city's dominance is always discernible; life in the small towns in Faulkner's fiction hangs on its relationship to the distant city" (184). Like Robin Molineux, Faulkner's two bumpkins come to this unfamiliar and potentially dangerous environment in search of economic advancement—in their case, to attend barber college. At first—as is consistent with the Dantean resonances of his name—Virgil assumes Robin's mantle of shrewdness by proposing himself as Fonzo's guide. In this role, Virgil ingeniously explains why all the plate glass in the Gayoso Hotel makes it an unsuitable hostelry for them: "Suppose somebody broke it while we was there. Suppose they couldn't ketch who done it. Do you reckon they'd let us out withouten we paid our share?" Fonzo bows to Virgil's specious reasoning, with consequences that Faulkner indicates in the next sentence: "At five-thirty they entered a narrow dingy street of frame houses and junk yards" (184). That is to say, the two rubes randomly wander the streets, like Robin, hoping to stumble onto their objective: a place to stay.

They further resemble Robin not only by wandering through town thirsty and hungry—Fonzo is tantalized by the smell of ham cooking— but also by having a Brother-Jonathan-like encounter with a loose woman, in their case, with Reba Rivers, the notorious madam who will reappear in *The Mansion* and *The Reivers*. The boys decide to put up at Miss Reba's place in consequence of another piece of bizarre reasoning, this time on the part of Fonzo, who argues that the whorehouse must be a hotel since, "Who ever heard of anybody just living in a three-storey house?" (185). This rationalization suggests that Virgil and Fonzo have traded roles and that Fonzo will now act the part of the "shrewd" youth. Fonzo's new role is emphasized when he calls out slangily, "Hold me, big boy; I'm heading for the henhouse" (187).Thus, it is Fonzo, not Virgil, who reasons, on the basis of the woman's undergarment he finds on the floor, that Reba must be "a dress-maker" (189). Fonzo's shrewdness also invents the excuse that they have been "to prayer-meeting" when a visit to another whorehouse has delayed their return to Miss Reba's (190). In imitation of the schemas proposed by structural analysts of narrative, we might say that the role played by Robin Molineux has been "displaced" and split between two characters in Faulkner's narrative, just as the part played by the girl in the scarlet petticoat is displaced partly into Miss Reba and partly into the prostitutes whom Virgil and Fonzo later patronize.

In *Reading for the Plot,* Peter Brooks maintains that such variations within a frequently used structural pattern are only to be expected. According to Brooks: "The names that an individual tale will assign to these agents—and the way it may combine or divide them—are relatively unimportant, as are their attributes and motivations. What counts is their role as vehicles of the plot." While rejecting the doctrinaire categories established by Vladimir Propp because of the "relatively simple and formulaic nature of the narratives" that Propp uses as evidence,[9] Brooks still argues that "something like the concept of 'function' may be necessary in any discussion of plot, in that it gives us a way to think about what happens in narrative from the point of view of its significance to the course of the action, as a whole, the articulation of narrative as a structure of actions" (15-16). In considering *Sanctuary* especially, this proposition seems likely. In the light of the intertextual context provided by Hawthorne's story, one can see that Virgil and Fonzo go to Memphis not so much to develop the themes or advance the plot of Faulkner's novel as a whole, but to perform their functions in an individual, imbedded, narrative based on a popular American myth.

Other elements of displacement also lend support to this proposition. Just as Robin Molineux's naiveté provokes laughter throughout his quest, the boys' innocence is laughed at by Miss Reba: "Then she began to laugh, her hand at her breast. They watched her soberly while she laughed in harsh gasps" (187). This displaced laughter probably accounts as well for the later episode in which State Senator Clarence Snopes reacts to Virgil's confession that they have been sneaking out of Miss Reba's to visit prostitutes by saying, "I'll be durned if you aint the biggest fool this side of Jackson" (192). That Clarence is a displacement of the kindly stranger in Hawthorne's tale also seems likely. Both older men manifest an experienced grasp of the ways of the world that is laughably absent in the rustic protagonists. In both narratives, furthermore, experience involves some measure of corruption. In Hawthorne's tale, a mature grasp of the political facts of life leads to accepting "the foul disgrace of a head that had grown grey in honor" (229): the Major's barbaric tar-and-feathering. In Faulkner's chapter, the worldly view consists of an easy acceptance of prostitution. While the rustic Fonzo cannot get over the fact that such sexual abundance flourishes in Memphis— "And to think I been here two weeks without never knowing about that house" (190)—to the worldly-wise Clarence, sex is no more than a financial transaction. To explain the economic advantages of patronizing black prostitutes, Clarence "wave[s] a banknote in his cousin's face," and explains, "This stuff is color-blind" (192). Faulkner need not add that the only important color is green.

It should perhaps be no surprise that Flannery O'Connor's story "The Artificial Nigger" has been the object of considerable critical inquiry since its original publication in 1955—and not just because of its aggressively provocative title.[10] Like the rest of O'Connor's fiction, "The Artificial Nigger" has occasioned vast and varied thematic commentary, predominantly devoted to the story's congruence with select points of Christian doctrine, most recently as these Christian teachings bear on issues of race.[11] However, none of this commentary recognizes how clearly "The Artificial Nigger" echoes the narrative structure of Faulkner's Chapter 21 and, consequently, of Hawthorne's tale. The metropolis in which O'Connor's narrative unfolds is Atlanta, a setting that Ted R. Spivey has shown to be as provocative to O'Connor as Memphis was to Faulkner or Boston to Hawthorne. In "Flannery O'Connor, James Joyce, and the City," Spivey writes, "[E]ven from the beginning of her real awareness of the city, Atlanta would take on [for O'Connor] the semblance of the modern megapolis, the New South city Southern writers have, at least since World War II, often hated and yet have been drawn to" (93).

The role of the shrewd rustic traveling to Atlanta is filled by Mr. Head, a character as appropriately named as Faulkner's Virgil Snopes. To stress the connection, O'Connor's narrator observes about Mr. Head early in the story that "He might have been Vergil summoned in the middle of the night to go to Dante" (250). Mr. Head is also Virgilian in serving as a guide for his equally rustic grandson, Nelson. In fact, Gilbert H. Muller claims in "The City of Woe: Flannery O'Connor's Dantean Vision" that "the affinities between [O'Connor's story] and Dante's passage through the Inferno are striking enough to permit an allegorical reading of her tale" (206).[12] Although readers of Hawthorne probably recognize the dangers attendant on allegorical readings, there is still merit in Muller's suggestion. Surely, for example, O'Connor intended to suggest Dante by the episode in which Mr. Head explains to Nelson that "a man could slide into [the city sewer system] and be sucked along down endless pitchblack tunnels," and Nelson "connected the sewer passages with the entrance to hell" (259).[13]

This pattern of literary allusions is revealing. In addition to Muller, readers as various as Frederick Asals and Louis Rubin have recognized thematic parallels between Dante's work and O'Connor's story.[14] Since Lance Lyday has drawn a similar parallel between the *Inferno* and *Sanctuary*,[15] and, according to Lea B. Newman (221-22), several critics— including herself—have done the same for Hawthorne's tale, one suspects that the mythic American narrative of a rustic's encounter with urban life may be merely one variant of an even more inclusive narrative structure, perhaps, as Muller suggests, "one of the classic exercises of rite de passage in Western literature" (206). Whether or not a search for such inclusive structures is pursued, it is clear at least that in several significant ways "The Artificial Nigger" intertextually encounters the other two narratives previously discussed.

First of all, Mr. Head is as deluded as his literary predecessors about his shrewdness. After Mr. Head makes an insulting remark about cockroaches to cover his embarrassment over being barred from the kitchen of the railroad dining car, the narrator ironically observes, "Mr. Head was known at home for his quick wit" (257). Armed, like Robin Molineux, with a false estimate of his quick wit, Mr. Head is confident that he can skillfully guide Nelson through the intricacies of urban life even though he has gotten humiliatingly lost on two previous trips to Atlanta. Before leaving the country, Mr. Head tries to assure this grandson of this competence with a question worthy of Robin: "Have you ever . . . seen me lost?" Nelson's response serves to alert the reader to the story's ironic tone: "It's nowhere around here to get lost at" (250). Another irony surfaces in O'Connor's displacement of the Benjamin-Franklin/Horatio-Alger-like motives that inspire Hawthorne's and Faulkner's protagonists to seek self-advancement. Mr. Head wants to manage the visit to Atlanta in such a way that Nelson can "see everything there is to see in a city so that he would be content to stay at home for the rest of his life" (251).

Despite these ironic displacements, O'Connor still follows the familiar structure. First, she causes the yokels to wander the city, hungry and thirsty, here tracing circles around the Atlanta railroad station because they left their sack lunch of sardines and biscuits behind on the train. As in the other narratives, Nelson and Mr. Head soon drift into the poorer, less secure part of town, here a black ghetto resembling the neighborhoods inhabited by Robin's strumpet, and Miss Reba. The boy's emotions dramatize their situation: "Nelson was afraid of the colored men and he didn't want to be laughed at by the colored children" (261). As in Hawthorne's and Faulkner's narratives, danger and laughter coincide.

Another element of this familiar narrative pattern surfaces when Nelson inquires directions from a black woman whom the narrator describes as follows: "Her hair stood straight out from her head for about four inches all around and she was resting on bare brown feet that turned pink at the sides. She had on a pink dress that showed her exact shape" (261). Clearly, this woman can be understood as a displacement of Robin's girl in the scarlet petticoat, Reba Rivers, and the prostitutes, white and black, in *Sanctuary*. In O'Connor's treatment, however, the character goes beyond the simple narrative function fulfilled by Brother Jonathan's "young gentlewoman" to take on considerable tonal complexity, as is shown again through Nelson's response:

He suddenly wanted her to reach down and pick him up and draw him against her and then he wanted to feel her breath on his face. He wanted to look down and down into her eyes while she held him tighter and tighter. He had never had such a feeling before. He felt as if he were reeling down through a pitchblack tunnel. (262)

In addition to a reminder of the Dantean allusion in the last few words, this passage creates a rich mixture of erotic and maternal suggestions, which shows that, although the structure largely controls the shape of O'Connor's story, she exercises great individual creativity in filling out this pattern. Ben Griffith thought, in fact, that the episode might have evinced too much creativity, causing O'Connor to respond in a letter, "You may be right that Nelson's reaction to the colored woman is too pronounced, but I meant for her in an almost physical way to suggest the mystery of existence to him . . ." (*Habit of Being* 78).

The authority of the structural pattern is shown, however, not only by O'Connor's eagerness to defend the episode, but also by the tale's subsequent unfolding. Soon Mr. Head follows Robin's example by seeking assistance from a kind stranger, a "man, who was bald-headed and had on golf knickers" (267), who provides directions to the suburban train station. This structural influence may be felt also in O'Connor's insistence that Mr. Head and Nelson should displace the same narrative function as "shrewd" rustic.[16] Although this point is made several times, as when the narrator says that two "looked enough alike to be brothers and brothers not too far apart in age" (251), the definitive passage appears when Nelson and Mr. Head encounter the plaster statue of the watermelon-eating Sambo which gives the story its title. It seems clear that in the passage O'Connor is trying to fulfill the thematic intention she expressed for the story in a 4 May 1953 letter to Ben Griffith: "What I had in mind to suggest with the artificial nigger was the redemptive quality of the Negro's suffering for us all" (*Habit of Being* 78). The narrator first observes: "It was not possible to tell if the artificial Negro were meant to be young or old; he looked too miserable to be either. He was meant to look happy because his mouth was stretched up at the corners but the chipped eye and the angle he was cocked at gave him a wild look of misery instead." Then the narrator writes about the story's chief rustics: "The two of them stood there with their necks forward at almost the same angle and their shoulders curved in almost exactly the same way and their hands trembling identically in their pockets" (268). Obviously, the two characters fulfill the same narrative function as dual displacements of the "shrewd" rustic on a visit to the big city. And so, the inter-structurality of the Hawthorne-Faulkner-O'Connor narratives emerges as clearly as does O'Connor's individual thematic intention.

In another variant on the familiar pattern, Mr. Head's interpretation of this purely urban phenomenon echoes Robin Molineux's preposterous misinterpretations and the bizarre rationalizations of Fonzo and Virgil.[17] Earlier in the narrative Mr. Head explained away the discrepancy between the weight of 98 pounds supplied by a public scale and Nelson's assumed weight of 69 pounds by saying that "that the machine had probably printed the number upside down, meaning the 9 for a 6" (259). With equally ingenious wrong-headedness, Mr. Head now patiently explains to Nelson: "They ain't got enough real ones here. They got to have an artificial one" (269). Foolish though the explanation is, O'Connor insists that the exchange is crucial to the vital connection between Mr. Head and Nelson: "He looked at Nelson and understood that he must say something to the child to show that he was still wise and in the look the boy returned he saw a hungry need for that assurance. Nelson's eyes seemed to implore him to explain once and for all the mystery of existence" (269). As in the earlier cases created by Hawthorne and Faulkner, this correct, worldly-wise view entails moral corruption, here a contrived rationalization of institutionalized racism.[18]

Even smaller elements of O'Connor's tale suggest that it shares intertextual properties with the narratives written by Faulkner and Hawthorne. The sewers in Atlanta, for example are frightening not only because they look like entrances to the Inferno. They also maintain a steady noise that disturbs Nelson with its urban insistence: "He drew [his head] back quickly, hearing a gurgling in the depths under the sidewalk" (259). Virgil and Fonzo also find the sounds of the city disconcerting: "They didn't go to sleep for some time that first night, what with the strange bed and room and the voices. They could hear the city, evocative and strange, imminent and remote; threat and promise both—a deep steady sound upon which invisible lights glittered and wavered" (187-88). Faulkner's scene continues: "The house appeared to be filled with people who did not sleep at night at all" (189). In Hawthorne's version of this narrative, Robin tells the kindly stranger, "Truly, if your town is always so noisy, I shall find little sleep, while I am an inhabitant" (226). Even in such secondary matters, the three narratives interact intertextually, most probably because of their common mythological origin.

A final striking similarity among the three narratives is suggested in Louis Rubin's essay "Flannery O'Connor's Company of Southerners: Or 'The Artificial Nigger' Read as Fiction Rather Than Theology." After discussing the Dantean allusions that shadow Mr. Head and Nelson's journey, Rubin emphasizes that O'Connor "does not hesitate to invest their trip to Atlanta and their experience there with a meaning and significance that are very much in excess of any possible interpretation the two characters themselves would know how to articulate" (128). Surely we might observe the same about Faulkner's presentation of Fonzo's erotic fantasies: "[He] thought of himself surrounded by tier upon tier of drawn shades, rose-colored, beyond which, in a murmur of silk, in panting whispers, the apotheosis of his youth assumed a thousand avatars" (188). In the same way, it can hardly be Robin who compares his search for the Major through the streets of Boston to that of "the philosopher seeking an honest man" (215-16) and the night watchman to "the Moonshine of Pyramus and Thisbe, [who] carried a lantern, needlessly aiding his sister luminary in the heavens" (218). Discrepancies of this sort are not stylistic flaws, according to Rubin, because "in a story like [O'Connor's] . . . there is a deliberate and carefully constructed distance between narrator and character, which is embodied in the language but goes beyond that into viewpoint and attitude" (130).

Most likely, we can discover in this last similarity the principal attraction of this structure for these three writers. To narrate a "shrewd" rustic's encounter with the complexities of American urban life necessitates not merely the two conventional perspectives of innocence and experience, or of conservatism and progressivism, but a third level of irony from which the writer may endorse neither but criticize both. It probably should go without saying that this is a level at which fiction inevitably exceeds interpretation. Consequently, critics have been unable to agree on precisely where Hawthorne stands regarding authority and autonomy in "My Kinsman, Major Molineux."[19] By the same token, readers of Faulkner have uncovered conflicting evidence in *Sanctuary* concerning the author's views of sexuality, economics, and the power of historical change.[20]

O'Connor's critics have become embroiled in similar disputes when interpreting "The Artificial Nigger," as Mary Neff Shaw helpfully explains in her essay on the story in *Flannery O'Connor: New Perspectives* (139-51). Experienced readers of O'Connor's work will probably expect that much of the critical dispute hinges on theological matters. As Sarah J. Fodor has explained: "After she announced, 'I see from the standpoint of Christian orthodoxy,' in her 1957 essay for Granville Hicks's *Living Novel* (162), critics increasingly quoted O'Connor to explain religious meanings in her work. Typical of reviews in the 1960s, this conjunction of biography and evaluation illustrates the waning power of W. K. Wimsatt and Monroe C. Beardsley's interdiction against the 'intentional fallacy'" (23-24). Even apart from the intentional fallacy, critics' eagerness to engage in theological interpretation is understandable when O'Connor gives Mr. Head thoughts such as the following: "He saw that no sin was too monstrous for him to claim as his own, and since God loved in proportion as He forgave, he felt ready at that instant to enter Paradise" (270). Despite their sincerity, however, it may finally turn out that these theological interpreters have, like Robin and his country cousins, been going about their searches in the wrong way, since the passages thematically crucial for most of them occur after—or at least outside of—the structure that is central to all three narratives.[21] In the antepenultimate paragraph of the story, Mr. Head and Nelson step off of the train back onto their own rural soil. In the final sentence of the final paragraph of the story, Nelson says, "I'm glad I've went once, but I'll never go back again!" (270). In between these passages, Mr. Head has his spiritual epiphany. As O'Connor explained in her 4 May 1955 letter to Ben Griffith, in the "last two paragraphs [of "The Artificial Nigger"] I have practically gone from the Garden of Eden to the Gates of Paradise," and she adds that "I am not sure it is successful" (*Habit of Being* 78). Critics are disposed to pronounce O'Connor successful or not depending in large measure on their a priori critical commitments. Each critic is probably "correct" enough in his or her own way, but all of these readings occupy critical territory outside the ground on which "The Artificial Nigger" encounters Faulkner's Chapter 21 and "My Kinsman, Major Molineux" through structural intertextuality.

Other views of these textual encounters are, of course, possible. In fact, Michel Gresset distinguishes inter-structurality from other forms of intertextuality in a manner that easily legitimates other angles. In "Of Sailboats and Kites: The 'Dying Fall,' in Faulkner's *Sanctuary* and Beckett's *Murphy,*" Gresset justifies external intertextuality by writing, contra Julia Kisteva, "If intertextuality is to be understood in the rather strict sense of 'a mosaic of quotations,' if, in other words, one should be able to prove that a text inserts, or incorporates, direct identifiable borrowings from another text before calling it 'intertextual,' admittedly my topic lies outside the scope of these proceedings" (57). Having rejected the more familiar alternative, Gresset then goes on to compare Faulkner's novel intertextually with Beckett's, rather as I have done with three different narratives in this chapter. Following Kristeva rather than Gresset, however, might have led to a greater emphasis on the allusions to Dante in each of the texts that I have discussed.

Alternatively, another critic might choose to link these three narratives by applying Mikhail Bakhtin's theory of the "carnivalesque," a sense, as he says in *Rabelais and His World*, of "temporary liberation from the prevailing truth and from the established order . . . the suspension of all hierarchical rank, privileges, norms, and prohibitions" (10). It seems highly likely that someone could examine all three of the texts considered in this chapter in the light of what Bakhtin goes on to call "carnival laughter" (11-12), "legalized carnival licentiousness" (13), and "abusive language, insulting words or expressions" (16). Robin's nightmare experiences leap immediately to mind, of course, especially the scene in which he finally encounters his kinsman in an atmosphere heightened by "a band of fearful wind-instruments, sending forth a fresher discord . . . a redder light . . . and a dense multitude of torches . . . concealing by their glare whatever object they illuminated" (227). Fonzo and Virgil seem equally subject to these carnivalesque forces as they "stopped at a house with red shades in the lighted windows. . . . [and] could hear music inside, and shrill voices, and feet" (192). To represent the carnivalesque in literature, it is necessary, as Bakhtin says, to emphasize "degradation, that is, the lowering of all that is high, spiritual, ideal" (19). Obviously, this is the imaginative setting in which Robin and the apprentice barbers encounter the challenges of the big city, and it is also the environment surrounding Nelson and Mr. Head, at least after they realize that they are lost. Many passages from O'Connor's tale might suffice to illustrate, but one seems especially apt to me: "The women were milling around Nelson as if they might suddenly all dive on him at once and tear him to pieces" (265). And yet, I have not chosen to approach these narratives through the avenues provided by Bakhtin.

Neither have I found the possibilities of imitation or influence compelling, although others might adopt this intertextual line. In an essay entitled "Flannery O'Connor's Devil," for example, O'Connor's friend and fellow-novelist John Hawkes, uses a letter in which O'Connor confesses her attachment to Hawthorne's mode of romance [*Habit of Being* 457] to compare O'Connor and Nathanael West.[22] Elsewhere in these letters, O'Connor writes that "my opinion of Hawthorne is that he was a very great writer indeed" (*Habit of Being* 70) and that "Hawthorne interests me considerably. I feel more of a kinship with him than with any other American . . ." (*Habit of Being* 457). Since O'Connor lists both Hawthorne and Faulkner in another letter (*Habit of Being* 99, 98) as influences, a suitably disposed critic might be off in pursuit of these personal affiliations, despite O'Connor's disclaimer in another letter: "I keep clear of Faulkner so my own little boat won't get swamped" (*Habit of Being* 73). O'Connor notwithstanding, Malcolm Cowley connects Faulkner and Hawthorne in his Introduction to *The Portable Faulkner* (3-4), as does Joseph Blotner in *Faulkner: A Biography*.[23] Surely these actual and putative biographical connections tell us something significant about these three authors, but a study of the intertextual encounters among three of their texts also tells us something significant about the authors' common attraction to the same set of mythic attitudes.

Northrop Frye remarks about a similar attraction in his essay, "Myth, Fiction, and Displacement": "Writers are interested in folk tales for the same reason that painters are interested in still-life arrangements: because they illustrate essential patterns of storytelling" (27). Like the structurally simple folk tale, the narrative of an innocent rustic's encounter with urban life seems to offer creative freedom to a variety of artistic talents. Different as these talents and the artists' intentions may be, however, they have in common the same narrative structure, and this narrative structure may be used as an intertext to read fictional variants comparatively, even though obvious surface differences among the texts might lead others away from intertextual analysis. Having accepted such an inter-structural approach, however, we must concede that the widely divergent thematic readings proposed by incisive critics for all three works of fiction require that we guard against an over-determined search for structural parallels. As Wallace Martin wisely points out in his *Recent Theories of Narrative*: "Obviously, we can make stories appear more similar than they actually are by omitting all features that make them different" (93). Even with Martin's warning in mind, however, it is possible to see that the essential narrative pattern illustrated in these three narratives can dominate at times even over theme. Hawthorne does not fully resolve the ambiguities clouding Robin's future, for example. Faulkner interpolates Fonzo and Virgil's journey to Memphis into *Sanctuary* without organically relating it to the larger themes of the novel. O'Connor addresses Mr. Head's supposed salvation only within the closing paragraphs of her story.

The mythical intertext of the inexperienced rustic's first encounter with the complexities of urban life thus dominates each of the narrative variants discussed in this chapter, despite the generally acknowledged literary genius of their three authors. The explanation for this conflict lies, I would suggest, in the complexity of the mythic forces underlying all three narratives. As native-born American authors, Hawthorne, Faulkner, and O'Connor were inescapably steeped in Jeffersonian confidence about the salubrious qualities of rustic living. As sophisticated thinkers, all three authors were disposed to reject most simple answers: about the virtues of rural living, the evils of the city, and the inevitable consequences of encounters between the two. As creators of fictional narratives, all three authors relished the riches of irony and ambiguity, the possibility of eating their cake while still having it. Thus, Robin and his country cousins take the same journeys, face the same challenges, and respond to them in substantially the same ways, despite the three authors' various thematic intentions. One suspects that if a fourth American narrative genius were to undertake a similar story, the resulting narrative would be inter-structurally similar to the three examined here.

3

THE "MATTER" OF THE ROSENBERGS
AND OTHER INTERTEXTS
IN NOVELS BY E. L. DOCTOROW AND ROBERT COOVER

In the ninth chapter of his *Poetics,* Aristotle writes that poetry is "a more philosophical and a higher thing than history" because poetry tells "what is possible according to the law of probability or necessity," while history is restricted to "what has happened."[1] Recognizing that Aristotle's "poetry" includes all imaginative writing should help us understand why certain historicized, but still problematic, incidents of the past would engage the attention of inquiring American novelists. The trial and execution of "atom" spies Julius and Ethel Rosenberg constitute such an incident, and E. L. Doctorow and Robert Coover are two such novelists. In an interview with Larry McCaffery,[2] Doctorow tells how he approached his subject matter in his novel, *The Book of Daniel* (1971): "I would not write a documentary novel but quite clearly and deliberately use what had happened to the Rosenbergs as *occasion* for the book" (46; Doctorow's emphasis). According to Raymond A. Mazurek, Coover's creative approach was similar in *The Public Burning* (1977): "Insofar as it is an historical novel, *The Public Burning* makes use of actual historical materials, and its irony is often predicated on the reader's awareness of those documents" (30). Some of the terms circulating in these remarks—*historical novel, Rosenbergs, documents*—clearly suggest that these two novels can be productively examined in terms of their intertextual encounters with historical events attached to the historico-cultural phenomenon identified with the names of Julius and Ethel Rosenberg.

For the record, the Rosenbergs were arrested in New York City during the summer of 1950 for conspiring to commit espionage by transferring the "secret" of the atomic bomb—supposedly known only by the American sources responsible for the Manhattan Project and the subsequent bombings of Hiroshima and Nagasaki—to foreign agents, thereby allowing the Soviet Union to detonate its own atomic device unexpectedly in September, 1949. On March 29, 1951, following a four-week trial, the Rosenbergs were found guilty of the charge and were sentenced by Judge Irving R. Kaufman to death in the electric chair. After a series

56

of appeals and legal motions, including several refusals by the Supreme Court of the United States to review their case, the Rosenbergs were electrocuted in Sing Sing prison on June 19, 1953.

These bare bones of the case hardly suggest the complexity of response and interpretation that the case elicited at the time and has continued to elicit until the present day.[3] Knowing how a person regarded the guilt or innocence of the Rosenbergs, the justice or injustice of their trial, and the legitimacy or cruelty of their capital sentencing, was often assumed in years past to serve as a reliable guide to that person's orientation as a political liberal or conservative. Naturally, there were factions within the ranks of the two larger political groups, organized around fine legal distinctions and Byzantine subtleties of judicial interpretation. Despite such subtle differences of opinion, however, we may generalize that—like the Fugitive Slave Law, the gold standard, and entry into the League of Nations—the Rosenberg case served for its time as a popular measure of Americans' political dispositions. As Michael Dobbs writes in *The Jerusalem Post* (10 Apr. 1997): "Executed by electric chair in Sing Sing at sundown on June 19, 1953, the Rosenbergs rapidly became a potent political symbol. To the left, they were martyrs of the McCarthyite 'hysteria' then sweeping America. To the right, they were leaders of a communist fifth column that had betrayed America from within."[4]

It should therefore be no shock to discover that the Rosenberg case has occasioned a great deal of interpretive commentary. As David Thorburn has observed, "More than four decades after their execution, Julius and Ethel Rosenberg are irretrievably mythic figures, the subject of journalistic and scholarly studies in many languages, the inspiration for plays, novels, poems and a remarkable range of visual art—heroic martyrs on the Left; false-speaking ideologues who betrayed their country, their young sons, and their own humanity to many on the Right" (171). As Dobbs's and Thorburn's characterizations suggest, the indisputable "facts" of the Rosenberg case have been interpreted, arranged, and narratized by countless critics in accord with the thematic intentions of each. To borrow a term from the scholars of medievalism,[5] we may say that although the central "matter" of the Rosenbergs surely exists, interpreters' ideological dispositions have usually served to construe this "matter" in widely diverse directions. And this is true of creative writers as well as of politicians and political historians. In *The Book of Daniel* and *The Public Burning,* in particular, the "matter" of the Rosenbergs serves primarily as an intertext for novels devoted to the writers' larger purpose of interpreting the American spirit. Because Doctorow and Coover are highly creative writers, moreover, the "matter" of the Rosenbergs is forced to encounter in these novels other intertexts derived from literature, history, and popular culture.

The "matter" of the Rosenbergs appears in the two novels in various ways. A prison letter from Paul Issacson (Doctorow's fictionalized version of Julius Rosenberg) to his wife, Rochelle (Ethel), remarks on "how many of the characters in this capitalist drama are Jewish" and goes on to list: "The defendants, the defense lawyer, the prosecution, the major prosecution witness, the judge" (213). In Doctorow's novel, these roles are filled by Paul and Rochelle Isaacson; their lawyer, Jacob Ascher; Howard Feuerman, the government prosecutor; the Isaacsons' friend and principal accuser, Dr. Mindish; and Judge Barnet Hirsch. In the actual Rosenberg trial, the corresponding characters were the Rosenbergs; their lawyer, Emanuel H. Bloch; the prosecutor, Irving Saypol; Ethel's brother and self-confessed co-conspirator, David Greenglass; and Judge Irving R. Kaufman. Although no one on this second list is specifically named by Doctorow, they encounter the characters in his novel intertextually. As Doctorow explains in an interview with Larry McCaffery, "I felt people would know about the Rosenbergs and that was all I needed to write a book about Paul and Rochelle Isaacson" (46). Although Coover's strategy is quite different from Doctorow's, his intertextual assumptions are the same. Coover's judge is ostentatiously named Irving R. Kaufman, and this character speaks and writes words that match words to be found in the trial records. Even so, Kaufman becomes just as fictionalized as Doctorow's Barnet Hirsch. To justify imposing the death sentence on the Rosenbergs, for example, Coover's Judge Kaufman says, "I believe your conduct in putting into the hands of the Russians the A-bomb years before our best scientists predicted Russia would perfect the bomb has already caused, in my opinion, the Communist aggression in Korea with the resultant casualties exceeding fifty thousand" (25), just as the actual judge said at the trial.[6] However, Kaufman's words are set up as blank verse in Coover's novel, a typographical signal of fictionality that can hardly be ignored. It is apparent that, while the "matter" of the Rosenbergs is variously transformed in the two novels, it continues to function as a significant intertext.

Coover uses the Rosenbergs' prison letters much as he uses Kaufman's speech. During the early section of the novel focused on the Wednesday and Thursday just before the Rosenbergs' execution, Coover juxtaposes an actual letter from Ethel to her two sons with discursive passages detailing some historical and political events of the early 1950s (42-43). Typography serves to signal fictionality here since passages from the letter are offset slightly and divided from the historical passages with white space. Thus, while historical and fictional texts encounter each other, both are finally absorbed into the fabric of Coover's novel. Later, in the section of the novel devoted to the public celebration preceding the electrocutions—the "Public Burning" of the title—another of Ethel's letters intertextually encounters the purely fictional when Chico Marx reads it aloud to the crowds gathered in Time Square "in his Jewish-Italian accent as Groucho goes stalking relentlessly about the set in his famous bent-kneed crouch, puffing a cigar and bobbing his eyebrows" (454). Once again, words lifted from a verifiable document intertextually encounter the fictional. It is probable, of course, that most Americans at the time of the execution had not read the Rosenbergs' prison letters, and so would have failed to recall these words even if Coover's fictional event had actually occurred. It is even more probable that most readers of Coover's novel today will not have read these letters. They operate as an historical intertext even so—in part because Coover sets up the textual encounter by saying that "Harpo (Ethel) [is] sitting in the electric chair and writing desperate letters to Groucho (Julius)" (454) and in part because the letters differ so strikingly in their rhetoric from the surrounding passages of Coover's diegesis.[7] As a result, even if we have never read any of the actual letters, our normal response to this scene is most likely the conviction that Coover's fictionalized Chico is reading words actually written by the woman named Ethel Rosenberg who was executed as an "atom" spy.

Doctorow creates a similar form of intertextuality when he interrupts his diegetic narrative with an extended discursive passage entitled, "True History of the Cold War: A Raga" (248-54). Although the section is not comprised entirely of historical quotation, its rhetorical effect is that of scholarly summary or paraphrase (probably constructed by the novel's protagonist): "In March 1946, Churchill makes a speech in Fulton, Missouri, with Truman on the platform applauding vigorously. Churchill finds provocative menace in the 'iron curtain' the Soviets have dropped in front of Eastern Europe" (253). Probably most readers will be sensitive enough to the editorializing implied by Doctorow's phrase, *applauding vigorously,* to realize that history is being filtered through the novelist's ideological commitments. At the same time, most readers know that the term *iron curtain* must have come from someone, somewhere, and almost as many will know that Winston Churchill was its author. Fulton, Missouri, may not be on the tips of as many tongues, but it still rings true or at least as probable. This aura of authenticity extends even to more questionable elements of this segment of the novel, as when Secretary of War Henry Stimson explains the importance of the Yalta Conference to President Harry Truman by saying, in implied indirect discourse, "Harry, listen to me. This is the movement for remaking the world" (250). Once again, few readers would have access to original documents associated with this conference, and most might wonder whether this was exactly the tone that Stimson habitually used when addressing the President. Even so, the surrounding context sounds thoroughly grounded in research.[8] The resulting sense for the reader is—as in Coover's novel—of an intertextual encounter between history and fiction. After all, Doctrow signals his intentions by subtitling this "historical" essay, "A Raga."

At times, Doctorow's use of verifiable historical documents resembles Coover's. To set up the Moscow Purge Trials of 1938 as a context for the Isaacsons' trial, Doctorow directly quotes (62-63) Edward Hallett Carr, author of *History of Soviet Russia, 1917-1923* (1951). David A. Shannon's *The Decline of American Communism: A History of the Communist Party of The United States Since 1945* (1959) serves a related function when this historical study encounters speculations by the novel's protagonist, Daniel Isaacson, about the political myths usually accepted by his parents and their associates (294-95). The text of Nathaniel Weyl's *Treason: The Story of Disloyalty and Betrayal in American History* (1950) is used similarly (183-84) to provide background for Daniel's thinking about the crime of which his parents were accused: Was it treason? Conspiracy? Non-conformity? Weyl's verifiable text about the legal definition of treason provides the intertext. In Coover's novel, the intertext for this discussion is the Constitution of the United States, which is quoted and analyzed in terms of its legal interpretations by Coover's character Richard M. Nixon (76-77). The words of the Constitution are verifiable, and the legal interpretation probably is too, but even without such verification it sounds authoritative. On the other hand, these words are uttered by an indisputably fictional character, even if the character shares many traits with a former Vice-President (1953-1961) and President (1969-1973) of the United States. The verifiable and the fictional thus encounter each other productively. The same may be said when Doctorow invents *Spies on Trial* by Sidney P. Margolis to represent the conservative interpretation of the Isaacson case and *The Isaacson Tragedy* by Max Krieger to represent the liberal side. The second title probably signals its fictionality to the reader by using the names of Doctorow's fictional characters, but the author of the invented book still sounds enough like the liberal newspaper columnist Max Lerner to make such an identification somewhat complicated. It is probable that, as far as most readers are concerned, the two invented books are just as effective intertexts as the actual books by Carr and Shannon that could be fetched from the library and toted home. In the same way, Richard Nixon and his audience, Uncle Sam, probably sound as capable

of interpreting the Constitution as the actual Supreme Court Justices—
Earl Warren and Chief Justice Fred Vinson—that Coover depicts in his
novel.[9]

Such intertextual encounters between the historical record and the
novelist's inventions energize both books. An especially telling case
arises when Coover's character, Richard M. Nixon, deliberates on the
Rosenbergs' guilt or innocence. As he sits on the floor of his Vice-Presi-
dential office, surrounded by most of the available documents relevant to
the case, Nixon concludes that "the Rosenbergs were guilty of something, all right, but not as charged" (367-68). In this passage a fictional
character based on an historical person engages in the form of action that
has characterized most responses to the "matter" of the Rosenbergs from
the early 1950s until the present day—interpretation. Earlier in the book,
the fictional Nixon has interpreted the case as "*a little morality play for
our generation*" (119; Coover's emphasis). In a 1995 essay, "Arbitrary
Convictions? The Rosenberg Case, the Death Penalty, and Democratic
Culture," an actual scholar, Karl E. Klare, writes with equal conviction
that "The Rosenberg case was massive, brutal act of political terrorism
carried out by the government in order, among other things, to frighten
the Left of the early 1950s into submission" (276). In Robert Coover's
view of the "matter" of the Rosenbergs, such conflicting interpretations
are only to be expected. While writing a highly negative review of Louis
Nizer's legal memoir, *The Implosion Conspiracy* (1973), Coover concedes that "Americanists . . . prefer to celebrate the [Rosenberg] case as
one more episode in the legendary watchdog exploits of the F. B. I., a triumph of Anglo-Saxon jurisprudence, a moral lesson on the virtues of the
'middle way' and the malignancy of foreign ideologies, and a touching
love story" (4). The same "facts" are available to all interpreters, including Coover, Klare, and Nizer, but their interpretations differ radically.
Even so interpretation will—must—continue.[10]

Doctorow is of a like mind on this issue. By choosing *The Book of
Daniel* for his title, first of all, he clearly intends his readers to use the
Biblical Book of Daniel as an intertext for his novel. Paul Robeson, who
figures prominently in the novel as an aesthetic and political icon of the
American 1940s, is quoted at one point singing a spiritual with the lyric,
"Didn't my lord deliver Daniel?" (143), an ironic reminder that neither
the narrator of the novel nor his Rosenberg-like parents will find deliverance. In another, discursive, section of the novel entitled, "The Nature
and Function of God as Represented in the Bible," Doctorow's narrator
establishes the relevance of this Biblical character: "Daniel is apparently
able to soften the worst excesses of the rulers against his people by
making himself available for interpretations of dreams, visions or appari-

tions in the night" (21). As in Coover's novel, *interpretation* is the key. Finally, Doctorow concludes his novel with an extensive quotation from Daniel 12: 1-4, 9 in which the ambiguity of all interpretive activities, including this conclusion, is stressed: "Go thy way Daniel: for the words are closed up and sealed till the time of the end" (319). It is only to be expected, then, that Doctorow's narrative will abound with interpretations of all kinds, an expectation strongly supported by one of Daniel Isaacson's own theories of writing narrative: "the novel as a series of analyses" (296).

Interpretations, analyses, theories—these are the paradigms by which we attempt to make sense of experience, including the form of experience that I have been calling the "matter" of the Rosenbergs. The problem is, as Coover's character Richard Nixon says, that each of these interpretations, paradigms, and analyses is "Too pat somehow" (113). Even so, as Nixon also says, we cannot help interpreting events: "After all, history is never literal. If it were, it would have no pattern at all, we'd all be lost" (203).[11] Therefore, Coover provides his own interpretation of the "matter" of the Rosenbergs by means of subtle narrative touches. For example, he juxtaposes passages from Ethel Rosenberg's letters with a diegetic account of the event. Thus, we read "I die 'with honor and dignity'—knowing my husband and I must be vindicated by history" in italics, just before we read, "Joe McCarthy is grinning broadly in frank admiration" in regular type (513). In light of this stylistic and typographical contrast, it is easy to decide—in the words of the folk song quoted by Doctorow (170)—"Which side are you on?" Coover is on that side too, as is clear when he has the Warden of Sing Sing say about Ethel, "Funny, that smile. I can still remember it. She seemed to be trying to say she forgave us for what we were unjustly doing to her. She seemed proud and sure of herself, yet frightened at the same time" (408). When the crucified Jesus encounters the historical Ethel Rosenberg in a work of fiction, the intertextual levels are assuredly rich and multiple. At the same time, the final effect is to ally us with the Rosenbergs and against the government, as Coover obviously intends. Even Nixon must agree with Coover: "Well, poor Ethel—let's face it, she hadn't had it easy either. I'd envied her her equanimity at the end: she'd died a death of almost unbearable beauty" (524).

Ethel Rosenberg's intertextual encounter with Jesus perhaps may help us appreciate Linda Hutcheon's claim, in *A Poetics of Postmodernism*, that "In Coover's *The Public Burning*, the history of the Rosenbergs' execution is mediated by many different textualized forms" (133). In addition to the legal, historical, and mythic texts that we have noted, a wide variety of intertexts drawn from American popular culture proliferate on almost every page. As we have already seen, a routine by the Marx Brothers interacts with the Rosenbergs' executions (454-56). During this same portion of the novel, this "public burning" also encounters routines by the cast of *The Jack Benny Program* (447-50) and by Edgar Bergen and Charley McCarthy (451-52). Perhaps these episodes are responsible for the criticism voiced by some reviewers that Coover's novel is "tasteless." On the other hand, Coover's evocative capturing of American culture of the early 1950s can be seen as crucial to his fictional enterprise, a fictional encounter with the—surely tasteless—electrocutions of Julius and Ethel Rosenberg a quarter century before.[12] Issues of taste aside, it is clear that Coover's narrative is brought into direct intertextual encounter with the American popular culture of those times in this section. In addition to the extended descriptions of skits and routines, briefer mentions of familiar cultural touchstones abound. Fred Astaire and Ginger Rogers are present in Times Square for the executions, as are Bud Abbott and Lou Costello, Fibber McGee and Molly, Andy Divine and Marjorie Main, and Ozzie and Harriet (425-26). This allusive inclusiveness extends beyond Bob (Hope), Bing (Crosby), and Dottie (Lamour) (427) to include

all the thrills, tears, and laughter of the acts that follow: everybody from Veronica Lake and the Duke of Paducah to Yogi Berra and the Dragon Lady. Boris Karloff and Elsa Lanchester work a Frankenstein act with all the electrical paraphernalia, then Dean (Ethel) Martin drags Jerry (Julie) Lewis around the Death House set by his lower jaw while singing "One Fine Day" from *Madame Butterfly* in a drunken falsetto. Amos 'n' Andy turn it all into a blackface minstrel show, with Kingfish doing the lawyer's part, very wily, but bungling things up as usual, then Jimmy Durante and Garry Moore come out and play it for pathos, using the letters to the children. (428)

Coover's indictment of capital punishment is patent, especially as applied in the case of the Rosenbergs, but this indictment emerges through an intertextual encounter of the "matter" of the Rosenbergs with the cultural environment in which the events occurred. From the point of view of literary realism, we should recognize that most Americans living at the time of the Rosenbrgs' executions (1953) would recognize all—or most—of Coover's allusions in this passage. Even when the novel was first published in 1977, the recognition factor would probably be very high. And if we may postulate readers as culturally alert as Coover himself, the same can be said today.

Other intertexts derived from American popular culture operate throughout *The Public Burning*, including some easily recognized films.

Nixon fantasizes about a youthful sexual encounter with Ethel Rosenberg by comparing their imaginary experience to "a movie in which Clark Gable and Claudette Colbert spent a night together in a hotel room with a blanket up between them" (318). Later on, during a conversation with Uncle Sam (332), Nixon recalls that the movie was *It Happened One Night*, one of Frank Capra's wildly popular assurances that romance can solve all social problems. Andre De Toth's *House of Wax* (1953) provides a more complex intertext not only because it belongs to the genre of horror films—an apt analogy for publicly sanctioned executions—but also because the film was released in 3-D format, thus requiring members of the audience to wear distorting paper eyeglasses—an apt analogy for Red hysteria. An elaborate description of the film's plot concludes: "Finally, of course, Sue and her boyfriend are rescued as they must be, Professor Jarrod himself perishes in his tub of hot wax, and his crazy assistant gets busted" (283)—the sort of reassuring resolution unavailable to the Rosenbergs. After one man forgets to remove his 3-D glasses in this section of *The Public Burning*, he lurches through a nightmare version of New York City that ends with his being beaten and anaesthetized by the police before they cart him away to a mental hospital (283-88). Most probably Coover intends this highly fanciful development of an actual element of early 1950s American popular culture to support his confused character's fleeting impression, "It strikes him that he is perhaps the only sane man left on the face of the earth" (287), since it is clearly Coover's view that a culture that acquiesces in the Rosenbergs' execution cannot be sane. To argue directly to this conclusion, however, is to join the hundreds of other political interpreters of the "matter" of the Rosenbergs whose interpretations multiply contentiously only to cancel each other out. By using popular culture as a fictional intertext, however, Coover can fulfill the intention that Thomas LeClair attributes to him in a 1982 article: "to defamiliarize important subjects, to break through the moderating haze of conventional wisdom and media knowledge" (6).[13] Popular films help Coover to make this breakthrough in *The Public Burning*.

High Noon (1952), directed by Fred Zinnemann, is an even more significant intertext. Coover's Chapter 16 (236-44) is entitled "High Noon" to signify parallels between the political conflict involving the U.S. government and the Rosenbergs in the historical America of 1953, and the fictional conflict between Marshal Will Kane and his adversary, Frank Miller in the cinematic town of Hadleyville. Coover sets up this intertextual encounter by presenting parts of the review of *High Noon* published in *Time* magazine (14 July 1952) typographically as a musical lyric to be sung to the tune of the title song written by Dimitri Tiomkin

(236-37), and he secures the parallel by printing some of Ned Washington's actual song lyrics later in the chapter (241). Beyond the limits of the song, Coover invokes this intertext by writing, "The lives of the A-bomb rustlers are now in the hands of that gangly wire-tough old general, Ike (Swede) Eisenhower, who's seen a lot of border action in his day, in Eisenhower's hands and the hands of the old clock on the wall" (237). By the latter detail, Coover develops another parallel—between the eighty-minute real-time limit that controls Zinnemann's film and the arguably undue haste that marked the government's march toward the executions.[14] By depicting President Eisenhower as a cowboy, Coover recalls the biographical details of Eisenhower's early life already introduced through Richard Nixon's narrative, and he reinforces an element of the fictional Eisenhower's characterization, also introduced by Nixon, the fact that *High Noon* is "one of the few [movies] that seemed to keep [Eisenhower] awake." As Nixon reports, Eisenhower "generally snored through" most other films (31). Given the dense texture of film references throughout *The Public Burning*, Eisenhower's usually sleepy response can only count against him in the reader's judgment. And yet this "cowboy" President functions as adversary to the Rosenbergs, just as Marshal Kane does to Frank Miller in *High Noon*. As Coover problematizes the intertextual encounter, however, the reader is encouraged to transpose the film's poles of value. Are the Rosenbergs more like Frank Miller, Coover asks, or more like Will Kane?

Coover also draws intertexts from the field of American drama. Richard Nixon recalls his youthful appearance as, appropriately enough, the District Attorney in *The Night of January 16th*, a courtroom drama written, appropriately enough, by Ayn Rand (120-21). Nixon reads in Ethel Rosenberg's FBI file that she appeared as the sister of a man unjustly executed in a play entitled *The Valiant* (110-11). Even more significantly Arthur Miller's play, *The Crucible*, functions as a continuing intertext. As *The Oxford Companion to American Literature* economically explains, this celebrated drama "treat[s] the Salem witch trials of 1692 as a parable for America during the era of McCarthyism, as the play probes into the problems of individual conscience and guilt by association."[15] This characterization is accurate, as Coover's direct quotations from the play (103, 107, 490) demonstrate, especially the Reverend John Hale's hysterical observation that "No man may longer doubt the powers of the dark are gathered in monstrous attack upon this village. There is too much evidence now to deny it!" (103). Coover clearly intends his readers to hear the voices of Judge Kauffman, President Eisenhower, and J. Edgar Hoover in concert with Hale's. The parallel is made explicit when Nixon first thinks that tickets to *The Crucible* might be an ideal thirteenth wedding anniversary gift for his wife, Pat, and then decides fearfully, "but we couldn't risk giving it any kind of official sanction, and besides, Edgar was probably photographing the audience for his files" (202). Ethel Rosenberg also dreams of going to see this play (99), but in Coover's narrative the only actual spectator is Arthur Miller himself, who sits in the Martin Beck theater alone watching the play while the carnival of the public burning goes on outside the theater (490).

Books of various sorts supply other intertexts in Coover's novel. *The Power of Positive Thinking* by Norman Vincent Peale (11) probably functions primarily to create verisimilitude, as in Coover's citations of popular figures like Nat King Cole (280) and Doris Day (287) elsewhere. The same may be said for the parodic speech delivered by the Nobel prize-winning "Billy" Faulkner to the crowd assembled for the executions (420-21). However, Coover's most sustained use of a literary intertext involves the works of Horatio Alger, Jr. Richard Nixon is the source of most of these references, but Uncle Sam tells Nixon that Julius Rosenberg read Alger as a child (92), and *Time* magazine applauds Nixon for his Horatio-Alger-like rise in the world (295). *Time*'s characterization is so accurate that Nixon habitually invokes Alger's name to explain all sorts of things: the streets of New York City (181), a little boy with a runny nose (209), a quotation that he just can't get out of his mind—"Over and over again, I shall sob out the last heartbroken wracking good-byes and reel" (434). More of Nixon's Algerine analogies concern the Rosenbergs, however, as when he speculates on Ethel Rosenberg's upbringing (315) or when the Rosenbergs' older son succeeds in the fifth grade: "Was he on his way to a Horatio Alger-like career, too?" (297). The apartment in which Julius grew up was "Like something out of a Horatio Alger story, except that Harry [Julius's father] was a socialist. . . . Also, Judaism was not the prevailing faith of the Alger heroes" (129). According to Nixon, Alger Hiss was like "the millionaire gone sour in the Horatio Alger novels, the evil nephew trying to con his rich uncle out of his cousin's inheritance, the wily traitor in a plain respectable man's troubled business. Rosenberg, on the other hand, had been born into a true Horatio Alger family, poor but honest, he should have made a fortune" (303-04). Naturally, Nixon agrees with *Time* about his own Algerine credentials, and even uses this parallel (259) to ally himself with President Eisenhower, whom he usually detests. Obviously Coover shares F. Scott Fitzgerald's and Nathanael West's familiarity with the works of Horatio Alger, Jr., and also their confidence that this familiarity may be exploited intertextually to create a more perfect union with American readers.

Doctorow also shares a pattern of intertextual allusion with Fitzgerald—at least as far as Hopalong Cassidy is concerned. At the turn of the century, a young Jay Gatz read books about Hopalong Cassidy's exploits and used the back of one to record his list of life resolutions. In the early 1950s, Daniel Isaacson and his sister, Susan, watch Hoppy on TV (157-58). Of course, Hopalong Cassidy is not Doctorow's only effort to provide a cultural intertext for his treatment of the "matter" of the Rosenbergs. Like Coover, Doctorow often resorts to Whitmanesque listings of cultural touchstones: Marlon Brando, Babe Ruth, Shirley Temple, FDR, Marilyn Monroe, Mickey Mouse, Fred Allen, Susan B. Anthony, Paul Robeson, Sammy Baugh, Calvin Coolidge, Wendell Wilkie, Elvis Presley, *Gone with the Wind* (150). Doctorow resembles Coover also in his use of actually published texts. As we have seen above, Doctorow introduces real books about American leftist politics and fictional books about the Isaacsons into his narrative. He also compiles a list of reliable liberal touchstones at one point: *Jews without Money* by Michael Gold, *The Iron Heel* by Jack London, *State and Revolution* by V. I. Lenin, *Gene Debs, The Story of a Fighting American* by Herbert Marais and William Cahn, *The Price of Free World Victory* by Henry A. Wallace, *The Great Conspiracy* by Michael Sayers and Albert E. Kahn, and *Who Owns America* by James S. Allen (129). These titles seem to be arranged in descending order of familiarity, but it is likely that most readers will recognize one or more titles or authors in any case, and they will consequently understand the narrow mindset of the FBI agents who confiscate all of these books as evidence of the Isaacsons' subversive tendencies. This understanding will then probably extend to the longish quotation from *The Story of the Five Year Plan,* a Soviet children's book by M. Ilin, which follows this list (129-30). Surely few readers will have actually read this book. Perhaps, we may conjecture, Doctorow just made it up! Because of the convincing context that Doctorow establishes beforehand, however, such doubts probably never take shape. *The Story of the Five Year Plan* thus ends up sounding plausible as part of this fictional world, along with Paul Robeson and *Jews without Money*—and that is the purpose of Doctorow's carefully constructed intertext.[16]

Whatever they might know about the works of M. Ilin, Doctorow's probable readers in 1971 could be expected to know that *Franny and Zooey* (1961) was an actual book by J. D. Salinger, about the unusually close brother and sister named in the title. Therefore, when Daniel recalls that he was forcibly separated from Susan on opposite sides of a public orphanage during their childhood, it makes perfect sense that he should entitle the sad memory, "Alone in the Cold War with Franny and Zooey" (177). These same readers would surely know about Martin

Ritt's 1965 film about Cold War espionage, *The Spy Who Came In from the Cold,* starring Richard Burton. However, just as the privileged Glass children are unlike the Isaacson children because they live more or less happily with their secure parents in Salinger's book, so the sad fact of life for the Isaacson family is that "life is never [as] well plotted" as in Ritt's film (277). In other words, Doctorow's intertexts must often be read as encountering his diegetic narrative ironically. Looking for irony is certainly the most effective approach to Doctorow's supposedly indifferent accounts of exquisitely cruel methods of capital punishment, including: drawing and quartering (86), smoking (122), knouting, and burning at the stake (143-44). Typically, Doctorow supports his discussion of knouting with references to *Traveling Sketches in Sweden and Russia* by Sir Robert Porter and *Arakcheev Grand Vizier of the Russian Empire* by Michael Jenkins. The horror of contemporary death by electrocution is obviously the moral intended by these cool but horrifying historic accounts of man's inhumanity to man.

As *Franny and Zooey* and *The Spy Who Came In from the Cold* demonstrate, Doctorow contextualizes his narrative through references to the world in which it was published as well to as the world in which the Isaacsons were executed. While it is apparent that Coover expects his readers to bring their knowledge of post-Rosenberg Nixon and America to bear while reading his account of the American 1950s,[17] the conjunction of past and present is even more important to Doctorow. Daniel is the son of leftist American activists, and he is a similar activist himself. Perhaps for this reason, Daniel is beaten by police during the March on the Pentagon in October 1967: "Daniel drank his own blood. It was Pentagon Saturday night. He swallowed bits of his teeth. And he was lifted by the limbs and he was busted on Pentagon Saturday Night" (273). It is important therefore that Daniel encounter historical persons known to have been present on that historically significant occasion. Daniel's thesis advisor, Professor Sukenick, is in Washington for the March, but so are Dr. Benjamin Spock, Yale Chaplain William Sloane Coffin, Jr., Norman Mailer, and Robert Lowell—all characters associated with the anti-war movement in the public mind at the time Doctorow's book was published and all easily traceable today through news banks or books like Norman Mailer's *The Armies of the Night.*[18] Doctorow intends Daniel's experience during the March on the Pentagon to interact with the experience of earlier American leftists, including his parents who are modeled on the Rosenbergs. To establish this parallel, Doctorow has Artie Sternlicht, spokesman for the politics of the 1960s, say, "You want to know what was wrong with the old American Communists? They were into the system. . . . They thought politics is something you do at a meeting" (166). While Sternlicht's insight is perhaps valid, Paul Isaacson demonstrates a foolish idealism that might be articulated by almost any visionary of the 1960s while standing outside a factory during the 1930s distributing pamphlets: "The people are uniting, offering a common front against the spread of Fascism" (210). In the same way, it is probably true, as Daniel says after being beaten by the police, that "It is a lot easier to be a revolutionary nowadays than it used to be" (274). Even so, Doctorow's use of history suggests that being an American revolutionary in the 1960s is no more likely to bring about substantive change than it was in the 1930s when Paul Issacson was distributing pamphlets or in the 1950s when the Rosenbergs were tried and executed.

The insoluble problems attending these political matters is most likely responsible for one of Doctorow's more radical stylistic stratagems in this novel: his decision to supply three endings. In the first, Daniel returns to the house where he lived with his parents and finds everything so much changed that there is no way for him to bring closure to his story through action (315). In the second ending, Daniel provides an account of his sister's funeral which provokes a sort of catharsis that permits him finally to mourn (315-18). In the third ending, student activists shut down the Columbia University Library in which Daniel has been composing his narrative, his "Book of Daniel" (318). Since this last ending combines political activity with profound ambiguity—what does the closing of the Library actually mean in terms of the Isaacsons/Rosenbergs?—it is not only the last ending but also the most appropriate. It is also Doctorow's testimony to the difficulties inherent in his subject. Because the Rosenberg case is so complex, it can be narratized only through some radical imaginative leap, even if the writer takes advantage of all the intertexts in the world.[19]

This discovery is consistent with Linda Hutcheon's view in *A Poetics of Postmodernism*: "those uninnocent, paradoxical historiographic metafictions situate themselves within historical discourse, while refusing to surrender their autonomy as fiction. And it is a kind of seriously ironic parody that often enables this contradictory doubleness: the intertexts of history and fiction take on parallel status in the parodic reworking of the textual past of both the 'world' and literature" (124). Desperate cases require desperate measures, such as Coover's making Uncle Sam a fictional character or using actual details recounted in Richard M. Nixon's self-serving memoir, *Six Crises* (1962), to develop the character of the fictional Richard M. Nixon in *The Public Burning* (1977).[20] In fact, both Coover and Doctorow adopt highly ingenious forms of alternative stylistics. Doctorow has Daniel describe the party that took place after his parents' conviction:

After the sentence was passed there was a big party. At the party, drinking champagne, was Judge Barnet Hirsch, defense attorney Jacob Ascher, Robert Lewis the son of Ascher's former law partner, the writers Margolis and Krieger (who got drunk and sang the *Internationale*), the Jewish prosecuting attorney Howard "Red" Feuerman, the President of B'nai B'rith, Thomas Flemming known as Talking Tom because he testified for the government at no less than four different spy trials, Boris Brill the famous anti-Communist expert, Mindish, and my parents. A late arrival who came to pay his respects was V. Molotov. (244)

Since this guest list mixes actual authors with invented ones and historical characters with characters invented by Doctorow, it perfectly epitomizes his technique in *The Book of Daniel*, perhaps especially so since no corresponding event—however displaced—appears in the historical records. By an equally radical stylistic device, Coover breaks up his narrative with three Intermezzos, the first a blank verse conflation of Dwight Eisenhower's 19 May 1953 radio address to the nation and his 20 January 1953 Inaugural Address (149-56),[21] the second a "Dramatic Dialogue by Ethel Rosenberg and Dwight Eisenhower" composed of published documents (247-54), and the third "A Last-Act Sing Sing Opera" featuring both Rosenbergs, Federal Prisons Director James V. Bennett, and a supporting cast of minor voices (381-94). Style so radical draws attention to itself as a means of alerting readers to the complex issues underlying a narrative. Quite obviously this is the kind of style that is adopted by both Coover[22] and Doctorow in their efforts to convey the "matter" of the Rosenbergs. As a result, the original, textualized, historical "matter" of the Rosenbergs and the political environment in which these two people were embedded thus ends up encountering the highly ingenious narratives composed by Doctorow and Coover intertextually, within the even wider intertext constituted by the American culture which the Rosenberg case can be understood both to epitomize and to challenge.

PART II

INTERTEXTUAL ENCOUNTERS IN FILM

In a 1997 article in *Film Criticism* Walter Metz clearly presumes the efficacy of intertextual film criticism in his essay, "Toward a Post-Structural Influence in Film Study: Intertextuality and *The Shining*." In light of the points I wish to raise in this section of the book, it is probably less important that the films Metz discusses—*Bigger Than Life* (1956), *Psycho* (1960), and *The Shining* (1980)—actually relate to one another in the ways that he claims as that making intertextual cinematic connections of this sort can be taken as an assumed critical good in 1997. Given the approach that I have adopted in this book, I might naturally be expected to agree that such assumptions are valid, and I accordingly make three sorts of intertextual assumptions about films in the following three chapters.

One assumption is that some films deliberately carry on an intertextual dialogue with the literary sources on which they are based, rather as *The Book of Daniel* and *The Public Burning* interact with the textual matter of the Rosenberg case. Any filmgoer can easily supply a long list of supporting examples, ranging from *The Grapes of Wrath* (1940) and *Beloved* (1998) to *Gone with the Wind* (1939) and *Peyton Place* (1957). It is probably only to be expected that the first examples that leap to mind are movies based on novels. As Brian McFarlane explains in his book, *Novel to Film*, "As soon as the cinema began to see itself as a narrative entertainment, the idea of ransacking the novel—that already established repository of narrative fiction—for source material, got underway, and the process has continued more or less unabated for ninety years" (6-7). The process has, as one might predict, resulted in both successes and failures. Jeffrey Sapperstein, for example, speaks for many in writing negatively about Barry Levinson's 1984 film adaptation of Bernard Malamud's 1952 novel, *The Natural*: "Where Malamud keeps carefully intact the fine line between desire and achievement, Levinson obscures the difference and falls back on the most meretricious means of persuasion—slow motion and Randy Newman's uncharacteristically pious soundtrack" (84). Again I would suggest that the central issue is not so much the accuracy of this particular film critic's judgment as the intertextual assumptions that underlie his deliberate moving back and forth from film to novel and vice versa.

One especially ripe opportunity to test such assumptions about the intertextual relations between novels and their filmed adaptations is provided by the many cinematic versions, filmed between 1904 and 1995, of Nathaniel Hawthorne's 1850 romance, *The Scarlet Letter.* Mark Axelrod explains in a 1996 essay, "It would appear . . . that particular texts are preferable for standardization and exploitation within the Hollywood film industry because of the way they are written" (204). Hawthorne's classic work of fiction certainly supports Axelrod's inference. From "artistic" silents, through studio entertainments obviously aimed at a mass audience, high-minded public television productions, and European art films, all the way down to a starring vehicle for Demi Moore, Hawthorne's romance has elicited many sweet and sour echoes. Since each film version also clearly echoes its contemporaneous culture, intertextualities multiply richly.

Films can also carry on other sorts of intertextual dialogues, including those with what we must call film genres. Many critics reject the very concept of film genres, arguing that the specific examples on which any generic definition is based must themselves have been originally selected because of their presumed correspondence to some (unstated) a priori definition. Even so, other critics (including me) operate as if film genres may be assumed and used provisionally—even if they are epistemologically open to strong contestation. Andrew Tudor, for one, writes that "We can only meaningfully talk of, for instance, an *auteur* breaking the rules of the *genre* if we know what these rules are" (122). Clive Thomson seems to make greater concessions to the doubters while still accepting that genres exist: "Genres, therefore, . . . are not to be viewed as abstract constructs but as literary forms closely influenced and determined by historical forces" (35). Since Thomson's remark arises in the context of his explication of Mikhail Bakhtin's critical ideas, it might be useful to say that many intertextual encounters between individual films and the film genres to which they seem to belong can best be described in Bakhtinian terms. As Thompson explains: "Bakhtin maintains . . . [that] each new example of a given generic type is in fact a new performance, a new text, a new event. . . . The implications of such an epistemological position for genre study should be clear: the validity of abstract generic typologies that hypostasize a group of texts synchronically is denied in favour of a diachronic perspective where the operative factor is transformation" (32). Most especially when the "new performance" seeks to vary the genre in some significant way—as by changing the gender of the principal actors—rich Bakhtinian intertextual dialogue results.

This is John Cawelti's point in his 1997 essay, "The Question of Popular Genres Revisited," where Cawelti writes: "One of the most significant recent phenomena to emerge in connection with these developments is what might be called the regendering and reethnicizing of contemporary popular genres. What I'm referring to here is the tendency of current popular writers to take genres that used to be largely oriented to white male fantasies and rewrite them with women, African American, and ethnic hero-heroine figures" (80). As most film critics recognized in 1991, *Thelma & Louise*, written by Callie Khouri and directed by Ridley Scott, performs such a generic transformation. Reading this film against the intertexts provided by the traditional "white male fantasies" enacted by the genre composed of male-buddy road-pictures therefore provides new insights into *Thelma & Louise* and into the film genre to which it eccentrically belongs.

Still a third form of intertextuality develops when a cinematic text ostentatiously advertises its own textuality. Such advertisements have long been common in popular films. Bob Hope and Bing Crosby, for example, were highly self-referential during the 1940s in their "road" pictures with Dorothy Lamour, as when Hope says to Crosby early in *The Road to Morocco* (1942), "I'll lay you eight to five that we'll meet Dorothy Lamour." Woody Allen's *Stardust Memories* (1980) tells the story of Sandy Bates, a short, balding, Jewish maker of highly successful comic films who wants to be taken more seriously as a cinematic artist, along the lines of his heroes, Federico Fellini and Ingmar Bergman. Since Bates was created and played by Allen, whose own professional situation in 1980 closely approximated Sandy's, the self-referential intertext was obvious to most viewers. Rob Reiner's 1984 parodic documentary, *This Is Spinal Tap*, also insistently demanded that viewers compare the film on the screen, recounting the exploits of a fictitious rock band called Spinal Tap, to similar films like Martin Scorsese's *The Last Waltz* (1978), which recounted the last concert of a rock band called The Band. Christopher Ames discusses other examples of this sort of cinematic intertextuality in his book, *Movies about the Movies* (1997). As Ames shows, films like *A Star Is Born* (1937, 1954), *Sullivan's Travels* (1941), and *Singin' in the Rain* (1952), deliberately highlight their representations of the very Hollywood film industry responsible for their production and release. The results are thus highly intertextual

The two "Hollywood Pictures" that I wish to discuss in the third chapter of this section follow equally self-referential strategies. When films take filmmaking as their principal subject, viewers are required to bring all their previous experience of filmgoing to bear on the present case. We have all seen enough films about Hollywood to know—or think we know—how the great studios operated, how movie careers are developed, and how movies are made. We are thus prepared—even compelled—to compare any new film on this subject to what we have learned from our prior cinematic experience. That is to say that viewing such a film necessarily involves our recognition of the allusive, intertextual, self-referential dimensions of the present cinematic text. Joel and Ethan Coen's *Barton Fink* (1991), for example, enters into a complex intertextual dialogue with all the films we have all seen already about "Hollywood" as well as with the American culture for which Hollywood functions metonymically. Robert Altman's *The Player* (1992) maintains this same intertextual dialogue and also extends it to include the cult of mediated culture that constitutes the discourse of contemporary American popular culture. Both of these films also engage in technical intertextuality by reproducing metadiegetic films within their primary diegeses.

Thinking about the highly varied intertextualities apparent in these films can, perhaps, help us think more productively about these films, their relations to the medium of film more generally, and our relations as viewers to all of these entities.

4

THE SCARLET LETTER ON FILM:
NINETY YEARS OF INTERTEXTUALITY

Upon its release in 1995, Roland Joffé's filmed version of *The Scarlet Letter*, starring Demi Moore, received nearly universal condemnation from reviewers of all persuasions.[1] In *Entertainment Weekly*, Owen Gleiberman spoke for many popular reviewers in calling the film a "clunky, dawdling literal-minded . . . movie that doesn't so much adapt the book as give it an expensive makeover" (44). In other words, the 1995 *Scarlet Letter* is glitz rather than substance. In *Newsweek*, David Ansen agreed that the film is awful, but for different reasons. Ansen objected that, in his "stupifyingly wrong-headed movie," Joffé anachronistically "pillories his 17th-century villains on the rack of 1990s sexual politics" (87). The generally outraged tone adopted by these popular reviewers was wittily echoed by Anthony Lane. Writing in *The New Yorker*, Lane explained that Joffé's opening credit claiming that the film was "freely adapted from the novel by Nathaniel Hawthorne" should have been extended to read "in the same way that methane is freely adapted from cows" (114). More seriously disposed reviewers raised more serious objections. The conservative political columnist Linda Chavez, for example, concluded that "The film version of *The Scarlet Letter* is a perfect Hollywood amorality tale for our time" (13A). From a more hieratic aesthetic viewpoint, James M. Welsh concluded in *Literature/Film Quarterly* that Joffé's film is "an insult to literature of the highest order" (299).

The unusual unanimity among these critics would seem to raise several questions about the suitability of Nathaniel Hawthorne's 1850 romance for cinematic representation. One especially challenging question is why anyone would dare to make a movie in the first place out of the book that Sacvan Bercovitch called in 1991 "our most enduring classic" (xxii). Jean Normand offers a provocative answer in his much earlier (1970) study of Hawthorne, when he writes that "Hawthorne invented the visual techniques of the cinema on a literary level before the camera even existed" (311).

The text of *The Scarlet Letter* forcefully supports Normand's argument. The narrative proper opens with a chapter entitled "the Prison

75

Door," which provides a detailed picture of the people of seventeenth-century Boston, their clothing, their public institutions, their landscaping, and their physical relations to an exhaustively described prison door. The visual setting for the main characters' entrances is thus pre-established as in a film scenario. Twenty-four chapters later, the romance ends with a precisely drawn picture of a gravestone and its heraldic carving. No human characters are present as the novel fades to black with the words "ON A FIELD, SABLE, THE LETTER A, GULES." In between these pictures, there are several striking visual tableaus: Hester on a raised scaffold, holding the infant Pearl, with Dimmesdale looking down from a balcony and Chillingworth looking up from ground level; Hester, Pearl, and Dimmesdale, hand in hand on the scaffold at midnight, as Chillingworth looks up at them; Dimmesdale dying in Hester's arms in an ironic pieta framed by Pearl and Chillingworth. These are the three great scaffold scenes that prompted Malcolm Cowley to call *The Scarlet Letter* a play in five acts.[2] Obviously these scenes are equally well suited to treatment on film. This list of cinematic opportunities could easily be expanded: Chillingworth's visit to Hester in prison in Chapter 4; Hester and Pearl's visit to Governor Bellingham's mansion in Chapters 7-8; Hester and Pearl's walk along the seashore in Chapter 14; Hester's meeting with Dimmesdale in the forest in Chapters 17-19; Chapter 21, called "The New England Holiday." It would appear that Normand is more than correct about Hawthorne's cinematic potential. At least a surprising number of film-makers have arrived at this conclusion, some long before Roland Joffé (b. 1945) and Demi Moore (b. 1962) came along. And yet, each of these film-makers finally discovered a different story in Hawthorne's book, and each felt called upon to enhance even this story with extra-textual characters, incidents, and themes. Reviewing these films helps us to see how successive generations have intertextually revisioned Hawthorne's work in accord with the values and prejudices of their own times.

According to Julian Smith, there were at least five silent screen adaptations of *The Scarlet Letter* "stretching back to 1904" (108). Little documentation exists about the first three adaptations,[3] and the 1917 William Fox production, directed by Carl Harbaugh and starring Mary Martin, was the first to receive much critical attention. A 16 February 1917 reviewer in *Variety* apparently found this version rather subdued, resulting in a judgment that the film was acceptable if unexceptional. However, this reviewer may have established a dangerous precedent by suggesting that Hawthorne's story should have been expanded for the cinema: "A wide latitude could have been employed in the witchery or witchcraft scenes from the early Puritanical days that the tale speaks of to make this picture outstanding. . . . It would seem 'The Scarlet Letter' could have been made 'big' if there had been less fidelity to the story and more attention to possibilities." It would be nearly eighty years before Roland Joffé doggedly followed this advice in his much-condemned 1995 version.

In the next version historically—the much-admired 1926 silent film featuring Lillian Gish as Hester—the director, Victor Seastrom,[4] followed Hawthorne's lead in downplaying the resonances of the Salem Witch trials. Perhaps as a result, a contemporaneous review in *The New York Times* (8 Aug. 1926) by Mordaunt Hall called this picture "as faithful a transcription of the narrative as one could well imagine." While conceding that *The Scarlet Letter* was "not a hot weather picture," *Variety* (11 Aug. 1926) agreed that the film was "gripping," because "the story would make it that." Even a half-century later, Mark W. Estrin writes in *The Classic American Novel and the Movies* that this version "entertains by providing bright images to remember—particularly in Gish's luminous performance" (29). And, according to Pauline Kael, Gish's Hester "is one of the most beautifully sustained performances in screen history—mercurial, delicate, passionate" (345).

Despite most reviewers' praise of Lillian Gish and some reviewers' praise of Seastrom's textual fidelity, the film's scriptwriter, Frances Marion, must be conceded to have expanded Hawthorne's original narrative. Chiefly, the additions concern a comic subplot involving the textually derived Mistress Hibbins and the purely invented Giles the barber. In this version, Mistress Hibbins serves to articulate the most censorious female attitude toward Hester. Since, as Hall wrote in the *Times*, Lillian Gish's performance provides "an excellent conception of the courage of a young woman in the face of sneering, scorn and tittle-tattle," we can easily imagine that Hibbins would win few viewers' hearts. Thus, Giles seems justified when he contrives to get Hibbins into the sort of trouble with the authorities that results in her ducking in the village pond.

Even if we are fairly sure that this ducking episode does not appear in Hawthorne's book, we may begin to feel that there is some basis for the reviewers' overall statements about Seastrom's version. In the judgment of the *Times*, "The prudery of the ignoble bigots in Puritanical days is adroitly put forth in this picturization," while *Variety* affirms that the film makes "a strong plea against intolerance, for it makes the laws of the Colonies seem highly ridiculous and laughable, as judged by our present day standards." Then, again, we may suspect that this is not exactly what Hawthorne's *Scarlet Letter* goes to show after all. Perhaps we may remember the judgment of Hawthorne's narrator that the Puritan elders "had fortitude and self-reliance, and, in time of difficulty or peril, stood up for the welfare of the state like a line of cliffs against a tempestuous tide" (238). Perhaps we will then conclude that reviewers of the 1926 film were responding to the values of their own anti-Puritanical times— the 1920s of H.L. Mencken and *The Sun Also Rises*—rather than to the times of the Puritans or of Hawthorne's America. Perhaps we will finally agree with Kael that Marion's script is less an "adaptation" of the book than a "diminution" (345).

This would seem to be the case also of the next filmed version of the romance, the 1934 talkie directed by Richard G. Vignola, with Colleen Moore as Hester and Henry B. Walthall reprising his 1926 role as Chillingworth.[5] In this version, Hawthorne's text is also expanded by a comic subplot, here the Miles-Standish-John-Alden-like courtship of Abigail Crakstone by Samson Goodfellow and Bartholomew Hockline. The widow Crakstone here fulfills the function assigned to Mistress Hibbins in the previous version, that of articulating female criticism of Hester. Admittedly, this function is textually derived. When Hester first appears before the people of Boston in Hawthorne's second narrative chapter, an "autumnal matron" articulates the feelings of the "wives and maidens" in the crowd that the magistrates have been too lenient in forcing Hester merely to wear a scarlet letter on her bosom. "At the very least," this woman says, "they should have put the brand of a hot iron on Hester Prynne's forehead. Madam Hester would have winced at that" (51). This lack of sympathy from most members of her own gender is another sword in Hester's heart both in Hawthorne's romance and in these two filmed versions. In Vignola's film the lack of sympathy is exacerbated by Crakstone's obnoxious children, Diggery and Humility, who persecute Pearl, knock her down, and throw mud at her and her mother.

Just as Mistress Hibbins's intolerance was opposed by the more forgiving male heart of Giles the barber, so Crakstone and her crone-like associates are balanced somewhat by Bartholomew, who even gets to articulate a line attributed to "a young wife" in Hawthorne's text (51): "[L]et her cover the mark as she will, the pang of it will be always in her heart." This change typifies the war-between-the-sexes tone of the 1934 version. Although Bartholomew offers to intercede for his friend Samson with Abigail Crakstone, Bartholomew has no personal romantic designs on the widow's heart. He is happy in his bachelor life, as happy perhaps as Oliver Hardy, whom the actor Alan Hale physically resembles. In fact, the comic by-play between the looming Hale and the diminutive William Kent, who plays Samson, closely resembles the routines with which Laurel and Hardy were accustomed to amuse audiences in the early 1930s.[6] As in the Laurel and Hardy shorts also, the "boys" are continually menaced and browbeaten by the more mature women. After Bartholomew is dragooned into proposing to the widow Crakstone, he immediately becomes henpecked, followed to the tavern by his soon-to-be stepson Diggery and threatened with the displeasure of his wife-to-be. The sailors who represent a wild alternative to the Puritan community in Hawthorne's text here commiserate with a fellow male caught in the trammels of domesticity. As a reviewer for *Variety* (25 Sept. 1934) concluded, "Another venerated classic is wrecked on the rocks of comic relief."

Colleen Moore's Hester fits into the gender patterns of the 1930s as well as the beleaguered males. Perhaps for this reason, the *Variety* review continues that "It would be difficult to imagine a more happy choice for Hester than Colleen Moore." She is all melting eyes and nurturing instincts. Moore's successful silent screen experience is evident in the long, full-screen close-ups with which she greets bad news—Chillingworth's promise to identify her lover, for example, or Bellingham's plan to remove Pearl from Hester's custody and turn her over to the widow Crakstone. When Dimmesdale says to Hester, "We must marry," Moore's Hester replies as Joan Crawford might, "No, Arthur, it cannot be. . . . Our lives must be a living penance." Later, when a dying woman named Allison apologizes to Hester for years of intolerance, the 1934 heroine dismisses her guilty confession with, "Oh, hush!"[7]

Because of the mushy center at the heart of her character, this Hester does not command Dimmesdale to intercede with Bellingham to keep Pearl with her mother. Hawthorne's Hester says, "Look thou to it! I will not lose the child! Look to it!" (113). The Vignola/Moore Hester only looks beseechingly. This Hester also does not say to Dimmesdale in the forest, "Preach! Write! Act! Do any thing, save to lie down and die!" (198), because such decisiveness might strike a too Jean-Arthurish tone. Vignola's Hester does say—more or less textually—to Dimmesdale, "You shall not go alone!" (Cf. 198), but she says it with fluttering eyelashes and with romantic string music in the background.

In other words, this is not exactly Hawthorne's story either, and not only because of the interpolated characters and subplot. This is a *Scarlet Letter* for the mid-thirties, as close to a romantic comedy as the material will allow. Even Pearl, played by Cora Sue Collins, comes across as a b-grade Shirley Temple. Imagine what Vignola and Moore could have done if only Dimmesdale didn't have to die in the end! It will be another sixty years before Roland Joffé and Demi Moore decide that he doesn't have to die after all.

The gender conflicts handled so conventionally in Vignola's *Scarlet Letter* reappear in a more politically aware form when Hawthorne's romance next undergoes cinematic representation in Wim Wenders' 1972 German version, *Der Scharlachrote Buchstabe*. As would be appropriate at that time, Hester's situation takes on gender-inflected counter-cultural resonances. Wenders' Hester is a young, sexy, independent woman opposed by older, repressed male authority figures. Wenders' principal additions to Hawthorne's narrative support this thematic emphasis organically. As James M. Welsh explains in his *Magill's Survey of Cinema* essay, Wenders originally intended to cast the gorgeous Yelena Samarina as Hester, but the money men demanded that the starring role of Hester go to the equally gorgeous, but better known, Senta Berger. Wenders complied with their orders but cast Samarina as Mistress Hibbins. According to Welsh, whereas Hawthorne made the historical Mistress Hibbins older to suit his fictional design, Wenders made her younger.[8] Wenders also made Hibbins much dishier and gave her a slave named Sarah, played by the equally delectable Laura Currie. Since Mistress Hibbins alone among the Puritans sympathizes with Hester, Wenders creates opportunities to show at least some form of female solidarity by filming Hester, Hibbins, and Sarah together in scenes cut contrastingly against shots of the joyless, sexless, Puritan male elders.[9] The striking visuals support Wenders' vision thematically without introducing extra-textual dialogue.

That Samarina is the apple of Wenders' eye is clear when Hibbins—who seems in this version to be Bellingham's daughter rather than his sister—dons the governor's ceremonial robes and wig and parades in silence to the scaffold on which Hester has earlier stood. There she unsuccessfully attempts suicide by burning herself at the stake—without dialogue. In the following scene she does speak, relating to Chillingworth and Dimmesdale a disjointed tale about society, the prophet Jonah, and menstrual blood. Dimmesdale cannot bear to hear this speech and rushes from the room, reinforcing the viewer's sense of his weakness as a character and as a male. Later, Hibbins gets to wear her own scarlet letter to church on the occasion of Dimmesdale's election sermon, and she gets to laugh maniacally when Dimmesdale reveals the literal letter "A" on his breast. Though largely without textual basis, these developments in Hibbins's character may be seen to fit effectively into the thematic program of Wenders' film.

Thematic effectiveness is also the result of some other liberties that Wenders takes with Hawthorne's text. Because the money men also dictated that the film should be shot in Spain rather than in New England, the natural scenery available to Wenders called for some ingenious reinflections of Hawthorne's imagery. For example, after Hester is released from prison in Hawthorne's text, she goes to live in "a small thatched cottage" located "[o]n the outskirts of the town, within the verge of the peninsula, but not in close vicinity to any other habitation." This location is symbolically appropriate, Hawthorne says, because "[a] clump of scrubby trees, such as grew on the peninsula, did not so much conceal the cottage from view, as seem to denote that here was some object which would fain have been, or at least ought to be, concealed" (81). Because of his location shooting on the Spanish seacoast, Wenders was probably unable to find the right sorts of trees. Instead, he chose to situate Hester's dwelling on a hilly island. He also added a non-speaking watchman to assure that no one would breach Hester's isolation without permission of the magistrates. Clearly this location is symbolically effective. Furthermore, it creates a subtle comic opportunity when the beadle slips down this treacherous hill toward the cold water early in the film.

Another effective use of scenery occurs during the episode called by Hawthorne "A Forest Walk." The occasion is Hester's "resolve to make known to Mr. Dimmesdale, at whatever risk of present pain or ulterior consequences, the true character of the man who had crept into his intimacy" (182), that is, the fact that Chillingworth is her husband who is seeking revenge for his cuckoldry. The best place for this disclosure, Hester feels, is a secluded path in the forest. This location seems appropriate because the forest "hemmed [the path] in so narrowly, and stood so black and dense on either side, and disclosed such imperfect glimpses of the sky above, that, to Hester's mind, it imaged not amiss the moral wilderness in which she had long been wandering" (183). Without the forest primeval at his disposal, Wenders could not appropriate Hawthorne's symbolic location. Even so, he was able to represent Hester's conviction that "she would need the whole wide world to breathe in, while they talked together" (182) by means of location shots on the seashore showing the sea over Hester's shoulders and the rocky coast behind Dimmesdale. Since Hester will leave the community by sea and Dimmesdale will die ashore in the town, the shots are effective in foreshadowing the plot. The symbolism also effectively represents the wildness of Hester's character and the emotional rigidity of Dimmesdale's. All in all, Wenders makes a virtue of necessity in his use of scenery without compromising the thematic direction of Hawthorne's narrative.

Another change is more problematic since it concerns plot rather than setting. After Dimmesdale has confessed his guilt to the congregation and revealed the literal scarlet letter on his breast, he collapses. He is then carried back into the sacristy as Hester and Pearl make their way to the waiting ship. When Dimmesdale recovers from his faint, he tells the new governor, Fuller, that he can now rejoin Hester and Pearl with a clear conscience. Since Fuller has consistently articulated the most severe male judgment against Hester in this gender-inflected film, he cannot be pleased to hear that the Hester-Dimmesdale romance is about to have a happy ending. And so, he strangles Dimmesdale. The camera then cuts from the cruel and guilty Fuller to a saddened but departing Hester, and the political and gender conflicts animating the film are visually restated. Although the film might easily end with these shots, Wenders chooses to show Chillingworth and his faithful Indian companion[10] apparently returning to the wilderness. Wenders achieves thematic closure in any case.

Although *Der Scharlachrote Buchstabe* was produced in 1972, it was not released in the United States until 1978. This release date indicates that the late 1970s were flush times for *The Scarlet Letter*. Most impressively, 1979 brought an ambitious four-night, four-hour PBS filmed version of Hawthorne's romance. It would seem, however, that the primary motivation for this project did not derive from Hester Prynne or Hawthorne. As David Gelman and Cynthia H. Wilson wrote in *Newsweek* at the time, there was considerable nationalistic embarrassment in the late 1970s that all the classy television programs seemed to be made in England. As the reporters suggested in their title, this *Scarlet Letter* was intended to be a "Masterpiece of Our Own." In the end, Gelman and Wilson were willing to concede, this adaptation was "a flawed but striking production" (94). This was pretty much the opinion also of *Variety*, whose television reviewer pronounced the film "a respectable and literal, but far from compelling . . . adaptation" (11 Apr. 1979). In *The New Yorker* Michael Arlen wrote in summary: "Public television's version of 'The Scarlet Letter' was not terrible; it had a few decent moments. . . . Nor was it much good . . ." (129).

The cause of these tepid critical responses would seem to be the reverse of what damaged the Seastrom and Joffé versions. As the *Variety* reviewer explains, "Rick Hauser, the producer-director, and his adapters, Allen Knee and Alvin Sapinsley, have managed to cram all the major incidents of the novel into the latest version, but they haven't re-thought the material as a film." As a result, an excess of literal fidelity on the part of these sincere PBS adapters seemed capable of damaging a cinematic representation of *The Scarlet Letter* as much as an excess of adaptive originality on the part of others.

Whereas Seastrom's Hester counter-textually says "Hush!" to the repentant Mistress Abigail, and Joffé's Hester says to a potential rapist, "You bastard, get out!" Hauser's production is riddled with direct quotations from Hawthorne's text. This is the main problem, according to Larry Baker, who has written the most exhaustive analysis of this production. According to Baker, "The narration, dialogue, and off-camera screen directions may be the literal words of Hawthorne, but they are not Hawthorne intact" (220). Arlen objects on the same grounds that "sometimes the dialogue is genuine Hawthorne, and sometimes it is genuine television, but more often than not it is a strange composite of the two," resulting in a *Scarlet Letter* with "the stately lethargy of a becalmed galleon" (130, 129). As we might anticipate from these remarks, even textual idolatry will not necessarily produce a faithful cinematic representation of Hawthorne's work.

Baker explains that this production—like its predecessors—was too rooted in the time in which it was produced to do justice to a nineteenth-century tale about seventeenth-century characters. A "1970s American audience already saturated with supernatural motifs and radical feminism" (226) could not help revisioning in contemporary terms Hawthorne's words and the pictures they inspired. Thus, for example, the symbolic dimensions of Chillingworth's demonism tend to become literalized. Hawthorne writes that "it grew to be a widely diffused opinion [among the common people in Dimmesdale's congregation] that the Reverend Arthur Dimmesdale, like many other personages of especial sanctity, in all ages of the Christian world, was haunted either by Satan himself, or Satan's emissary, in the guise of old Roger Chillingworth" (126). In his characteristically indirect style, Hawthorne himself says nothing about Chillingworth's demonism one way or the other. As many critics—including F. O. Matthiessen and Yvor Winters—have observed, someone else always has to take responsibility for authenticating the more preternatural elements in Hawthorne's fiction.[11] Thus, when Chillingworth later discovers something on the breast of the sleeping Dimmesdale, Hawthorne's narrator slyly says, "Had a man seen old Roger Chillingworth, at that moment of his ecstasy, he would have had no need to ask how Satan comports himself, when a precious human soul is lost to heaven, and won into his kingdom" (138). The narrator will not say directly that Chillingworth is Satan or even Satan-like. An unidentified "man" might have said something like this if he had been present at the scene, but this man wasn't present, and so said nothing of the sort.[12] On screen, such indirection is impossible. Thus, as Baker explains, "a twentieth-century audience, preconditioned by a spate of cinematic demon-children, will be very apt to see Pearl as the nineteenth-century version of a child literally possessed by a literal devil, Chillingworth" (222). This would be a definite plus in a cinematic representation of *The Exorcist* but rather a disadvantage in *The Scarlet Letter*.

Other elements of the production also attracted the attention of critics. Several commented on what Gelman and Wilson called "its seemingly off-center casting" (94). Meg Foster's Hester came in for the largest share of abuse, although John Heard's Dimmesdale ran a close second. As was the case with Henry B. Walthall's 1926 Chillingworth,[13] some critics praised the acting of Kevin Conway as the possible demon and some found him definitely over the top. The television critic for *Variety* had it both ways, describing Conway as "a road company Richard III," but still calling the performance "wittily malignant, and a delight to watch." Baker sarcastically suggests that Christopher Lee would have been even better in Conway's role (226).

It is probably significant that Baker, who indicts the 1979 version most strongly for its immersion in the contemporary milieu, presents part of his criticism through an allusion to a contemporary star of b-grade horror movies. As has been true of earlier adaptations, this PBS cinematic version of *The Scarlet Letter* drew its audience appeal and its narrative defects from the same source: the contemporary scene. This is even more the case with the Joffé/Moore version.

In regard to the 1995 film's fulfillment of the developmental program first outlined in *Variety* in 1917, many reviewers were archly censorious. Beginning with the premise that "life is not long enough to watch Demi Moore playing Hester Prynne," David Denby writes that he watched only the first hour of the film. That was apparently enough: "What I saw in that dismaying and languid hour was a big swooning, 1955-style drama about repressed passion, nude bathing, and, finally, sex among the corn kernels (in the barn, you know)" (57). On a similar note, Owen Gleiberman writes that the sex-in-the-barn scene is "not the image I'll remember most. No, that would be Hester's teenage mulatto slave, who's hidden in the adjacent house, pleasuring herself in the tub as she enjoys a kinky communion with . . . a bird. A scarlet bird. You heard me" (43). One might answer Gleiberman that the mulatto slave can most likely be traced back to Wenders' film and that the bird probably derives in some strange way from Hawthorne's text. When Governor Bellingham first sees Pearl, he says, "What little bird of scarlet plumage may this be?" (109). Later, while Dimmesdale is inside delivering the Election Sermon, Pearl dances through the market place, making "the sombre crowd cheerful by her erratic and glistening ray; even as a bird of bright plumage illuminates a whole tree of dusky foliage by darting to and fro, half seen and half concealed, amid the twilight of the clustering leaves" (244). To Denby's criticism, one might answer that there was probably as much sexual repression among the Puritans as among any other group of human beings. By the same token, some sort of sex surely took place between Hester and Dimmesdale, or Pearl would not be dancing in the market place or anywhere else. At the same time, we must conclude that—any remote similarities to Hawthorne's text notwithstanding—the Moore/Joffé version is the clearest evidence to date that film-makers continually re-vision *The Scarlet Letter* in the terms provided by their own cultures.

For one thing, Joffé's Hester and Dimmesdale could have stepped right out of a music video. When, more than half-way through the film, Hester finally stands in ignominy on the scaffold, she is wearing discrete but fetching earrings and the only attractive gown in the whole community. Her trademark side-curls have returned also, canceling out the signals of childbirth sent by her stringy, damp hair in the previous scene. Hester has to look so terrific in order to get away with her speech to the Puritan elders: "I believe I have sinned in your eyes, but who is to know if God shares your views?" The same rule apparently applies in the later scaffold scene in which Dimmesdale rescues Hester from the hangman. Standing in a great looking pair of boots, using his leather gloves to brush his long, clean hair out of his eyes, Dimmesdale looks like he could front an unthreatening heavy-metal band. Instead of writhing about with a microphone, however, Dimmesdale shouts, "I love this woman. I am the father of her child, and in God's eyes, I am her husband." This is Hollywood glitz, 'Nineties style.

As the two speeches just quoted suggest, this film also provides a 'Nineties version of Christian theology. Hawthorne's Dimmesdale says to Hester in the forest, "Were I an atheist,—a man devoid of conscience,—a wretch with coarse and brutal instincts,—I might have found peace, long ere now. Nay, I should never have lost it! But, as matters stand with my soul, whatever of good capacity there originally was in me, all of God's gifts that were the choicest have become the ministers of spiritual torment" (191). The Dimmesdale played by Gary Oldman in 1995 is less bothered by spiritual issues because he is less capable of distinguishing theologically between good and evil. When Hester asks him, "Do you believe we've sinned? Dimmesdale can answer only, "I know not." Hawthorne might find Oldman/Dimmesdale's theological confusion suitable punishment for his flirtatious quip to Hester earlier in the film: "And here I thought comprehending God was going to be my greatest challenge." Clearly the film-makers feel the quip demands no punishment, since they end their film with a voice-over in which the now-grown Pearl asks, "Who is to say what is a sin in God's eyes?" One suspects that Hawthorne would happily volunteer an answer.

Then, again, Hawthorne would probably not feel comfortable on the *Oprah Winfrey Show*, as most characters in Joffé's film would. A glossy advertising insert from *Entertainment Weekly* (4 Feb. 1994) demonstrates that the television tabloid echoes are hardly accidental: "As relevant today as when Nathaniel Hawthorne wrote it almost 150 years ago, 'The Scarlet Letter' stars Demi Moore as Hester Prynne, a spirited and sensual young woman who is branded an adulteress and cast out by a harsh Puritanical society that seeks to punish her for being human. . . . 'The Scarlet Letter' is a story about the corrosiveness of fear and how it breeds racial and cultural hatred. But it is ultimately a tale of the redemptive power of love." In other words, the 1995 *Scarlet Letter* was conceived and executed as an over-long, dramatized talk show about sex, multi-cultural tolerance, and sexual politics.

The sexual aura that disturbed reviewers including David Denby and Linda Chavez is inseparable from the film. Mituba's autoerotic scene in the tub clearly derives from her spying on Hester doing the same thing earlier on. That Mituba's scene is intercut with the scene showing Hester and Dimmesdale in the barn is just as clearly intended to show that everyone in the Puritan community is doing something sexual most of the time, as American popular culture today assumes. Thus, in Joffé's film Brewster Stonehall tries to rape Hester, Chillingworth wants to sleep with Hester as soon as he returns from Indian captivity, the women of the community are interested primarily in whether a character named Mary was sexually abused during her Indian captivity, and the community elders reveal obvious sado-masochistic tendencies as they brutally question Mituba about Hester's possible involvement in witchcraft. A comparable list of sexual activities might be gleaned from the daytime television listings during sweeps week.

Joffé's film is equally up to date in terms of multiculturalism. Dimmesdale's first sermon segues easily from the need for the Puritans to establish a city on a hill to the need to love their neighbors irrespective of race or religion. Hester is unconvinced that the Algonquins really need Dimmesdale's translation of the Christian Bible or that Christian morality is superior to what the tribes already practice. In support of this suspicion, the redeemed captive, Mary, says that civilized communities can be more cruel than the Indians, a point forcefully reiterated by Chillingworth in a later scene: "I find true savagery to reside elsewhere." After these bells of multiculturalism have been appropriately rung, however, Dimmesdale engages in the climactic fight with the Indians as energetically as Burt Lancaster would.

The Puritan elders in this film see Indians, Quakers, dissenters, and independent women as variations of the same problem—nonconformity. In a totally fabricated incident, Chillingworth tells these elders that his former community in Virginia came to ruin through these agents of "Otherness," and the terrified white males accept Chillingworth's analysis without question. False charges, suborned testimony, a jack-booted posse—all the modes of phallocentric totalitarianism familiar to watchers of television documentaries—soon follow. Since none of this political subtext seriously threatens the love plot involving Hester and Dimmesdale, viewers are encouraged to condemn oppression and bask in their own unchallenged tolerance without intellectual distraction. Easy answers are Joffé's specialty.

This is true also of the film's central feminist message. The community of women embracing Hester and Mistress Hibbins is clearly preferable to the male power structure that includes Chillingworth and Governor Bellingham—as Wim Wenders has already told us. Hibbins— usually called *Harriet* in this version—naturally assists Hester during Pearl's birth, Demi Moore's most demanding, least quaffed, scene. Appropriately, Hibbins encourages Hester to sit up during the delivery, following recent female recovery of birth techniques repudiated by the male medical profession. Even among the Indians, women's greater wisdom is evident. After the captive Chillingworth goes more native than the natives, it is the elder women of the tribe who decide—in subtitles—that he should be sent back to the white community. When Dimmesdale naively assumes that some sort of accommodation can be worked out between the male elders and the women accused of witchcraft, Hester asks, "What has happened to the man I love?"

Hester is in the right, of course, as we might expect on the basis of Demi Moore's name above the film's title.[14] And yet, Hester's triumph is mixed. Despite her professed self-reliance, Hester is well on her way to being hanged when the dashingly attired Dimmesdale finally arrives to declare his love and save the day. Significantly, Hester and the other accused women are gagged as well as bound in this scene. Significantly also, final victory arrives not through Dimmesdale's confession but through the *deus-ex-machina* device of an Indian attack just at the crucial moment. Shades of *Cat Ballou!* Joffé thus both strikes a note of feminism and sings the lyrics of a violent finale, proving to his 'Nineties audience that—despite Puritanical hang-ups suggesting the contrary— you really can have it all.

In her opening day story on this film in *USA TODAY*, Susan Wloszczyna writes, "As the film's star Demi Moore has bluntly declared, 'Not very many people have read the book'" (1D).[15] As we have seen, Moore was greatly mistaken in this assumption. Ninety years of cinematic representations of *The Scarlet Letter* have clearly demonstrated that generations of directors and screenwriters have read Hawthorne's original text—and also that each has done so under the ruling assumptions of a different social context. These acts of interpretive revisioning can perhaps be better understood in light of a principle enunciated in *The Implied Reader* by Wolfgang Iser: "With all literary texts . . . we may say that the reading process is selective, and the potential text is infinitely richer than any of its individual realizations. This is borne out by the fact that a second reading of a piece of literature often produces a different impression from the first. . . . This is not to say that the second reading is 'truer' than the first—they are, quite simply, different . . ." (280-81). Following Iser, we may therefore suppose that we have not seen the last filmed version of *The Scarlet Letter*, and we may further suppose that—whether the later versions are "truer" or less "true" than their predecessors—they will be deeply rooted in their own times, and they will not exhaust the potential of Hawthorne's text.

5

GENDERING GENRE:
THELMA & LOUISE AS A FEMALE ROAD FILM

Steve Neale has very cogently observed that "Genres do not consist only of films: they consist also, and equally, of specific systems of expectation and hypothesis that spectators bring with them to the cinema and that interact with films themselves during the course of the viewing process" (160). Thus, when we go to the movies to see a Western, or a musical, or a Chuck Norris film, we enter the theater with certain expectations, based on our past experience, which will inevitably serve as an intertext for the specific film we are about to see. This sense of how genre creates various intertextualities is especially apparent in the critical reception accorded *Thelma & Louise* (1991), written by Callie Khouri and directed by Ridley Scott. When *Thelma & Louise* was released, virtually all reviewers recognized that the film derived from some readily identifiable tradition, genre, or formula. Kathleen Murphy takes the high cultural ground in *Film Comment* when she writes, "Thelma and Louise and the Thunderbird light out for the mythic territory, their trajectory as tragic and magnificent as Ahab's" (29). In *Films in Review*, Edmond Grant first compares the principal characters' odyssey to the adventures of Huckleberry Finn and Jim and then descends the cultural staircase to establish other parallels between *Thelma & Louise* and *Easy Rider* (1969). Grant warns in his review that "Just about the worst way to describe *Thelma & Louise* is to sum it up as a female 'buddy movie'" and proposes instead that we think of the film as "a road movie of a very special sort" (1461). That is to say, even in denying the validity of a generic formula, Grant encourages us to recognize this film's resemblance to movies that do conform to formulaic description. In *New Statesman & Society*, Anne Billson follows a similar line along the way to a negative conclusion: "Not only is it not controversial; it's not even terribly original. *Thelma & Louise* is a 1970s Buddy Road Movie, but with Susan Sarandon and Geena Davis instead of, say, Jack Nicholson and Warren Oates" (1463).

Kenneth Turan calls the film a "neo-feminist road movie" in his *Los Angeles Times* review. David Denby goes Turan one better in *New York* by hailing the arrival of the "first feminist buddy-buddy movie," a complex generic description rivaled perhaps only by Brian Johnson's identification of *Thelma & Louise* as an "outlaw-buddy-road movie." These positive and negative judgments demonstrate the validity of Thomas Sobchack's proposition: "Consciously or unconsciously, both the genre film-maker and the genre audiences are aware of the prior films and the way in which each of these concrete examples is an attempt to embody once again the essence of a well-known story" (103). Specifically, we may say that, like all movies, *Thelma & Louise* must be watched with a double vision that sees both the film itself and the other films it resembles and departs from. In other words, Ridley Scott's film carries on its own generic dialogue, as earlier films such as *Butch Cassidy and the Sundance Kid* (1969) did. In the case of the Khouri/Scott film, however, the dialogue is not with the Western but with the buddy film or the road picture, that is to say, with the—primarily male—narrative in which two companions abandon the constraints of civilization to "light out for the territory."[1]

The ideological underpinnings of the genre can be seen in this description by Jack Boozer: "[C]lassical outlaws of the road film begin as members of society who seek escape from or revolt against it. Their reactive travel odyssey is an effort to overcome their disenfranchised status within the community, and to locate a better alternative outside it" (189). If we add the perhaps overly-obvious addendum that this odyssey takes place outdoors, we probably know all we need to know if we are trying to determine whether a specific film belongs to this genre. *Thelma & Louise* identifies itself as a road picture even as the opening credits roll. We first hear Charlie Sexton's slide guitar on the soundtrack playing the "Badlands" theme as black-and-white shots of sky and wide open country mutate into rich color. Our initial impression is thus of unconfined space, the natural world, viewed against the sort of wailing musical background that signals regret, missed chances, paradise lost. We might be forgiven for expecting to see something like David Lynch's *Wild at Heart* (1990). We at least know that we will see some sort of road picture.

This "Badlands" theme reappears later in the film as Thelma Dickinson (Geena Davis) trots into a rural grocery store on her way to pull her first armed robbery. Crime and other antisocial activities performed against an outdoors background are the incidents defining this genre, incidents connected here by music as well as by plotting. Significantly, the musical theme appears again when Thelma and Louise Sawyer (Susan Sarandon) stop at an ostentatiously rural gas station to buy gas, not to rob the place. Out in the middle of these psychological badlands, Louise trades her watch and earrings for the elderly, white-bearded proprietor's straw cowboy hat, perhaps invoking other echoes of David

Lynch in the process. It is certain, though, that by swapping away tokens of social feminization, Louise re-enforces one of the film's gender themes, and by appropriating the classic sign of the social outsider, Louise connects this scene to the beating heart of the genre. Meanwhile, "Badlands" plays in the background.

Other examples of what Rick Altman calls the "semantic elements" of this genre appear throughout the film. Just before Thelma and Louise have their first unpleasant encounter with a swinish oil-tanker driver, the camera lovingly traces the complete outline of their green 1966 Thunderbird convertible, ending with a close-up of the model name. From its introduction in 1955, through the Beachboys' "Fun, Fun, Fun," and into the "outlaw-buddy-road movie" mythology of *Thelma & Louise*, this model of car has metonymically represented the freedom and excitement of the open American road. Whether because the brand name carries echoes of its natural wild ancestor, or because a '66 Thunderbird is "just such a bitchin' car," experienced viewers must recognize that Thelma and Louise could drive no vehicle more semantically appropriate to their generic quest.

Every time the convertible is shot from above against a ribbon of road stretching into the distance through hills or desert flatlands, these same viewers must filter the shot through so many others in so many other films derived from the same formula. As Altman writes in his essay, "A Semantic/Syntactic Approach to Film Genre," "Spectator response . . . is heavily conditioned by the choice of semantic elements and atmosphere, because a given semantics used in a specific cultural situation will recall to an actual interpretive community the particular syntax with which that semantics has traditionally been associated in other texts" (38). Driving freely and happily along is thus recognizable as a necessary syntactic link to the film's probable tragic resolution. Another familiar link appears when Louise's inspired driving allows the pair to escape temporarily from a large posse of state police cars. As the Thunderbird twists, turns, and corners with a screech of tires, members of the viewing audience cannot avoid memories of so many other chases in so many other movies, especially when the cop cars overturn to the tune of banjo music on the soundtrack, a la *Bonnie and Clyde* (1967).

At the film's end, these generic echoes return with considerable force, and with some interesting variations. Just as Huck Finn and Jim erringly go further south down the Mississippi to escape slavery in *Adventures of Huckleberry Finn*, and just as Captain America and Billy go east instead of west in search of the American Dream in *Easy Rider*, so Thelma and Louise go west instead of south to get to Mexico. It is inevitable, therefore, that their journey will end tragically, despite their temporary escape from the posse and despite the gorgeous Grand Canyon scenery that they soon enter. When a police helicopter containing Hal Slocumbe of the Arkansas State Police abruptly flies up from the canyon in front of the Thunderbird, absolute escape is clearly out of the question. Because we are probably rooting for the lovely outlaws and against the police, however, we may nurture secret hopes of some sort of escape. This is, after all, how we feel when the heroes run out with six-guns ablaze to confront overwhelming odds at the end of *Butch Cassidy and the Sundance Kid*. As in the earlier film, however, only imaginative escape is possible. With the massed forces of the law behind them and the telescopic gun-sights of the police trained on their backs, Thelma proposes to Louise that they just "keep going" over the edge into the Canyon. This is what they do. Like Butch and Sundance, they accept death rather than accommodation with the forces of society. Unlike the two cowboy bank robbers, Thelma and Louise kiss each other with tears in their eyes and join hands before meeting death. Thus, although the film clearly establishes its generic credentials, it also demands that we listen to its continuing dialogue with the genre.

One familiar semantic element of the road adventure is the central characters' conviction of transformation. Transformation occurs in *Thelma & Louise* also. As Louise tells Thelma early in the film, "Things have changed. Everything's changed." Thelma's equivalent transformation becomes clear later on when she tells Louise, "Something's like crossed over in me, and I can't go back. I mean, I just couldn't live." In this respect the two characters resemble many others who realize how good it feels to be bad only after they have violated the margins of acceptable social behavior. In terms of their motivations, however, Thelma and Louise significantly differ from the characters with whom viewers have grown familiar. Shortly before Louise announces that everything has changed, she has shot and killed Harlan Puckett, the man who was trying to rape Thelma. Just after Thelma says that something has crossed over for her, she and Louise decide to lure the offensive tanker truck driver who has subjected them to continuing verbal abuse to his well-deserved punishment. Like their generic ancestors, Thelma and Louise have been driven outside the law by the unacceptable standards of everyday society. Unlike these—usually male—predecessors, Thelma and Louise have experienced the injustices of society largely in terms of gender. As so many reviewers recognized, *Thelma & Louise* is a familiar story defamiliarized through a shift in gender. The changes in generic semantics resulting from such a shift have been less remarked upon, however, and are very important in terms of the dialogue they introduce between this film and the film genre of which it is part.

Before Harlan Puckett (Timothy Carhart) turns ugly at the Silver Bullet dance hall, he and Thelma dance romantically. At one point the camera shoots the dancing couple from behind so that we can see Harlan's arm draped possessively around Thelma's shoulder, his hand holding a beer bottle by the neck. The shot clearly signals that Harlan is some sort of jerk. When he feeds Thelma too many drinks and twirls her aggressively around in order to make her drunk, Harlan emerges as the sort of jerk who tries to take unfair sexual advantage of women. This is the message of the film's first emotional plateau when Harlan tries first to cajole Thelma and then physically to force her to have sex with him in the Silver Bullet parking lot. When Louise arrives to break up the attempted rape, her angry speech to Harlan reveals that this incident is intended to be representative rather than unique: "In the future, when a woman's crying like that, she isn't having any fun!" Louise is, of course, sincerely concerned for her friend, but by emphasizing "a woman" rather than Thelma, Louise's speech suggests the typicality of Harlan's behavior. Later on, the waitress at the Silver Bullet tells officer Slocumbe (Harvey Keitel) who is investigating Harlan's death that she hopes Harlan's wife was the murderess. The speech helps us to accommodate this man's violent death, to see his cruel behavior toward Thelma as typical of his usual dealings with women, and to suggest perhaps that Harlan is not the only man who fits in this category. Louise's continuing discourse about the law's gender bias in rape cases tends to re-enforce this last suggestion.

While Thelma and Louise sit in a coffee shop some time between the killing and the waitress's comment, the jukebox plays Tammy Wynette's version of "I Don't Want to Play House," demonstrating that sexual exploitation is a social phenomenon common enough to furnish recognizable material to popular culture. The rest of *Thelma & Louise* supports this demonstration. Thelma's husband Darryl (Christopher McDonald) is playing around with another woman long before his wife goes off with Louise. Darryl is clearly more interested in his personal appearance and his muscle car than he is in Thelma or any other woman. Consequently, the other woman in the case is never even specifically mentioned. It is consistent with these signs that when Louise calls Darryl after having been missing for several days, he ignores her voice on the telephone in order to watch a play in the football game on television. His half-hearted threat, "Get your butt back here, Thelma, now!" merely confirms what experienced witnesses like the waitress have to say about most men in the social main stream.

Even Louise's lover Jimmy (Michael Madsen), who undergoes a certain amount of personal growth in the film, is blame-worthy. When

Louise desperately calls asking Jimmy to draw out her life savings and wire them to her, she also asks him, "Do you love me?" Jimmy pauses much too long and takes a drag on his cigarette before saying that he does. As we learn from a conversation between Thelma and Louise, commitment is Jimmy's problem. Obviously, he cannot be Louise's salvation, and so the song playing on the soundtrack during this scene— "Part of You, Part of Me"—is about Louise and Thelma not about Louise and Jimmy. Jimmy *can* function to represent romantic possibilities that might ripen under other conditions, and so he says to Louise before going out of her life forever, "I just want you to be happy." When this speech is followed by a long, lingering soul kiss delivered in a public setting, we can see, perhaps, how Louise and Jimmy might have lived happily ever after in another form of heterosexual bourgeois romance. Not in this story, however, and so Jimmy is earlier shown displaying his violent temper by throwing furniture around a motel room in Oklahoma City, and he also reveals his inability to imagine that Louise could have problems that have nothing to do with their sexual relationship. This kind of male behavior, rather than the kind that only wants a woman to be happy, is apparently the social norm against which the female outlaws must define themselves.

By including Jimmy along with Darryl and Harlan, the film is able to highlight the two women against a social background rather than situating them solely in the particulars of specific sexual relations. Further support for this proposition comes from the scene in which Max, the FBI agent (Stephen Tobolowsky), advises Darryl how to keep his wife on the telephone long enough to allow the police to trace the call. "If she calls, just be gentle," Max says, "you know, like you're really happy to hear from her, like you really miss her. Women love that shit." Darryl is slime, of course, and Max is an unappealing character, especially in contrast to Harvey Keitel's character, Slocumbe. Even so, these three men bind together in this scene when Darryl wonderingly repeats Max's closing remark, "Women love that shit," and they all share a good laugh. This lack of respect across the gender line resurfaces later in the film when a brief shot of the FBI surveillance team shows one of the agents reading *Boudoir* magazine.

In the semantics of the road film, the police are stereotypically the road outlaw's adversaries and—given the audience's tendency to identify with the outlaw—the audience's adversaries. In the case of *Thelma & Louise*, the police further epitomize the more oppressive qualities of the white male power structure. As Patricia Kowal notes, most of the film chronicles "a flight from both the law and the constraints of a patriarchal society" (400)—structurally inseparable entities. Therefore, when a highway patrolman chases and catches the Thunderbird, the ensuing encounter must be inflected in terms of gender as well as of social conflict. The cop first talks to Thelma and Louise through his p.a. system rather than face to face. Then he carefully adjusts his uniform cap before swaggering toward their car. Any member of the audience might identify with the scared, confused driver in such a scene. Because of the film's systematic association of white male behavior with social oppression, however, this identification must take on gendered dimensions. Probably for this reason, Thelma and Louise are shown smiling, flirting, and looking respectfully up at the self-important bully. While he addresses the two women with a calculated "official" language, they respond with warm charm and excessive politeness. Thelma is the soul of politeness even while holding a gun on the surprised cop and forcing him to climb into the trunk of his patrol car. That this scene derives from gender politics as well as from the semantics of the genre is made clear when Thelma tells the cop to "be sweet" to his wife and children. "My husband wasn't sweet to me," she says, "and look how I turned out." Darryl and all that he stands for resonate throughout this scene. In fact, we can almost see Darryl in uniform, strutting in front of the women and then cowering in the trunk of his car. The gender message implicit in the sequence concludes with Thelma throwing the keys to the patrol car trunk off into the desert. Significantly, she "throws like a girl." No wonder the policemen in the final scene keep Thelma and Louise firmly anchored in their telescopic sights!

One other gendered variant on the road movie deserves attention. Three times during the film, Thelma and Louise encounter a disgusting, sexually abusive truck driver who makes Darryl seem like Alan Alda. The first time, Thelma has just held up the grocery store, and the two female outlaws are riding joyfully along, relishing their antisocial freedom. The second time, Thelma and Louise seem particularly well suited to the freedom of the open road as they ride along propelled by Marianne Faithful's "The Ballad of Lucy Jordan" on the soundtrack. On both occasions, the trucker violates the asexual freedom of Thelma and Louise's community with the lewdness tolerated by society as a form of "harmless sexual play." While patently offensive, this truck driver is unlikely to threaten Thelma and Louise in terms of the plot. He is too broadly defined for that. On the other hand, our past experience tells us that a minor character who has appeared twice in the film probably will acquire some greater significance later on, and he does.

Just after Thelma says, "I feel awake . . . wide awake. I don't ever remember feeling this awake. . . . Everything looks different," the truck driver appears for the third time. By this point in the film, the outlaws have realized that Slocumbe and the FBI are beginning to close in on them and that, consequently, the end of the road is approaching. As they drive on despite this realization, they appropriately bop along, head-dancing to B. B. King's version of "Better Not Look Down" on the radio. Then the trucker comes along again, shouting obscenities, making lewd gestures, illegitimately infringing on their freedom as characters in a road movie. Understandably, the two women decide to turn the tables on this chauvinist pig and coax him into a secluded side road for his due punishment. Viewers must agree that this punishment is richly deserved because they can see, as the trucker cannot, that only a lustful fool blinded by a delusion of male superiority could believe that two such gorgeous women would be sexually interested in a fat, ignorant, low-comedy stud.

When the driver sneakily removes his wedding ring before climbing down out of his rig, perhaps viewers recognize that Harlan and Darryl probably did the same thing in their roles as disgusting adulterers. When the driver refuses to apologize and instead launches a torrent of verbal obscenities, we cannot fail to remember Harlan, at least. Harlan might be alive today if he hadn't told Louise to "Suck my cock!" The last verbal straw from the driver comes when he concludes his refusal to apologize by saying, "Fuck that!" Just how common such verbal abuse is in American society is anybody's guess. That it is widespread seems certain, however, and so the two women shoot out this pig's very expensive truck tires as a legitimate balancing of the scales for many probable earlier incidents. Shooting at his truck until the gasoline explodes seems somewhat more problematic. To some, the explosion brings the episode to its dramatic and legitimate close. Others have suggested that Ridley Scott just likes big explosions and is usually willing to push any sequence over the top to get one. Until this explosion, however, there should be general agreement that Thelma and Louise's encounters with the obscene truck driver combine the generic familiarity of legitimized violence and the gendered innovation of sexual harassment as provocation.

Another generic innovation involves the women's—especially Thelma's—sexual behavior. In *The Dialogic Imagination*, Mikhail Bakhtin notes that "The road is especially . . . appropriate for portraying events governed by chance" (244). King Arthur's meeting with the Black Knight in *Monty Python and the Holy Grail* is a good illustration of Bakhtin's point, as is Ulysses' meeting with Calypso or Tom Jones's meeting with Mrs. Waters. In the last two cases—and, generically, in the road picture—male heroes encounter desirable females, largely by chance, enjoy their favors, and move on to further adventures. The woman's role is to be loved and left. When road heroes travel in male-female pairs, their roles are as a rule just as generically determined. As Jack Boozer explains: "Female road outlaws have usually been represented either as innocent girlfriends and wives, who stand beside their man and suggest the hope of peaceful family alternatives, or as *femmes fatales*, who betray the male protagonist and the family ideal out of greed" (189). When female characters enact the sexual roles usually allotted to male heroes, however, the genre is both re-enforced and challenged.

This is definitely the case when Thelma meets the hitchhiking J. D. (Brad Pitt) during a refueling stop. Just before J. D. appears, Darryl has revealed his indifference to Thelma by ignoring her voice on the telephone in favor of a televised football game, and Darryl's subsequent lame threats have provoked Thelma to uncharacteristic defiance and obscenity and to characteristic tears. Then she sees the undeniably hunky J. D. in the rearview mirror. Because viewers have sided with Thelma during her nasty marital encounter, we probably see J. D. as a viable romantic alternative for her. Louise is less starry-eyed and more aware of the problems attached to giving a single male hitchhiker a ride while fleeing the police, and so Thelma must regretfully turn down J. D.'s request. In keeping with Bakhtin's theory about chance meetings, however, the two female outlaws soon see J. D. sitting by the side of the road farther down the line. Thelma whines and pants like a puppy until Louise agrees to give J. D. a ride only as far as Oklahoma City, where they anticipate picking up the money wired by Jimmy.

Unexpectedly, Louise finds Jimmy waiting in Oklahoma City along with the money. Jimmy has extended himself considerably to get there, he is sincerely concerned about Louise, and he claims to want to help her in any way possible. Despite the temporary threat to Louise's plan posed by Jimmy's unexpected appearance in the motel lobby, then, this narrative sequence seems to be playing out positively, perhaps even with the suggestion that Jimmy can help the two women out in some more traditional (male) way. The very possibility leaves Thelma alone in another motel room with no narrative function. To fill this narrative vacancy, J. D. soon appears at Thelma's door, standing in the rain and wearing a sheepish grin. J. D. looks irresistible—and is! Thelma invites him into her motel room, and the stage is set for a female displacement of the generic sexual road encounter.

In this scene, the influence of gender is patent. Although J. D. eventually turns out to be a criminal, thief, and liar, his sexual overtures to Thelma are sweet and unthreatening. In a female re-sexualization of movie sex, the lovers begin by playing games. Smiles and laughter then give way to gentle foreplay in which Brad Pitt's body—rather than Geena Davis's—is the object of the camera's gaze. As a full body shot of J. D.'s naked upper torso and partly unbuttoned jeans pans to the bed, we see only Thelma's legs being gently extended to full length by J. D.'s hands. A brief shot of Thelma's panties confirms that they are cute rather than ostentatiously erotic, a confirmation also of her diegetic character. The shot may be intended to invoke as well an earlier shot of Harlan with his jeans unbuttoned and Thelma's panties hiked up while she is bent over the rear of a car. Because Harlan and Darryl are all that Thelma has known about sex previously, J. D. represents the new possibilities now available to her. No wonder she dreamily reports to Louise the next morning that "I finally see what all this fuss is about!" The sequence overall is erotic, pleasant, unthreatening—a dual recognition that sexual encounters on the road are part of the genre and that these encounters must be re-inflected to suit female protagonists.

The sequence enters into other intertextual relationships also. Even as Thelma and J. D. have been making Edenic love in one motel room, Louise and Jimmy have been discovering next door that sex has nothing to do with what's the matter with them or with the world they live in. By morning, Louise and Jimmy are much more nearly the compatible 'Nineties heterosexual couple that happy movie endings require, but this development merely prepares for their permanent separation. In the morning too, Thelma discovers that J. D. has stolen all their money. Sex leaves a bill for Thelma to pay, as it seldom does for the male road hero. Thelma must begin to shoulder more responsibility for her and Louise's situation. She must act as a woman rather than as a child or a puppy. Specifically, she must use the techniques J. D. has taught her in order to rob a store.

As this sequence makes clear, male and female characters enact the generic incidents of the road movie differently when it comes to sex. Other examples of these semantic variations on the genre abound. Before setting out on their road trip, for example, the two women smile into the camera for the polaroid picture that will serve as the film's logo. Butch and Sundance might be photographed, but they could not allow themselves to acknowledge the camera's presence or—especially—to smile. If Butch and Sundance, or any other male road warriors, downed some "shooters" at the Silver Bullet, they could not allow themselves to wince afterwards, as Thelma and Louise do. Nor would male characters sing along with the Temptations' version of "The Way You Do the Things You Do" or unashamedly head-dance along with B. B. King. After Louise kills Harlan, she becomes physically ill. We can imagine a male character badly beaten and bleeding after such an encounter. He might even appear shot in some non-disgusting way. We can't imagine him vomiting. Thelma is addicted to chocolate when the film begins, but she switches to Wild Turkey after she has become an armed robber. A store owner is puzzled that Thelma prefers many miniature bottles of whiskey instead of a more economical pint, but in terms of the film's gender inflection, Thelma's choice makes sense. Like a male road hero, she prefers whiskey to chocolate bars, but the miniature bottles of Wild Turkey that she tips up enter into dialogue with and cancel out the upended fifths of rotgut and cans of beer that her male predecessors brandished.

In these and other ways, this Khouri/Scott version of a road film recognizes what Bakhtin calls the grotesque body of the world.[2] Thus, Thelma and Louise go into several ladies' rooms in the course of their adventures. In the Silver Bullet, Louise must practice contortions to see herself in the rest room mirror through a crowd of other women. In fact, Jami Bernard sees shots of this sort as responsible for the film's distinct difference from other examples of the genre. Bernard writes that men "may never know the breath of fresh air it is to see a throwaway scene out of women's own lives such as the one in a dance-hall ladies' room where women are stacked five-deep to get a look at their hair in a mirror" (1466). In a comparable scene, Louise, Thelma, and another woman are in the ladies' room at a coffee shop. The strange woman checks her appearance in the mirror and leaves. Then Louise talks to Thelma through the closed stall door before using the mirror herself to wipe off the blusher that signifies the residual traces of her social conformity. As when she later trades her earrings and watch for a straw hat, Louise signifies her increasing emancipation from society through specifically gendered signs. In the same way, it is surely significant that Thelma emerges from the gas station's primitive outhouse just after Louise has made her trade. In these scenes, the grotesque body of the world continues to occupy a prominent place in the film's discourse, but the signs of the body's presence change as the journey takes the protagonists farther away from their conventional social roles. Perhaps for this reason the two stars' faces are increasingly made up to appear gritty and un-starlike to accord with these other developments.

Gender enters dialogue with genre in another way when the protagonists cry. During their first motel stop, Louise implies that Thelma is largely responsible for their precarious situation, and Thelma begins to cry. A male hero probably would not cry in this situation, and his companion surely would not apologize and try to think of a way to distract his crying partner. Louise thinks of just the thing for Thelma to do: go out and sun by the motel swimming pool. For this reason, Margaret Carlson seems mistaken to me when she indicts the film because "The characters don't confide in each other as real-life women would" (57). The (especially female) dialogics³ through which Thelma and Louise try to understand each other's feelings throughout the film more than compensates, I would argue, for Louise's refusal to share the details of her earlier horrific experience in Texas. She shares much more with Thelma when she understands and forgives her friend for behaving thoughtlessly and thus for perhaps provoking her own tears. Thelma cries again after her unproductive phone conversation with Darryl—luckily so, as it turns out, because she first spots J. D. while refreshing her eye make-up in the rearview mirror. After Thelma allows J. D. to steal their money, Louise cries. Again tears produce an apology and, this time, a resolve on Thelma's part to take more responsibility for the pair's lives. Since tears are a culturally constructed sign of the female, Thelma and Louise are true to their gender in these scenes. Since the effect of these tears is to advance their journey, they are also true to their genre. The last tears in the film, though unshed, help establish the same point. Before plunging to their deaths, Thelma and Louise look at each other with eyes brimming with tears, they kiss, and then they hold hands. The scene works beautifully, but it could only function as gender parody if the actors were men, even if the men were Robin Williams and Nathan Lane.⁴

Within the community established by Thelma and Louise and vicariously joined by the viewers, all these signs of femaleness are semantically appropriate. This point is strongly re-enforced in the scene in which Jimmy and Louise finally part. As a sign of his character development, Jimmy is prepared to give Louise one long goodbye kiss even though they are sitting in a booth in a motel coffee shop. As this kiss lasts and lasts without suggesting any sort of pre-coital eroticism, a group of waitresses watch approvingly. The scene epitomizes another form of female fantasy in which the male is so involved in the female that he becomes unaware of other people and indifferent to their (especially, male) gazes. The waitresses are crucial to their scene's semantic effect. This is how a female road outlaw takes leave of her man, the scene says, and this is how the larger female community endorses the event. Perhaps many actual men and women kiss each other in public the way Louise and Jimmy do. Perhaps no one does. Perhaps many actual women would disapprove of such behavior in real life. Perhaps they wouldn't. In terms of this embodiment of this genre, however, the scene is clear evidence of how gender interacts with genre.

Another example is purely sartorial. As we have seen, Louise eventually begins to wear a man's straw cowboy hat. After they blow up the oil tanker, Thelma leans out of the convertible and grabs the driver's filthy cap up off the ground. In subsequent scenes, the two women drive happily along wearing signs of this film genre's male origins. Significantly, these hats blow off when Slocumbe's helicopter suddenly swoops up out of the Grand Canyon. After wearing men's hats for awhile, Thelma and Louise die unquestionably as women.

That this is the preferable choice is clear by contrast with the film's male characters. Even without Harlan and Darryl, the men of *Thelma & Louise* cannot be thought of positively. When the FBI agents come to Darryl and Thelma's house, for example, the sequence surely is intended to climax in the "Women love that shit" remark that helps the men bond so effectively. The sequence begins, however, with another extremely effective scene when the drivers of a long line of police cars turning into the driveway all use their turn signals. Even out of context, the scene is a satire on male driving habits. In contrast to the earlier scene in which Thelma has madly whipped the Thunderbird across several lanes of traffic to make a u-turn on a rain-slick highway, the turn signal scene further cements the gender superiority of Thelma and Louise.

When men are acting together in this film, the same judgment can be confirmed. As many reviewers observed at the time, Harvey Keitel's character, Hal Slocumbe, is the film's most sympathetically developed male character. When most of the police are striving to keep our heroines in their gun-sights during the film's climax, for example, Slocumbe begs, "Don't let them shoot those girls." Even an unprofessional feminist might object that Thelma and Louise are women, not girls, but the usage is consistent with Slocumbe's character. He is a sympathetic but realistic male character rather than a projection of ideological correctness. This is especially clear in the sequence in which the police arrest and question J. D. In terms of plot, the sequence represents restricting possibilities for Thelma and Louise. J. D. knows what they look like, he has talked to them recently, and he understood all the while that they were in some sort of trouble with the police. Whatever he tells the authorities can only work against the women's best interests. As the questioning begins, it briefly seems as if J. D. might hold his tongue. Affecting a James Dean cockiness, he is proof against Max and his FBI methods of intimidation. J. D. even seems to score some rhetorical points when he levels a joking homosexual accusation at Max and Slocumbe, thereby confirming his own role as stud. When Slocumbe gets J. D. alone, however, the tables of gender are soon turned. Slocumbe is not a nerd like Max, and he is not a blowhard. Like the heroes of traditional male narratives, Slocumbe says what he means and means what he says. J. D. is thus quickly cowed by this superior male force and cringes under Slocumbe's charge that, by stealing their money, J. D. has forced "those two girls" into a life of crime. Slocumbe even whips J. D. with his own cowboy hat, signifying a true masculinist triumph over the previously preening younger man. It is probably this defeat at Slocumbe's hands that provokes J. D. to taunt Darryl in the next scene about having slept with his wife. Darryl is, of course, no match for J. D., but J. D. is no match for Slocumbe. That Slocumbe finally fails to help Thelma and Louise in any significant way is an indictment both of the system and of the men who invented the system.

These judgments are represented symbolically throughout the film by some clever inflections of the road film's characteristic relations of indoor and outdoor space. Before Thelma and Louise set out on their journey, they are defined against indoor sets. Thelma bounces around her kitchen like Lucy Ricardo. Louise carefully rinses and dries the glass she has used for a drink of water. As American cultural critics have been observing since the mid-nineteenth century, women are semiotically associated with the home,[5] and that's where Thelma and Louise are departing from. After they have decided—in the neutral space of a motel room—to drive on to Oklahoma City as the first stage of their escape to Mexico, however, Thelma and Louise are increasingly filmed in outdoor settings. The change is semantically significant in that Scott simultaneously begins filming the police in indoor settings. The women have chosen to escape the inequities of society by going on the road, and so the protectors of these inequities must be visualized in settings symbolically opposed to the road. That this equation overturns our stereotypical ways of representing male and female experience is, of course, the whole point of regendering the road movie.

At the same time that Thelma is getting her first look at J. D., the male authorities are bending over their computer screens trying to track down these dangerous women. While Thelma is panting over J. D. and begging Louise to pick him up, Slocumbe is inside Thelma's house, interviewing Darryl. Later Thelma and Louise bask in the sun and fresh air of the great outdoors as they listen to Marianne Faithful sing about Lucy Jordan's fantasy of doing the same thing. Meanwhile, back at Thelma's house, the police sit in a darkened room in front of a television set, quibbling about whether to watch a Cary Grant movie or the football game. These viewing choices could represent conventional American constructions of gender, but here they are both allotted to men. The women have more exciting things to do than watch television.

One of these exciting things is locking a disarmed highway patrolman in his trunk. A remote overhead shot of their convertible pulling away from the scene of this crime onto the expanding ribbon of highway fades to a shot of an interior inhabited by Slocumbe and the FBI. In terms of plot, these cuts represent the simultaneous sequences of action that will coincide in the film's climax. In semantic terms, the shots also reinterpret the traditional associations of gender and landscape that viewers bring to this film from their previous experience of the genre. When Thelma and Louise soon encounter a herd of cows on the road, the topological translation seems complete. Even when their trip is temporarily interrupted, the interruption will occur in terms of outdoor experience. What could be more reminiscent of the typical American male picaro's condition than a herd of cattle? Perhaps for this reason, Thelma says during this interruption that she is glad she has come along with Louise, notwithstanding all their undeniable problems. If Louise hadn't taken the law into her own hands back at the Silver Bullet, Thelma says, "My life would have been ruined a whole lot worse than it is now. At least now I'm having some fun." She might add that she is having fun by living outside of society—literally as well as physically. As Thelma says shortly afterwards, after tasting this kind of freedom, "I can't go back. I mean I just couldn't live." Given the film's total dynamic, Thelma is entirely correct. There is no place for her or Louise back in the social world they have left behind. Moreover, when Louise agrees with Thelma, she also confirms the equation between female rebelliousness and the great outdoors. Louise says that she also cannot return to society because she does not "want to end up on the damn Geraldo show." Louise (and Thelma) don't want to end up crimped into the space of a television set, broadcast into millions of dens, living rooms, and kitchens, condemned to life indoors.

That is to say that they have escaped to some degree the gender constraints customarily imposed by the genre in which their story is told. Rick Altman reminds us in *The American Film Musical* that "genres are not neutral categories . . . rather they are *ideological constructs masquerading as neutral categories* (5; Altman's italics). In the case at hand, the genre of the road picture usually presupposes male action and female spectatorship or ancillary support. When Khouri and Scott change the protagonists' gender, they subvert these presuppositions. This subversion was clearly intended, as Susan Sarandon explained to Brian Johnson: "We respected him [Ridley Scott] and he respected us. But I'm not going to tell you that he's a *feminist*. . . . If this had been directed by a really serious feminist, it might have seemed too much like a political statement. And if Ridley had two bubbleheads, he might not have gotten some of the stuff that we added. If anything, this movie shows that people coming from completely different perspectives can create a third thing—something we haven't seen before" (65). As we have seen, this third thing can be called an intertextual cinematic dialogue.

This suggestion is altogether consistent with the approach that Dale M. Bauer and Susan Jaret McKinstry—following Bakhtin—call "a feminist dialogics." As they write in the introduction to their *Feminism, Bakhtin, and the Dialogic* (published in the same year that *Thelma & Louise* was released): "[T]he object is not, ultimately, to produce a feminist monologic voice, a dominant voice that is a reversal of the patriarchal voice (even if such a project were conceivable), but to create a feminist dialogics that recognizes power and discourse as indivisible . . . and narrative as inherently multivocal, as a form of cultural resistance that celebrates the dialogic voice that speaks with many tongues, which incorporates multiple voices of the cultural web" (4). This is, of course, what Bakhtin would himself hope the result of generic transformation to be, as he explains in his *Problems of Dostoevsky's Poetics*: "A genre is always the same yet not the same, always old and new simultaneously. Genre is reborn and renewed at every new stage in the development of literature and in every individual work of a given genre. This constitutes the life of the genre" (106). In the case of *Thelma & Lousie*, this also constitutes a variety of challenging intertextualities.

THE HOLLYWOOD PICTURE:
BARTON FINK AND *THE PLAYER*

As we have seen in connection with *Thelma & Louise*, films made in easily recognized forms and genres are always already intertextual, since they inescapably call up our previous film experience of that form. This is certainly the case with what we might call "The Hollywood Picture"—a movie about the movie industry. In *Hollywood in Fiction: Some Versions of the American Myth*, Joseph Spatz writes, "To average man and intellectual alike the word 'Hollywood' means more than sunshine and palm trees, mass art, or wealth and glamour. Like a literary symbol, it has acquired so many connotations that it has become far more than the sum of its parts. . . . Despite the great debate about its central significance, most people agree on one fundamental point. Hollywood in its social, economic, political, artistic, and moral atmosphere, is somehow a commentary on, or a microcosm of, contemporary Western civilization in general and American culture in particular" (9). It is totally plausible, therefore, that Hollywood not only has been the source of so many popular films but also has been their subject. Any experienced filmgoer can hardly have escaped seeing several of the classic Hollywood Pictures: *What Price Hollywood?* (1932), *A Star Is Born* (1937, 1954; 1976), *Sullivan's Travels* (1941), *Sunset Boulevard* (1950), *Singin' in the Rain* (1952), *Whatever Happened to Baby Jane?* (1962), *The Day of the Locust* (1975), *Who Framed Roger Rabbit?* (1988)—even *You Oughta Be in Pictures* (1940), the Warner Brothers cartoon in which Daffy Duck convinces Porky Pig to break his contract with Leon Schlesinger in hopes of starring in films with Bette Davis and Greta Garbo. In other words, we have all seen enough films about Hollywood to know—or think we know—how the great studios operated, how movie careers are developed, and how movies are made.

We are thus prepared—even compelled—to compare any new film on this subject to what we have learned from our prior cinematic experience, to witness the new film's intertextual encounter with the tradition. As Christopher Ames writes in his *Movies About the Movies: Hollywood Reflected*: "All Hollywood movies are about Hollywood: some just happen to be set there as well. That is, all Hollywood films contribute to the larger story of film and celebrity that gives 'Hollywood' its complex meaning. Film audiences read the literal plot of a movie simultaneously with that developing metanarrative of Hollywood to which each film contributes a piece" (2). Viewing a Hollywood Picture necessarily involves our recognition of the allusive, intertextual, self-referential dimensions of the present cinematic text.

In Joel and Ethan Coen's *Barton Fink*, for example, a Hollywood Picture produced in 1991 enters into an intertextual dialogue with Hollywood voices from the 1930s such as Clifford Odets and Nathanael West, as well as with film genres like "the wrestling picture." The innovative cinematic style of the Coens, which many authorities attribute to the brothers' deep immersion in film history, interacts intertexually with subject matter conventionally associated with more traditional stylistic practices. The same may be said for Robert Altman's 1992 film *The Player*. Altman's film is set in Hollywood, his principal characters work in the film industry, and the writers take it for granted that producers are their natural adversaries. *The Player* also alludes frequently to the viewer's previous film experience and makes use of highly self-referential stylistic devices, as when the acting styles of Whoopi Goldberg and Lyle Lovett are obviously out of key with the style adopted by the stars, Tim Robbins and Peter Gallagher. The plot of Altman's film also carries on an intertextual dialogue with earlier films. Our past experiences have probably led us to anticipate an Aristotelian connection between incidents and the overall plot. If someone is threatening Griffin Mill, we expect to learn who it is. If Griffin kills David Kahane under the mistaken assumption that Kahane is responsible for these threats, we expect the person actually responsible to be unmasked later. If Griffin thinks he can get away with murder because he is so shrewd, then the unlikely detectives—Goldberg and Lovett—should trip him up in the end. Our experience of earlier films has led us to understand that you can't get away with murder, that bad guys don't win. Griffin does get away with murder, however, and he lives happily ever after. Investigating the means by which Hollywood Pictures such as *Barton Fink* and *The Player* enter into intertextual dialogue with Hollywood and the American culture for which Hollywood functions metonymically can, therefore, help us think more productively about these films, their relations to the medium of film more generally, and our relations as viewers to all of these entities.

In *Barton Fink*, the title character, played by John Turturro, is an idealistic young playwright who goes to Hollywood in 1941 hoping to earn enough money as a script-writer to sustain his more serious work in the politically conscious world of the New York theater. Since his first successful play, *Bare Ruined Choirs*, told the inspiring story of the group of proletarian heroes that Fink calls "fish mongers," we may legitimately doubt his ability to write successfully for the audience that he calls "the common man." These doubts are re-enforced after Fink encounters a paralyzing writer's block when ordered by the head of Capitol Pictures, Jack Lipnick (Michael Lerner), to write a "wrestling picture" for Wallace Beery. Further confirmation comes from Fink's insensitivity to the actual common man who lives next door to him in the Hotel Earle, an insurance salesman named Charlie Meadows (John Goodman). Charlie repeatedly offers to tell Fink interesting stories about his life as a common man, but Fink ignores these offers. The problem with Fink is, as Charlie eventually charges, "You don't listen!"

Instead of listening to Charlie, Fink erroneously seeks instruction from a respected-novelist-turned-script-writer, W. P. Mayhew (John Mahoney). Mayhew is, however, too pickled in alcohol to provide much guidance, and so Fink begs Mayhew's secretary-lover Audrey Taylor (Judy Davis) to help him work up a story treatment before his early morning meeting with the tyrannical Lipnick. Since Audrey has written all of Mayhew's scripts—and his last two novels—she is well suited to become Fink's muse and lover. It is only after Fink awakens to find Audrey's murdered body beside him in bed that he finally turns to Charlie for assistance. Charlie disposes of Audrey's body. Fink goes to his story conference. Everything seems to be working out until two police detectives tell Fink that Charlie is actually Madman Mundt, a homicidal maniac who likes to decapitate his victims.

Suddenly Fink becomes inspired—perhaps by this horrifying story, perhaps by the mysterious box that Charlie has left in his care. After typing furiously for days, Fink finishes a script, rushes out to celebrate at a USO dance, behaves arrogantly, and is slugged on the jaw by the common men in uniform. Returning to the Earle, Fink is told by the police that Mundt/Charlie has killed and beheaded Mayhew and that Fink is considered an accomplice. Charlie reappears, murders the detectives, attacks Fink's intellectual pretensions, and resumes his own life as a common man. Fink brings a script based on Charlie's life to Lipnick, who rejects it as pretentious. A disappointed Lipnick tells Fink that, as punishment, he will be kept under contract until he "grows up," but that nothing he writes will be produced. Fink then takes Charlie's mysterious box for a walk along the beach, and the film ends with Fink gazing out on the Pacific.

Throughout *Barton Fink* a wide variety of thematic and stylistic textual voices interpenetrate, creating extremely rich intertextual encounters. One voice enters the film by means of graphic representations. Fink's drab hotel room has only one decorative touch: a wall hanging of a 1940s bathing beauty looking out to sea. The lovely woman in this scene is probably intended to represent everything Fink lacks—sex, beauty, social acceptance, innocence, the healthy outdoors, the appeal of the West Coast. Since the Coens have used a shot of sunny surf crashing on a rock to serve as a transition between New York and Hollywood, this fantasy woman is associated with these positive qualities even on her first appearance. During the earlier portions of the film, the dreariness of Fink's life is repeatedly emphasized by shots of this cheesecake reproduction. Later on, while Fink is working frantically on his wrestling script, his creative efforts are occasionally juxtaposed to this picture. By this point, though, the scene of the bathing beauty has been complicated by an inserted photo of Charlie, jauntily posing on the running board of an automobile during a sales trip to Kansas City, the scene of several murders. In terms of the film's principal action, Charlie is a real participant in Fink's life; the woman is purely a fantasy. Later on, though, Charlie walks through fire, serenely murders two policemen, and frees Fink from his handcuffs in an act of superhuman strength. Thus, viewers can only wonder how "real" Charlie is. By the same token, Fink actually meets this woman in the film's closing scene. She is dressed in a two-piece bathing suit exactly as she has been in the color reproduction that Fink has repeatedly gazed at in the film's earlier scenes, and yet she speaks pleasantly to Fink as if their encounter is a realistic, everyday meeting. In the film's final shot, Fink in the foreground stares at her in the background, sitting in the exact pose she held on the wall of Fink's room. Now viewers must wonder how "real" she is. The question leads to others: How real is Fink? Lipnick? Audrey? Mayhew? How real are films anyway?

The Coens also use literal textual voices to create intertextual encounters with their principal, cinematic form of representation. There is, first of all, the ominous slogan reproduced on the Hotel Earle's complimentary stationery: "For a Day or a Lifetime." (It is probably in this light that some reviewers interpreted the film as an allegory of damnation!)[1] There are also the few words of scene-setting that Fink types and retypes during his creative paralysis. Other words are invisible. After Fink has first encountered his writer's block, a new scene opens with fingers flying over a typewriter. The fingers do not belong to Fink, however, but to Ben Geisler's secretary. The scene helps establish that words are, in one sense, the principal commodity of the film industry. As Lipnick intones, "The writer is king here at Capitol Pictures." For a writer to be unable to write words in this environment is hellish indeed. As several reviewers pointed out at the time, this is a kind of hell with which the Coens were personally familiar. According to Jack Mathews, "The Coens have said they got the idea for 'Barton Fink' while suffering writer's block themselves and imagined Turturro and Goodman interacting in a sleazy hotel" (86). It is therefore to be expected that writing and the written word will figure so prominently and intertextually in *Barton Fink.*

J. P. Mayhew serves as an especially interesting source of textual voices. Obviously modeled on William Faulkner, the Mayhew character represents the authoritative voice of the hieratic literature taught in school—in opposition to the popular voice of film chosen by the Coen brothers. Mayhew's artistic burnout also represents the voices of other successful writers supposedly destroyed by their sojourns in Hollywood, for example, F. Scott Fitzgerald, William Faulkner, Nathanael West, Aldous Huxley, and James Agee, the writers discussed by Tom Dardis in *Some Time in the Sun* (1976). Richard Schickel explains in *Time:* "As this story is traditionally told, Hollywood is the great corrupter of innocent talent, luring it away from righteousness with false promises of easy money for easy work, then blunting and eventually ruining it with vulgar values and stupefying assignments" (59).[2] Naturally, the Coens refuse to tell the story traditionally. Mayhew's character is thus very complicated. During a picnic, he presents a copy of his novel *Nebuchadnezzar* to Fink with the hand-written inscription: "May this little entertainment direct you in your sojourn among the Philistines." Since we later discover that this novel was most likely written by Audrey rather than by Mayhew, the apparently simple ironies in this inscription take on great complexity. The distance between Mayhew's art and "entertainment" is not so absolute as he would pretend, and not all the Philistines are studio executives. The Coens emphasize the latter point by having Mayhew follow up the book presentation by singing "Old Black Joe," urinating on a tree, and smacking Audrey in the face.

The title of Mayhew/Audrey's novel also surfaces later. Caught in the grip of writer's block, Fink desperately opens the Bible provided by the hotel, hitting upon the second chapter of the book of Daniel, the narrative in which Daniel reconstructs and interprets the dream of Nebuchadnezzar, king of Babylon.[3] Fink's advanced political liberalism hardly seems compatible with a sincere search for Biblical assistance, and yet his desperation is real; Fink needs to find some way to unlock his own words. Turning from Daniel to the book of Genesis, Fink is horrified to see his own feeble sentences on the page in place of the opening verses. The Bible does not offer the way out of Fink's dilemma, and yet these scenes are surely intended to recall scenes from earlier films in which a passing remark or a casually glimpsed passage opened the blocked gates of creativity. In *The Great Waltz* (1938), Fernand Gravet's Johann Strauss is inspired to compose "Tales From the Vienna Woods" by listening to the incessant rhythm of carriage wheels. In *Night and Day* (1946) starring Cary Grant as Cole Porter, Porter hears the ticking of a grandfather clock and is inspired to write the title song. The Coens call up these echoes only to frustrate them. Fink is uninspired. What we have been led to expect continues to carry on an intertextual dialogue with what the Coens are willing to deliver. Moreover, since relatively few viewers in the Coens' probable audience would immediately recognize the Biblical reference to Daniel, we must conclude that the episode involves something more than a literary allusion directly connecting Fink to Daniel or Nebuchadnezzar.

Other forms of representation also acquire intertextual status. Fink's play *Bare Ruined Choirs* contributes to the film's intertextual polyphony even before he goes to Hollywood. The opening shots of *Barton Fink* present a realistic backstage environment in which we view Fink and several stage hands appropriately dressed in 1940s clothing. Playwright Fink looks ecstatic; the stagehands look bored beyond belief. These visual elements are contextualized by the soundtrack on which we hear actors reciting the final lines of Fink's play. These lines on the soundtrack help us understand what these people are doing backstage, but the inflated, proletarian-poetic diction of these lines conflicts with the level of representation before our eyes. The first speeches we hear in the film thus serve both to question the depth of Fink's talent and to remind us that representation is not necessarily reality.

After Fink arrives in Hollywood, the visual and oral components of the film continue their intertextual dialogue. Having been given his assignment to write a wrestling picture for Wally Beery, Fink immediately returns to room 621 of the Hotel Earle and gets started. After typing for a short while, he is distracted by a voice weeping or laughing in room 623. Unable to work in the presence of real-world emotion, Fink calls down to the desk to complain. When Charlie Meadows comes over to apologize, Fink is given another chance to listen to the voice of the common man. Charlie asks what he writes about, and Fink replies, "I guess I write about people like you, the average working stiff, the common man." Charlie responds, "And I could tell you some stories," but Fink dismisses Charlie's offer: "Sure you could." Instead of listening, Fink launches into a self-important lecture about the creative process. Perhaps as a result, he soon finds himself unable to continue with the script. This conflict between Fink's supposed aesthetic principles and his actual practice is echoed in a later scene. After learning from the police about Charlie's probable identity as Madman Mundt, Fink is inspired to go back to work on the wrestling script. Until this point, the camera has repeatedly represented Fink's writer's block by focusing on his unused typewriter or on the few opening sentences he has been able to grind out. Now the screen shows a driven Fink from behind, typing furiously, flying typewriter keys, Fink's eyes shining with energy. When the phone rings, interrupting this creative frenzy, we see Fink stuffing cotton in his ears. Again Fink refuses to listen to the voice of the common men who inhabit the real world. Instead, Fink and the audience listen to the interior voice of Fink's creativity—supposedly the voices of Charlie's life, actually the same inflated, poetic diction that opens the film and that Richard T. Jameson calls "Odets-speak" (32).

Many earlier films about creative geniuses have conditioned audiences to expect happy results from episodes of this sort. Experienced viewers might easily recall comparable scenes of inspired creativity in *Young Tom Edison* (1940) starring Mickey Rooney as the title character and *The Agony and the Ecstasy* (1965) with Charlton Heston as Michelangelo. The Coens work against the audience's expectations, however. Fink does not triumph over his own doubts as Edison and Michelangelo do, and thus he fails to win over the unsympathetic authorities. Lipnick is unimpressed by Fink's work: "This is a wrestling picture. The audience wants to see action, adventure, wrestling, and plenty of it. They don't want to see a guy wrestling with his soul." The triumph we have been led to expect by the pictures of creative activity on the screen has been canceled by the voice of Fink's creative pomposity on the soundtrack. That the crude, practically illiterate Lipnick gets to make this point is at once ironic and appropriate.

Of course, the most obvious intertextual encounters in *Barton Fink* result from the fact that this is a film about the industry that makes films. Seeing films discussed, made, and shown on screen eventually makes the audience aware that the embracing film probably went through similar processes. At least, the audience's willing suspension of disbelief is shaken by these reminders that films are not "life" but artistic constructions. Most reviewers addressed this fact at the time of release. Jami Bernard wrote in the *New York Post* that *Barton Fink* "is a vicious satire of how Hollywood grinds creative minds to pulp in the service of an audience it only barely understands" (85). Kenneth Turan agrees in his *Los Angeles Times* review:

Well, we all know what happens to scribes in Hollywood, and though the Coens, in a predictable burst of disinformation, have insisted that making a picture about screenwriters could not have been further from their minds, on one level "Barton Fink" is an enormously amusing crackpot take on the underside of the Hollywood dream. If John-Paul Sartre and Billy Wilder collaborated on a script of Scott Fitzgerald's Pat Hobby stories and handed it to Luis Bunuel to direct, "Barton Fink" would be close to what they'd come up with. (80)

Jack Mathews' judgment in *Newsday* is more tentative but similarly focused: "It's a highly stylized, constantly inventive and slowly evolving horror comedy that seems/might/could be spoofing both Hollywood and the left wing New York Intellectuals who found it both seductive and loathsome during the Golden Years" (85). Even though he considered the film "a failure," David Denby followed the same line when he observed in his *New York* review that the film "starts as a satire of Broadway and Hollywood a half-century ago, becomes a seriocomic exploration of the nature of creativity, and then, after a number of brilliant scenes, takes a disastrous turn into a fiery apocalypse" (128).

These reviewers' shared insistence that the film be seen as satire is perfectly understandable.[4] During Fink's first exposure to the picture business, Jack Lipnick tells him, "The writer is king here at Capitol Pictures." Even so, Lipnick gets all the lines, stunning Fink into silence by a torrent of show-business language. Despite his claim that "We do not make B-pictures here at Capitol," Lipnick does not commission Fink to create a coherent narrative with a beginning, middle, and end. Instead, he orders the new studio writer to bring "that Barton Fink feeling" to an obvious formula film: a "wrestling picture" for Wallace Beery. In *Film Comment* Richard T. Jameson praises "the surreal nuttiness of [the film's] deadpan proposition that there ever was such a genre as the wrestling picture" (26). Jameson is right on target about "surreal nuttiness," but as Ian Hamilton reports in *Writers in Hollywood, 1915-1951*, Sam Marx of MGM actually asked William Faulkner to produce such a script in 1932: "Marx had it in mind to assign Faulkner to a wrestling picture, called *Flesh*, with Wallace Beery in the lead. Faulkner claimed not to have heard of Beery, so Marx arranged a special screening of *The Champ*. After watching for a few minutes, Faulkner walked out—of the projection room and out of the studio's main gate" (195). Furthermore, as most film viewers already know from a variety of sources, genre films were a staple Hollywood product during the Golden Age. Audrey recognizes this generic influence later in the film when she tells Fink: "Look, it's really just a formula. You don't have to tie up your soul into it. We'll invent some new names, and a new setting." This is what Audrey did for

Mayhew, this is what she proposes to do for Fink, this is what many experienced pros did.

Since the Coens' awareness of film formulas is well attested, the intertextual function of film genres is apparent.[5] As Anne Billson typically writes, "The Coens know their conventions inside-out, and—this is important—they never forget that the Modern Cineliterate Audience knows them inside-out as well. The MCA can spot a plot reversal at 50 paces, but the Coens have managed to keep one step ahead" (82). This means that when members of the Coens' audience recognize familiar generic markers of style and theme, they cannot avoid experiencing an intertextual encounter between the familiar and the original. A brilliant example occurs when Ben Geisler (Tony Shalhoub) reserves a screening room so that Fink can watch some dailies from a wrestling picture called *Devil on the Canvas*—just as Faulkner was encouraged to watch *The Champ*. As far as Geisler is concerned, the sole purpose of this exercise is to familiarize Fink with the recurrent properties of the genre. When the projectionist asks which wrestling picture to screen, Geisler therefore screams into the telephone, "I don't give a shit which one! Wrestling pictures!" The formulaic camera angles and lighting of this black-and-white metadiegetic[6] film cannot help triggering the audience's memories of similar scenes. At the same time, the metadiegetic film inescapably enters into intertextual dialogue with the Coens' sophisticated production, especially since the numbered takes from *Devil on the Canvas* are intended to stress the repetitiousness of the filmic process.

As the previous example suggests, the Coens also involve their audience in an intertextual encounter between the familiar and the innovative on the stylistic level. The costuming and set design of *Barton Fink* are surely intended to call up the audience's experience of earlier films. Fink's heavy overcoat, his hat, his dark, drab suits come realistically out of the Thirties, but they come even more out of the films of the Thirties. So does the Hotel Earle. Sam Spade could stay there. So could any character played by Elisha Cook, Jr. Charlie says that he is a great fan of Jack Oakie, and this is no surprise because they wear the same kind of underwear. On the other hand, no film of the Thirties contains tracking shots like the ones in which Fink is first shown walking slowly down the Earle's long sixth-floor corridor toward the camera and is then shown walking a similar distance from behind. The cutting is pure Coen.

Technical self-references of this sort are, in fact, frequently mentioned as signatures of the Coens' cinematic style.[7] When Fink eavesdrops on some passionate next-door neighbors, he is shot from high above with his ear pressed to the wall of his hotel room. When Audrey and Fink are about to make love, the camera tracks from Fink's shoes to the bathroom to the sink to the drain, while moans of pleasure are heard in the background. When Fink awakes the next morning, he hears a mosquito and then sees it perched on Audrey's back. The camera zooms in until the mosquito fills most of the screen. When Fink swats the mosquito, blood explodes. In these highly original scenes our attention switches quickly—and intertextually—between realistic representation of the story and self-referential film technique. We must therefore interrogate both.

The Coens' challenges to the tradition of realistic cinematic representation emerge from both stylistic and thematic directions, a development that one might almost expect in light of Christopher Ames's remark in *Movies About the Movies*: "When we are reminded that we are reading a novel or viewing a film, the realist frame is temporarily broken. But self-reference in film typically does something that self-referentiality in literature does not: it foregrounds the circumstances of artistic production and reception, the dynamics of industry and audience" (8). That the same might be said about Robert Altman's *The Player,* we may see in—among other places—*One on One with Robert Altman*, a filmed interview packaged with the video release of his film. In this interview, Altman says simply, "This is a movie about movies." Obviously, then, we might expect *The Player* to share many features with *Barton Fink*, including an acute awareness of the stylistic and thematic opportunities afforded by a conscientious use of intertextuality.

Altman's film focuses on Griffin Mill (Tim Robbins), an apparently passionless "player" in the bottom-line world of contemporary Hollywood. Although Griffin is known in the studio as "the writer's executive," he has actually reduced all writers to groveling sycophants who pitch him script ideas "in twenty-five words or less," desperately seeking the approval that can make them enormously wealthy. When Griffin's life is anonymously threatened by a spurned writer, he tries to ignore the danger lest a scandal weaken him in his power struggle with an even more ruthless young adversary, Larry Levy (Peter Gallagher). When the threats continue, Griffin eventually deduces that they are coming from writer David Kahane (Vincent D'Onofrio), whom he then tries to buy off with the promise of a shot at the big time. After Kahane rejects this offer and threatens to expose Griffin's desperate strategy, a fight ensues and Kahane is killed. As it turns out, Kahane was not the one making the threats after all, and so the threats continue by postcard, by telephone, and by fax. Also continuing is Griffin's career pressure from Larry Levy. To counter the latter, Griffin tricks Levy into producing an anti-capital-punishment film written by Tom Oakley (Richard E. Grant), sure that the film will fail and that Levy will be blamed.

Meanwhile, police detectives Avery (Whoopie Goldberg) and DeLongpre (Lyle Lovett) pursue Griffin even as he pursues Kahane's former lover June Gudmundsdottir (Greta Scacchi). Griffin gets June, but the detectives fail to get Griffin. Instead, Griffin gets away with murder, wins out over Levy, becomes head of the studio, marries June, and lives happily ever after. To secure this last item, Griffin agrees to film a script written by the anonymous writer, who is now more interested in making a fortune than in killing Griffin. This script is called *The Player* and is focused on an apparently passionless player in the bottom-line world of contemporary Hollywood who gets away with murder. As Altman says in an interview with Richard T. Jameson in *Film Comment*, this ending is "like a lobster tail or shrimp tail that's turned back into itself. . . . At the end of *The Player* what we are saying is that the movie you saw is the movie you are about to see; the movie you saw is the movie we're going to make" (23).

It is clear from Altman's description that his film is highly intertextual in the sense that—as in *Barton Fink*—a primary film text closely interacts with subsidiary films. In addition to the thematic intertextuality resulting from the film's subject matter, *The Player* also resembles *Barton Fink* in drawing intertexts from a wide variety of media, including the literally textual. Griffin receives story pitches and threats over the telephone, but he also receives written threats by fax, in his office and while driving his Range Rover. Griffin realizes that he has killed the wrong writer only after he receives a fax at his office saying, "SURPRISE." Later on, a fax sent over his car phone says, "Look under your raincoat." Two faxed arrows point disturbingly down at his coat. When Griffin moves the raincoat, he sees a package and a card with the message "Do not open till Xmas." Opening the box, Griffin sees and hears a rattlesnake curled on the floor of his Range Rover. Of course, viewers also read all of these words on the screen, and so a literal text interacts with the visual text. In a related intertextual device, Griffin finds a postcard under the windshield wiper of his Range Rover with the text of another anonymous threat and a picture on the other side representing a movie still of Humphrey Bogart pointing a gun threateningly at the viewer. Similarly, the most threatening message that Griffin receives— "In the name of all writers, I'm going to kill you"—appears on the reverse of a flip-out postcard selection of Hollywood tourist sights. Viewers read the words, see the photos of Bogie and Hollywood, and watch Altman's movie—all at the same time. Throughout the film, moreover, sets are decorated with posters for old films. When Griffin's secretary Jan (Angela Hall) sits at her desk, she is framed against a poster for *Highly Dangerous*, starring Marius Goring. When Griffin lies to the police about his affair with June and his murder of Kahane, the scene is shot before a garish poster advertising *M*, with the slogan, "The worst crime of all." Altman clearly assumes not only that his viewers can read but also that they will recognize all, or at least some, of these references.

Other intertexts fit more obviously into the traditional formulas. After Griffin has escaped identification in a police lineup by an eyewitness to the murder, his lawyer Gar Girard (Kevin Scannell) says, "Everybody thinks you've gotten away with murder." Obviously engaged in dialogue here are two voices: one enunciating a cliche about escaping punishment in general and another commenting on Griffin's guilt in the matter of David Kahane. Echoing in the background is still another voice derived from our earlier experience of film. This one says that in the movies no one gets away with murder. All these voices are further complicated by the following scene: a blank screen with the title card "One Year Later." This voice moves the plot of *The Player* along to its ironic happy ending, but it also calls up the viewers' previous experience of such cards in other films. We are reminded that "One Year Later" conventionally brings the triumph of virtue in films. When we realize that the same is not necessarily true in life, we must also realize that we are watching a "movie."

As in *Barton Fink*, this emphasis on "filmness" lies at the heart of Altman's enterprise. When Griffin is questioned by Detectives Avery and DeLongpre at the Pasadena police station, Whoopi Goldberg and Lyle Lovett act in styles more suited to a film by David Lynch than to one directed by Altman. Goldberg's Avery is bizarre, obscene, menacing, as she twirls a tampon in Griffin's face. Lovett's DeLongpre is just plain weird, spelling and pronouncing *Gudmundsdottir* and inappropriately swatting a fly. The scene acquires a specific Hollywood intertext, however, when DeLongpre talks about the movie he saw last night—*Freaks*. With a character who looks like Lovett chanting "One of us, one of us" in the background, anything that happens in the foreground must be understood as being in intertextual dialogue with another film, Tod Browning's *Freaks* (1932). Altman uses a similar strategy in the much-discussed extended tracking shot with which *The Player* gets under way.[8] One step in the process is a monologue by the studio security officer, Walter Stuckel (Fred Ward), about the extended tracking shot by which Orson Welles opened *Touch of Evil*. In the *One on One* interview, Altman emphasizes the self-referential qualities of the scene: "I'll have characters in the shot—Fred Ward actually—talking about these shots. So we're telling the people what we're doing at the same time." What "we" are telling the people most of all is that they are watching a movie, and "we" are doing so by means of various cinematic intertexts.

Interestingly enough, this consciousness on the viewers' part does not erase the mimetic content of the film. The danger represented by Larry Levy operates as effectively in terms of Altman's plot as the dangers confronting characters in *Highly Dangerous* or *M*. At the same time, Levy's kind of danger definitely signals "Hollywood." Therefore, many reviewers discuss *The Player* not only as a film about film but as a film about Hollywood films. Marcelle Clements, for example, sets *The Player* in a context comprised of *The Big Picture, The Day of the Locust, Barton Fink*, and *Sunset Boulevard* (128). The last comparison is particularly apt since at one point Griffin's anonymous enemy uses the alias *Joe Gillis*. Perhaps we should expect that Griffin will not recognize the name. Someone tells him that Gillis is "the writer who gets killed in *Sunset Boulevard*." A dialogue thus develops among two dead writers— Gillis and Kahane—and a potentially murderous writer—the anonymous caller. *The Player* also enters into intertextual dialogue with *Sunset Boulevard*, a film about another Hollywood that is both different and similar.

Other cinematic intertexts also contribute to *The Player*. As Griffin explains to June, his job is to listen to writers pitching ideas for potential movies. In the earlier part of the film the satiric potential of these story pitches lies in their formulaic and imitative nature. A writer called Buck (played by Buck Henry) pitches *The Graduate, Part II*: "The three principals are still with us, Dustin Hoffman, Anne Bancroft, Catherine Ross, twenty-five years later, and so are the characters, Ben, Elaine, and Mrs. Robinson. Ben and Elaine are married still. They live in a big old spooky house up in Northern California somewhere, and Mrs. Robinson lives with them." Mrs. Robinson has had a stroke or "a malady of some sort" and cannot speak. Perhaps viewers begin to hear *Psycho* in the background. Since Ben and Elaine now have a college-age daughter, viewers at least should recall *The Graduate*, written by Buck Henry. When Griffin wants to know if the new story will be funny, Buck replies, "It'll be weird and funny and with a stroke." Buck also suggests that the daughter should be played by Julia Roberts, a casting suggestion repeated with variations throughout the film.

That everyone suggests casting Roberts can be taken as a sign that original thinking is rare in Griffin's Hollywood. That sequels and spin-offs figure so prominently in the pitches only re-enforces this suspicion.

A script intended for Goldie Hawn is described first as *The Gods Must Be Crazy*, but with a TV actress instead of a Coke bottle, and then as *Out of Africa* meets *Pretty Woman*. Another story described as *Ghosts* meets *The Manchurian Candidate* is characterized as "a psychic, cynical, political thriller comedy, but with a heart." Even if viewers have not seen all the films mentioned, it is probable that they have seen some of them and that they will consequently bring this earlier experience into intertextual dialogue with the actual and virtual scripts involved in *The Player*.

Viewers also cannot avoid acknowledging the popularity of sequels in the real Hollywood. In this way Altman establishes a dialogue between the real and the represented Hollywood. The parallels are re-enforced in various ways as when the subplot in which Larry Levy challenges Griffin's position is contextualized in terms of similar executive shakeups at two actual studios: Paramount and Columbia. At lunch later on, Griffin speaks to Joel Grey, Anjelica Huston, and John Cusack. At a party that evening, Jack Lemmon plays the piano for Steve Allen and Jayne Meadows. Meanwhile, Griffin's assistant Bonnie Sherow fawns over Harry Belafonte and pitches a story to Marlee Matlin. Bonnie is played by Cynthia Stevenson, but Belafonte and Matlin play themselves. At a star-studded benefit, Nick Nolte and Elliott Gould walk toward the *Entertainment Tonight* cameras arm in arm with their dates. These two couples are followed by Griffin and June, however, and preceded by Larry Levy and Cher. Lisa Gibbons tells us that even though everyone else has agreed to dress in black and white, Cher has defiantly worn a red gown. This probably accords with our sense of Cher's public persona, but we must somehow harmonize this celebrity gossip with our intertextual understanding that Cher's date is a fictional character.

However, the most significant intertexts for Altman's principal diegesis are a series of metadiegetic films. When Griffin meets David Kahane at a showing of *The Bicycle Thief*, we also see black-and-white scenes from Vittorio De Sica's classic film, and we hear the Italian soundtrack. When the sad ending of *The Bicycle Thief* is overlaid with the title FINE, we cannot help sensing the film's contrast with the kind of studio picture where, in Larry Levy's words, "You slap a happy ending on it, and the script'll write itself."[9] The intertextual effects created by the Italian film are heightened in a following scene, set in a karaoke bar in Pasadena. As Griffin and Kahane discuss the latter's unproduced film script, Japanese characters sing against a background of black-and-white music video shots. The screen behind the singers shows the song lyrics in both English and Japanese characters, while the characters sing mindless lyrics in heavily accented English. Another cinematic intertext enters Altman's film through *The Lonely Room*, a metadiegetic film starring Lily Tomlin and Scott Glenn. Altman explains in *One on One* that he had his assistant director direct Tomlin and Glenn in an improvised scene about a CIA operative and his lover while Altman's camera filmed the filming. The scene opens with the assistant director's clapper and proceeds through several clearly identified takes in which the actors reposition themselves and give different readings of the same lines. Tomlin and Glenn also speak out of character between takes, discussing Glenn's per-diem expenses, for example, and re-enforcing the impression that they are actors acting, not spies actually living sordid lives. Viewers cannot help suspecting that the characters watching this filming—Griffin, his assistant Bonnie Sherow, Larry Levy—are merely creations of other talented actors who probably went through similar takes and retakes for their director, Robert Altman. This intertextual dialogue between representation and self-reference is enhanced at the end of the scene. Lily Tomlin's character stands looking out a rain-streaked window. When we look out over her shoulder, we see through a window of the St. James Club, the setting for Griffin's encounter with Tom Oakley and Andy Civella.

The most extended of these metadiegetic films is *Habeas Corpus*, a serious indictment of capital punishment written by Tom Oakley and marketed by his agent Andy Civella (Dean Stockwell). When Oakley describes the film as highly unconventional—no stars and an unhappy ending—these signs of artistic integrity appeal to Griffin as the tools to bring about Larry Levy's downfall. Civella is stereotypically without ethics, even to the point of proposing Julia Roberts and Bruce Willis for the leading roles. Griffin assures Oakley that he can convince Levy to produce the film as written, however. In one of Altman's many ironic twists on the narrative of film-making, the final product ends up looking much more like Civella's craven sellout than like Oakley's original conception. Viewers thus cannot ignore the voice behind the narrative asking questions about the relation of the finished product to the original scripts of most Hollywood films, including *The Player*.

Oakley has insisted throughout that his film, *Habeas Corpus*, must end with the unjust execution of his heroine. However, when we see the ending of *Habeas Corpus* one year after Griffin has escaped identification as Kahane's murderer, we discover that Oakley's film has a new look and a new, upbeat ending. We know, first of all, that we are watching a film within a film because we recognize Peter Falk, Susan Sarandon, and Ray Walston in costumes appropriate for a prison film but not for *The Player*. Then we see that the unjustly accused victim is being played by none other than Julia Roberts, wearing a prison uniform and a prison haircut. As Roberts walks into the gas chamber, therefore, a dialogue naturally develops between the aesthetic integrity that we have earlier been promised by Oakley and the potential happy ending that Roberts's presence portends. It is barely possible, of course, that Roberts is going to reenact her melancholy demise in *Steel Magnolias*, and so a happy ending is not absolutely guaranteed. However, any possibility of an unhappy ending is shattered when none other than Bruce Willis erupts onto the screen to rescue Roberts at the very last moment. This scene in the metadiegetic film is clearly intended to represent contemporary Hollywood film-making, as is the two actors' final dialogue. "What took you so long?" the Roberts character asks anticlimactically. "Traffic was a bitch," Willis responds in his *Die Hard* persona.

When this ending is screened for the studio executives, only Bonnie objects to the reshaping of the original story. "What about truth? What about the reality?" she asks Oakley in shock. Oakley responds: "What about the way the old ending tested in Canoga Park? Everybody hated it. We reshot it and now everybody loves it. That's reality." Like *Fatal Attraction, Habeas Corpus* will have a happy ending,[10] and so will *The Player*. After Larry Levy has fired Bonnie for insubordination, Griffin drives his lovely car to his lovely home where he is greeted by his lovely, pregnant wife. "What took you so long?" June asks. "Traffic was a bitch," Griffin responds. Movie music swells and the screen fills with a card that says THE END rather than *FINE*. Altman's picture is carrying on a dialogue much more with Hollywood than with Vittorio De Sica. Just before his arrival at this happy ending, Griffin hears one last pitch on his car phone. The caller is the anonymous writer who threatened Griffin's life earlier in the film, and he is now pitching a story called *The Player*. The story we hear described contains all the characters and actions that we have just seen in Altman's film. Griffin is especially interested in whether the studio executive "gets away with it." The writer assures him, "Absolutely! It's a Hollywood ending, Griff. He marries the dead writer's girl and they live happily ever after." Griffin says, "You can guarantee me that ending, you got a deal." The writer makes this guarantee, and *The Player* ends with us watching this very ending unfolding before our eyes. In this conclusion, a fictional character talks to a fictional character, Hollywood writers talk to Hollywood producers, and movies talk to movies.

This conclusion calls to mind two critical judgments that apply equally to *The Player* and to *Barton Fink*. In "The Death of the Author," Roland Barthes writes, "The text is a tissue of quotations drawn from the innumerable centers of culture" (146), and Joseph W. Reed writes similarly in *American Scenarios: The Uses of Film Genre*, "Movies come from movies, and any given movie repeats things from hundreds of others" (8). The two films under discussion in this chapter clearly attest to the intertextual value of "quotations" drawn from a wide variety of sources and media as well as to the definite consciousness that we can only watch new films in the context of the films that we have seen already. Griffin Mill addresses these issues in *The Player*, in the scene in which he takes June to a romantic hideaway to escape police scrutiny. The episode fulfills the conventional function of getting the two romantic leads away from the action of the plot long enough to let them discover their true love for one another. In contemporary films, moreover, this discovery usually involves a steamy sex scene. This is what happens in *The Player* also. Griffin and June dress attractively, dine elegantly, dance romantically, and then make passionate love. The whole episode fits right in with our previous film experience. Then again, perhaps it fits in a little too well. As they dance, June asks Griffin, "Do places like this really exist?" He correctly answers, "Only in the movies." If June had asked, "Do things work out this predictably in real life?" Griffin could have given the same answer. This imaginary question does appear in displaced form when June goes on to ask about the ingredients of a successful movie. Griffin answers: "Suspense, laughter, violence, hope, heart, nudity, sex, happy endings, mainly happy endings." Since he could easily be describing *The Player*, we are struck by the self-referential quality of the film. Since, with minor adjustments involving the ending, he could also be describing *Barton Fink*, the intertextual point is decisive.

PART III

INTERTEXTUAL ENCOUNTERS IN POPULAR CULTURE

In his essay, "Innovation and Repetition: Between Modern and Post-Modern Aesthetics" (1985), Umberto Eco concedes that "The notion of intertextuality itself has been elaborated within the framework of reflection on 'high' art," but Eco goes on to illustrate the concept through specific examples drawn from the novels of Nero Wolfe, the TV series *Dallas*, and the film *Raiders of the Lost Ark* in order to show that "forms of intertextual dialogue have by now been transferred to the field of popular production" (176). Eco is certainly not alone in discovering intertextuality in popular cultural forms. In a 1998 music review, Knight-Ridder columnist Thor Christensen writes that the "chart-topping debut album, *No Way Out* [by the rapper Puff Daddy], is less an artistic statement than a hit parade of samples and interpolations of songs by the Police, David Bowie, Lisa Stansfield and Grandmaster Flash—to name just a few" (3D). Although Christensen does not use the term *intertextuality*, his recognition of the earlier musical texts present in Puff Daddy's current work involves a critical strategy as intertextual as Eco's. Geoffrey O'Brien operates from similarly intertextual premises in reviewing the 1998 reissue of Harry Smith's *Anthology of American Folk Music* album, first released in 1952: "Copies, parodies, reversals, deliberate distortions, whatever was required to tone down, jazz up, smooth out, mess around, or make over: this had been the process of American music, of American entertainment, for so long before anyone took note that the recorded history could never be about anything but mixes, hybrids, crossovers" (49). Eco thus can be seen to have a great deal of company when viewing popular culture through the lens of intertextuality, and this tendency is supported not only by trends in popular music.

In my book *Metapop: Self-referentiality in Contemporary American Popular Culture* (1992), I discuss numerous other examples drawn from a variety of popular media. During the 1950s, for example, Walt Kelly's comic strip *Pogo* often presented the strip's leading characters in a metadiegetic narrative called "Li'l Arf An' Nonny," based on Harold Gray's popular comic strip, *Little Orphan Annie*. In 1976, Jerry Lee Lewis, a country singer whose flamboyant high-living had been extensively reported by the popular media, recorded a song entitled, "My Life Would Make A Damn Good Country Song." Jim Henson's brilliant syndicated TV program *The Muppet Show* (1976-78) featured a recurring soap-opera parody called "Veterinarians' Hospital," constructed of a series of corny medical jokes, mostly delivered by Miss Piggy. Usually the sketch ended when an unseen announcer broke in, and all the Muppets in the sketch looked up at the ceiling in surprise, trying to figure out the source of the announcer's voice that was so much a part of radio soap operas. In all of these cases, a current text in popular culture presupposes its audience's familiarity with similar earlier texts—correctly so, as the success of each of these examples attests.

Some of the audience's familiarity with earlier texts may be explained in terms of technology. Mimi White, for one, notes the contributions of cable television to the creation of what Eco (172) calls our "encyclopedia" of intertextuality. According to White's essay "Crossing Wavelengths: The Diegetic and Referential Imaginary of American Commercial Television," the easy accessibility of old television events in the forms of reruns and compilations elides the historical distinctions that once restricted intertextual referencing, when only memory could give access to the past of television and film. When historical time is canceled in this way, the result, according to White, is the creation of "an all-encompassing present text" (60) in which nearly every television or film text is nearly always available as a potential referent. The willingness—in fact, the eagerness—of television programmers to erase generic boundaries, as when celebrities appear in commercials or in cameos on other shows, only contributes to this trend, in White's view. Although White does not specifically use the term *intertextuality*, the greater availability of old TV moments that she notes can only increase the possibility of intertextual encounters. According to Constantine Verevis, similar results follow from the increased popularity of videocassette players and recorders: "[T]he introduction of an information storage technology such as videotape radically extends the kind of film literacy, the ability to recognize and cross-reference multiple versions of the same property, that is inaugurated by the age of television" (10). Eco, White, Verevis, and a score of other commentators recognize that having nearly everything from the popular cultural past available in the here-and-now creates a rhetorical climate in which intertextuality can run free.

Standard practices in earlier forms of American popular culture demonstrate that the current rhetorical situation is a development more than a revolution. When American songwriters could presuppose their audience's familiarity with all the conventional properties of popular love songs, they felt free to exploit this familiarity within the context of their own songs. Lyricists including Cole Porter, Lorenz Hart, and Ira Gershwin could therefore write love songs like "I Get a Kick Out of You," "Thou Swell," and "What Can You Say in a Love Song (That Hasn't Been Said Before)" with a reasonable assurance that their listeners would be able to recognize the new lyric's ingenuity by comparing and contrasting it with the hundreds of other love lyrics familiar from their previous experience. Unanticipated cultural allusions and both overt and covert forms of textual self-referentiality created a rich intertexual web for these artists and their audiences, a condition that lasted until the audience's expectations changed in response to the different attitude toward song lyrics associated with rock music. These highly intertextual songs are the subject of the first chapter in this section.

Similar rhetorical assumptions can be seen to underlie many of the very popular animated cartoons produced by the Warner Brothers studio from the 1930s through the early 1960s. Since these cartoons were originally intended to be screened in movie theaters preliminary to the screening of feature films, the animators could assume their viewers' familiarity with various kinds of genre films, with Hollywood stars and personalities, with the movie business, and with other animated films. The intertextual possibilities of this rhetorical situation are obvious, and they were enthusiastically exploited. At one point or another, Bugs Bunny was a cowboy; Daffy Duck, a superhero; and Porky Pig, Friar Tuck, in cartoons that called on the viewers' memories of earlier cinematic moments for intertextual laughs. An animated Humphrey Bogart appeared in Bugs Bunny's *Eight Ball Bunny*, as a live-action Errol Flynn did in *Rabbit Hood*. A live-action Leon Scheslinger, producer of many of these Warner Brothers cartoons, appeared with an animated Porky Pig in *You Oughta Be in Pictures*, a feature in which Porky's status as a cartoon "star" was central to the plot. Daffy Duck got into a heated argument with the hand that was "drawing" him in *Duck Amuck*. After a series of mishaps postulated on cartooning conventions, it turns out that the hand belongs to Bugs Bunny. In all of these cases, the jokes are fully intelligible only to those initiated into the popular environment that embraces producers and consumers alike. The interactions between the specific case at hand and the familiar elements of this environment create a variety of intertextual encounters, and so these cartoons constitute the primary subject of the next chapter.

After changes in the film industry eventually eliminated the role of animated cartoons in the release and showing of feature films, cartoons produced during the golden age moved to television, where they continue to thrive today as parts of what White calls the "all-encompassing present text" of television. Younger Americans are thus often as familiar with these cartoons as their parents and grandparents were, not from seeing them at the movies but from seeing them—over and over again— on TV. At the same time and in the same way, these Americans are acquiring familiarity with other animated cartoons produced many years after the Warner classics. Chief among the later productions, according to many, is the animated anthology series produced by Jay Ward and usually referred to today as *Rocky and Bullwinkle*. On Ward's show, the wide referential scope of the Warner Brothers cartoons was happily duplicated, as was the earlier cartoons' self-referential awareness of themselves as deliberately created forms of popular entertainment. The adventures of Rocky, Bullwinkle, Boris Badenov, Dudley Do-Right, and Peabody and Sherman thus can be understood to take up, repeat, and complicate the intertextual encounters first exploited by the artists at Termite Terrace. By now, generations of Americans have watched both sorts of cartoons over and over, often on the same screens on the same Saturday mornings or school-day afternoons. This is, in fact, how Americans of the television generation have learned most of what they know about American popular culture. It is only to be expected, then, that comedians of this generation would root so much of their performance in the intertextual encyclopedia that we call television.

Dennis Miller and Jerry Seinfeld are therefore merely the most obvious examples of contemporary television comedians who assume their viewers' easy familiarity with contemporary American popular culture—especially as mediated by television—as the basis for much of their own humor. Like the song lyrics and cartoons of earlier eras, the jokes of Seinfeld and Miller rely on cultural allusion, generic familiarity, and self-referentiality to connect the present example with its presumed intertexts. Seinfeld's sitcom episodes sometimes derive intertextual resonance from their very nature as episodes in a continuing sitcom. In other episodes, familiar cultural narratives such as the Zapruder film of John F. Kennedy's assassination or the very successful film *Apocalypse Now* supply intertexts. Most often, *Seinfeld* exploits passing references to political events or popular material goods to situate the action realistically and to produce a sure laugh. This last strategy is also the key to Dennis Miller's comedy. Without a firm grounding in celebrity politics, popular music and film, consumer goods, and (especially) the "all-encompassing present text" of television, Miller's highly insightful jokes would be largely unintelligible. With this grounding, one of Miller's routines is practically a handbook of popular intertextuality. As we might expect by this point, moreover, Miller presumes his audience's familiarity with the nature of his funny business and exploits this familiarity as another intertext.

From music to television comedy, and from the 1920s to the 1990s, intertextualities appear throughout American popular culture. Given the extreme form of "presentism" fostered by cable television, successful film remakes, CD technology, and nostalgia marketing, we may expect these intertextual occasions only to increase in number and sophistication in years to come.

"MY INTERTEXTUAL VALENTINE":
READING THE CLASSIC AMERICAN POPULAR SONG

During the first half of the twentieth century, an enormously talented group of lyric writers and composers created the art form that we
might call the classic American popular song. Most of these songs were
produced in "Tin Pan Alley," a collection of music publishers gathered
around 28th Street in New York City.¹ Despite the condescending reference in its name, this popular entertainment industry made possible such
unforgettable songs as "A Pretty Girl Is Like a Melody" by Irving Berlin
(1919), "Bill" by P. G. Wodehouse and Jerome Kern (1926), "Dancing in
the Dark" by Howard Dietz and Dorothy Fields (1931), and "All the
Things You Are" by Oscar Hammerstein II and Jerome Kern (1939).
While Tin Pan Alley publishers were producing the sheet music that
made these and hundreds of other love songs, comedy numbers, tear-
jerkers, and patriotic anthems available to the vast American audience of
singers and piano players, some of the song writers already named were
also filling the Broadway stage with musical shows. Abetted by other
individual artists, including Otto Harbach and E. Y. Harburg, and song-
writing teams like (Betty) Comden & (Adolph) Green and (George)
De Sylva, (Lew) Brown, & (Ray) Henderson, these artists created
loosely assembled reviews and more tightly scripted "book shows" filled
with memorable songs. Most notably, the singular genius Cole Porter
and the teams of Richard Rodgers & Lorenz Hart and George & Ira
Gershwin were producing individual Tin Pan Alley songs, Broadway
musical shows, and scores for Hollywood musicals—on a level of excellence never equaled before or since.

As a result of this creative activity, American popular culture was
blessed with a distinct artistic commodity as recognizably American as
jazz, hot dogs, and decaf cappuccino. Quite naturally, such a high level
of achievement established a tradition of conventional practice, as well
as an intimidating standard of excellence. In his introduction to Alec
Wilder's invaluable study, *American Popular Song: The Great Innovators, 1900-1950*, James T. Maher perceptively addresses one intertextual
dimension of this situation:

One writing in the [musical] theater lives with that tradition, with its freedom and its penalties. Puccini, far off, Lehar in the middle distance, and Jerome Kern, Irving Berlin, George Gershwin, Richard Rodgers, Arthur Schwartz, and Harold Arlen close at hand are listening. (So, too, are P. G. Wodehouse, Lorenz Hart, Cole Porter, Oscar Hammerstein II, Ira Gershwin, Dorothy Fields, and John Mercer.) The newest song writer in the theater must answer to them, for they are the measure of what he does. Throughout his career he must stand up against the formidable witness of their best work. And he cannot wish them away for they have instructed the communal ear—their songs are part of the unconscious reflex of the common memory. (xxxiv)

In terms of lyric writing, the most accomplished practitioners of this art—particularly Porter, Hart, and Ira Gershwin—acknowledged this formidable tradition and welcomed its challenges. Especially through the lyric devices of allusion, self-referentiality, and textual self-consciousness, these writers deliberately engaged with their past and present competitors intertextually. By examining song lyrics written by Porter, Hart, and Gershwin—and a few others by their contemporaries—we can gain insight into the astounding creativity of these song writers and into the critical concept of intertextuality itself.

Let us begin with the lyricists' use of allusion, or, as we are inclined to say these days, with "referencing." Porter, Hart, Gershwin, and their colleagues were often inclined to reference the historical, geographical, literary, and cultural knowledge of their times, just as poets from the past did—in the Renaissance or eighteenth century, for example. In this sense, poets in all of these historical periods can be understood as practitioners of intertextuality. As Jonathan Culler explains in *The Pursuit of Signs: Semiotics, Literature, Deconstruction*, intertextuality can be best understood as "a designation of [a text's] participation in the discursive space of a culture: the relationship between a text and the various languages or signifying practices of a culture and its relation to those texts which articulate for it the possibilities of that culture" (103). To document this kind of cultural participation, modern editions of John Dryden's and Alexander Pope's works usually bristle with footnotes identifying the poets' references for twentieth-century readers who are participants in a very different culture.

No footnotes would be required, in 1916 or today, for Cole Porter's song, "Something's Got to Be Done" (Kimball 33). According to Porter's lyric, the debutante in this song is not a prime marriage candidate because she is too taken up with Browning, Ibsen, and Shelley—all identified by last name only. She would fare much better, according to the singer, if she concentrated on marathon dances, Palm Beach, and the

Four Hundred—all references assumed to be easily recognizable by the ordinary listener. The same sort of listener should feel right at home with Porter's allusive song from 1935, "A Picture of Me" (Kimball 134-35). The premise is simple enough: the singer—a prince in the song's original setting—cannot imagine life without his lover—in the original version, a young woman named Karen. Their separate lives would be as inconceivable as Henry Ford without an automobile, Huey Long without Louisiana, Mr. Bulova without a watch, and Sunday afternoon without Father Coughlin. Some listeners today might need a footnote here—I'm thinking in particular of my students—but members of Porter's original audience could easily bring their past cultural experience to bear on the current lyrical case and make all the intertextual connections necessary. In "Which Is the Right Life?" (Kimball 74-75), the female singer, identified as a "cloak room girl," considers her life choices through allusions including Sophie Tucker, Arcadia, Paul Whiteman, and Walt Whitman. This 1929 song may be more familiar to some of us—it's familiar to me from Jeri Southern's recorded version—but it operates intertextually along the same lines as the more obscure "Something's Got to Be Done" and "A Picture of Me." In each case, familiar romantic situations are reinvigorated by introducing unexpected but easily recognizable cultural references.

Probably the crowning jewel in Porter's allusive crown is the justly famous 1934 hit, "You're the Top" (Kimball 119-20). Once again the dramatic situation is unexceptional: the singer searches for compliments adequate to describe a loved one thought to be truly exceptional. Since most lyric poets in the Renaissance and the following centuries attempted the same task, the singer faces quite a challenge to be original and so chooses to proceed by enlisting the listener's assistance through extensive cultural references. Thus, the loved one is compared to the Tower of Pisa, the Louvre, and the Colosseum, as well as to Whistler's mother, Napoleon brandy, and the recently discovered cellophane. Mixing as it does the high and the low, the hieratic and the demotic, this list of metaphoric vehicles epitomizes Porter's technique. His fields of reference while drawing flattering comparisons are quite broad, embracing the steppes of Russia, Garbo's salary, a Shakespeare sonnet, and Pepsodent toothpaste. Particularly when the listing also involves clever rhyming—as when "Inferno's Dante" is rhymed with "the nose/On the great Durante"—Porter demonstrates that an ingenious use of references can convert a highly conventional occasion into an original creation. Clearly this is the grounding for Thomas Hischak's judgment in *Word Crazy: Broadway Lyricists from Cohan to Sondheim*: "List songs are sometimes the refuge of lyricists with nothing to say. Such songs rarely move forward, they simply catalogue until they wear themselves out. Porter wrote the most effective list songs because their energy was matched by their cleverness. 'You're the Top' is considered Porter's (or anyone else's) best list song" (60). Although it is not within Hischak's sphere of interest to say so, we might add that "You're the Top" is also one of the classic American song's most effective intertextual exercises.

During the same period in which Porter introduced these songs, Lorenz Hart followed a similar intertextual strategy in many of the popular works he wrote in collaboration with Richard Rodgers. An especially Porter-like command of reference characterizes Rodgers and Hart's first big hit, in 1925, "Manhattan" (Hart 42-43). Though his field of reference is confined to New York City, Hart's imagination ranges widely, visiting Central Park, Canarsie, Coney Island, and Greenwich Village, as well as specific streets including Delancy, Mott, and Fifth Avenue. Again, the occasion is less momentous than its intertextual treatment: the singer and his lover will "turn Manhattan/into an isle of joy" because their love is so deep. A Passionate Shepherd made similar promises to his love over three centuries earlier,[2] and he also did so intertextually, by evoking a pastoral tradition as familiar to readers in 1599 as the geography of New York would be to theater-goers in 1925. In this way, both writers succeed in transforming the predictable into the novel and arresting. Several other striking uses of referencing in lyrics by Hart are less extensive, including the singer's assurance in the probably tongue-in-cheek "The Blue Room" (Hart 45-46) that the successful lovers will be as protected from the everyday cares of the world in their blue room as Robinson Crusoe was on his deserted island. Listeners who want to be spared ironic shading probably choose to ignore parts of Hart's lyric such as "With your wee head upon my knee," but even they cannot help bringing the unlikely Crusoe to bear on the present (1926) situation. In "Johnny One Note" (1937), Hart again alludes only briefly to extra-textual material, here to Giuseppe Verdi and his opera *Aida* (Hart 102). The supposed justification is that the title character gets a part in this opera and sings his one note so resoundingly that all the critics just rave. Although the situation in this song falls outside the typical love lyric scenario, the writer's rhetorical intentions seem similar to those in the examples previously cited. This performative lyric allows the pop singer who is telling the story of Johnny One Note to hold a note long enough to elicit the same kind of praise from the listener that Johnny elicited from the critics—and to do so in an operatic context established by the lyric's intertextual referencing.

In "A Foggy Day (in London Town)" (1937), Ira Gershwin briefly references the British Museum in the same way that Lorenz Hart alludes to the Bronx and Staten Island in "Manhattan" (Kimball & Simon 218). Another brief allusion helps bring some original sparkle to Gershwin's lyric in "But Not for Me," a song based on the familiar situation of a disappointed lover. This lyric, first of all, strikes a self-referential note: "They're writing songs of love," the singer laments, " But not for me" (Kimball & Simon 128). More obviously along the lines we have been pursuing so far is the later observation that love has brought the singer only "more Clouds of Gray/than any Russian play/could guarantee." Although the allusion is not to a specific Russian play or playwright—as would probably be the case in a lyric by Cole Porter—the listener's prior cultural experience is still called into intertextual play. Unless we have some sense that Russian literature is more essentially melancholy than French or English literature, the second complaint makes little sense. But, of course, most listeners in 1930 and today have this sense, and so Gershwin's allusion refreshes a trite lyric situation. More extensive referencing appears in the Gershwins' "They All Laughed" (1936), perhaps because it is a kind of list song (Kimball & Simon 211). The premise is that although everyone predicted that these two lovers would never get together, they have happily done so, proving the skeptics wrong, as other distinguished persons have fooled the experts before. The list of these achievers includes the explorer Christopher Columbus and the inventors Edison, Marconi, Whitney, Fulton, and the Wright Brothers. Equally illustrative—and certainly more Cole-Porterish—successes are the developers of Rockefeller Center and the inventor of the Hershey bar. In this way, Ira Gershwin combines high and low cultural references to bring true novelty to a tired lyric situation. It may be said of Gershwin, as Samuel Johnson said of the highly allusive English metaphysical poets of the seventeenth century, that "nature and art are ransacked for illustrations, comparisons and allusions" (12). While Johnson was displeased by this intertextual practice, however, generations of listeners have praised Gershwin's ingenuity. The final example of Gershwin's allusiveness that space allows is "I Can't Get Started" (1935), which he wrote in collaboration with Vernon Duke (Kimball & Simon 197). Here the situation is very familiar: an unsuccessful lover laments his or her lack of romantic success. However, the development is original in that the singer contrasts the present failure with many previous successes in other realms. Gershwin's field of reference for these successes is quite broad, including exploring the polar Alps, being presented at Court, playing golf under par, selling short during the stock market crash—I still don't know what that means!—and settling revolutions in Spain. Samuel Johnson's remark about ingenuity seems apt once again, as does the sense that most listeners have the past experience necessary to contextualize this ingenious variation on a familiar theme, even if they don't quite understand the intricacies of the stock market.

The other two main forms of intertextuality in the classic American popular song can be distinguished according to the forms of "overt" and "covert" textual self-consciousness that Linda Hutcheon identifies in *Narcissistic Narrative: The Metafictional Paradox*. Artistic self-consciousness of this sort is likely to develop when painters, composers, and authors are acutely aware that they are working within well-established traditions which they can assume to be as familiar to their audiences as to themselves. The Renaissance painter trying to produce still another madonna and child, the Baroque composer trying to extract a morsel of originality out of the motet form, the gothic novelist trying to ring still another change on the locked attic room—all of these artists might adopt an intertextual strategy to remind their audiences of the open secret that conventions are made to be both obeyed and broken. Overt intertextuality in popular song lyrics may be compared to the literary techniques operating in works like John Barth's collection of short fiction, *Lost in the Funhouse* (1968). The title story of Barth's collection, for example, presents a narrative about a young boy named Ambrose who goes to Ocean City, Maryland, with his family. It also presents commentary on the art of fiction—including a diagram of Freitag's Triangle (95)—and on the current story, as in the following: "At this rate our hero, at this rate our protagonist [sic] will remain in the funhouse forever. Narrative ordinarily consists of alternating dramatization and summarization" (78). In this passage, the diegetic illusion is, at least temporarily, suspended to draw the reader's attention to the narrative's status as a literary text. In popular song lyrics the equivalent would be Hart's ostentatious self-reference in his love song, "But Not for Me": "They're writing songs of love,/But not for me." Hutcheon's covert category can be illustrated by works like William Faulkner's *As I Lay Dying* (1930), in which the brief—256 pages in the Vintage paperback—novel's fifty-nine minichapters cannot help attracting the reader's attention to their author's ingenuity, perhaps even more strongly than to the Bundren family's struggles to get Addie safely buried. The pop lyric equivalent here might be Cole Porter's rhyme of *Dante* and *Durante* in "You're the Top," surely an achievement more notable than any of the imaginary lover's perfections.

"You're the Top" can also be fitted into the overt category of intertextual lyric, particularly through the song's opening verse. Thomas Hischak observes that with most song writers "the verse is often the throwaway part of the song. But Porter loved writing verses and excelled at it" (60). Hischak's demonstrative example is "I Get a Kick Out of

You," but it could just as easily be "You're the Top" because the entire verse of this love song focuses on the difficulty of writing love songs. The singer confesses that she—Ethel Merman in the song's original version—is "pathetic" at writing "words poetic." Other terms specifically referring to song writing follow, including *serenading, a bar,* and *ditty.* Like Shakespeare's references to "lines" and "black ink" in his sonnets,[3] these references first clearly tell listeners what they are about to hear before the writer gets on with the traditional business at hand: praising a loved one. Porter's "I Love You" (245) evolves from a similar verse (Kimball 245). Once again the singer—in this case, originally Bing Crosby—confesses an inability to "write" a love song "with words and music divine" and is forced to settle for the lyric that follows, identified here as "my first love song." The lyric is much less impressive than the lyric for "You're the Top," perhaps because Porter reportedly wrote "I Love You" only to prove to Monty Woolley that he could write a song even when presented with such an unimaginative title (Kimball 245). Whatever the case, Porter's song is overtly intertextual, as is the better known and superior "It's De-lovely" (Kimball 146-47). In this song published in 1936, the verse again focuses on writing a "ditty," here explicitly by using the self-referential term "verse." Because this singer fears that his verse might turn out to be the "Tin-Pantithesis of melody," he resolves to "skip the damn thing and sing the refrain." This refrain is very catchy—as many can probably recall—and might qualify as an example of covert intertextuality because of its ostentatious playing with language, as in "It's dilemma, it's delimit, it's deluxe,/It's delovely." Covertness aside, the direct references to song writing in the verse connect "It's De-lovely" with the other overtly intertextual Porter lyrics we have been examining.

Lorenz Hart also wrote love songs overtly concerned with writing love songs. The verse to "Spring is Here" (1929), for example, contrasts the present situation, in which the singer is loveless, to earlier, happier times in which "the world was writing verses like yours and mine." That these verses were usually accompanied by music is made clear as the verse recalls when "All the lads and girls would sing," as opposed to the sad present in which the world is "sadly out of tune." "Spring is Here" probably could make its point even without this verse, but Hart's strategy clearly shows that he knew that he was writing within an established tradition of intertextuality. The refrain of the overtly titled "I Could Write a Book" (1940) confirms this observation. Although the technical terminology in this song is drawn from the print trade—*book, preface, plot*—the dramatic situation resembles those that we have examined already. The whole reason for the singer to write a book "Is just to tell them that I love you a lot" (Hart 147)—the rationale for most of the love songs ever written.

Ira Gershwin displays an understanding of this tradition that easily matches Porter's or Hart's. In "Sing Me Not a Ballad" (1945), written in collaboration with Kurt Weil, Gershwin's lyric denies the value of writing love songs even as four choruses and a verse celebrate love. The ancient goddesses Venus, Cleo, and Psyche inspire the female singer here because, as she says, they "Are melodies in my key" (Kimball & Simon 237), apparently the key of romance. Despite her commitment to making love, this singer doesn't care for "a ballad," "a sonnet," or a "rhyme." She begs her potential lover, "please don't vocalize," even though that is what she is doing herself. Sometimes the need to write still another love song inclines Gershwin toward parody. In "Blah, Blah, Blah" (1931), written with his brother George, Gershwin begins each line with the nonsense words of the title to demonstrate how conventional most love lyrics are. Then he concludes the lines with specific but predictable rhymes: *hair/care, eyes/skies* (Furia 136-37). In this song the fictional lover almost totally disappears, eclipsed by the song-writing tradition in which the writer is far more interested. As one might expect, "What Can You Say in a Love Song (That Hasn't Been Said Before" (1934), written by Ira Gershwin, E. Y. Harburg, and Harold Arlen, is also parodic and overtly intertextual. Instead of "blah, blah, blah," lines in this song begin with "Mn, mn, mn," but the endings are equally bland: *surrender/tender, sweetly/completely* (Furia 123-24). In both songs Gershwin professes the impossibility of writing a new love song after so many predecessors have completely worked over the available materials. Then he goes on to write such a song. Gershwin's overt use of intertextuality is clearly an important part of his lyric style.

Overt intertextuality also occurs in less obvious forms than explicit references to song-writing. Lorenz Hart, for example, is a master at evoking the conventional properties of love songs indirectly. "My Funny Valentine" (1937) invokes the tradition through the last word of the title even while subverting it with the adjective *funny* (Hart 104). As Shakespeare praises his mistress in Sonnet 130 by claiming that her "eyes are nothing like the sun" (*Norton* 190), Hart's singer admits that her lover's "looks are laughable," even "Unphotographable," while praising him as her "favorite work of art." Unlike most Adonis-like lovers, this man has "a figure less than Greek" and a weak-looking mouth. Even so, the singer feels that "Each day is Valentine's Day" with this admittedly imperfect lover, just as Shakespeare's speaker considers his mistress "as rare/As any she belied with false compare." The singer in "Bewitched, Bothered and Bewildered" (1940) also concedes that her lover has distinct limitations. She admits that he is "a laugh," "a pill," a "half-pint imitation," and yet she still feels like "sweet seventeen" again just knowing that he loves her (Hart 154-55). Since both of these songs have been sung, "interpreted," and covered by most of the major ballad singers of modern times, we must assume that the romantic sentiment of the lyrics comes across despite the songs' overt challenges to the tradition to which they both belong.

Hart's "This Can't Be Love" (1938) resembles "My Mistress' Eyes" also. By calling up so many conventional, and traditional, romantic elements—sighs, sobs, dizziness, a heart that stands still—the lyric deliberately reminds listeners of what love songs usually say (Hart 132), just as Shakespeare calls up the over-used conventions of his time including golden hair and snow-white skin. Hart's singer then denies the relevance of the tradition by saying that he feels "so well" even though he "love[s] to look in [his lover's] eyes." As in some of the songs cited earlier, the situation of the smitten singer is familiar—perhaps too familiar—and so the treatment must be original. Paradoxically, this originality is available only because Hart is willing to invoke convention overtly. He does this also in "My Romance" (1935), although the tradition invoked by this lyric derives more obviously from Tin Pan Alley rather than from Shakespearean England.[4] The singer in "My Romance" first of all denies the importance of the items necessary for a conventional romance—and even more so for a conventional romantic ballad—a moon, a blue lagoon, "twinkling stars," "soft guitars" (Hart 92). Even without these familiar properties, this singer can be totally happy because his lover makes his "most fantastic dreams come true." As Shakespeare might agree, the greatest compliment is that nothing is needed for a perfect romance but his lover's presence. Another of Hart's interesting lyric variations on the tradition is "It's Got to Be Love" (1936). Unlike the singer in "This Can't Be Love," this singer does not feel "so well." Like Romeo at the beginning of the play—and like many other love-sick literary characters—this singer feels just awful. Having decided that his problem is not tonsillitis, neuritis, fallen arches, or indigestion, he decides that "It's got to be love" (Hart 95), and another love song gets written by working against the conventions with which its listeners are already familiar.

It seems to me that this familiarity is responsible for Cole Porter's frequent insistence that his current lyric is not just the same old thing. This "same old thing" thus becomes the intertext for lyrics like "I've Got You Under My Skin" (1936), "I Get a Kick Out of You" (1934), and "Let's Do It" (1928). The first song is probably the most traditional in professing without irony the singer's total immersion in his lover. (Even the whiny Bono gets the point in his 1994 duet with Frank Sinatra on "I've Got You Under My Skin.") On the other hand, the slangy expression that gives the song its title forces the song to play intertextually against the hundreds of other love songs that express this idea more conventionally. This is equally true of "I Get a Kick Out of You," a song that expresses the very conventional idea of helpless enthrallment through the very unconventional device of understatement. Getting a kick out of something is a far cry from burning with passion, becoming a totally new person, or any of the more common situations in which musical lovers usually find themselves. "Let's Do It" also studiously avoids the customary language of love, this time in favor of an unexpected directness. Since the sexually explicit slang meaning of "doing it" cannot be part of a mainstream popular song in 1928, the lyric also swerves intertextually between a graphic invitation for sexual intercourse and a more conventional entreaty—"Let's fall in love" (Kimball 72). In all of these cases, Porter overtly invokes a well-established lyric tradition primarily in order to work subtle variations on the tradition.

"Let's Do It" also opens the way to a discussion of more covert forms of lyric intertextuality. This song not only plays with the audience's understanding of what is sexually proper in a popular love song, it also teases the audience's ear with clever rhymes.[5] The listing in this lyric mostly involves animals and people of various nations who "do it." The former category includes birds, bees, sponges, and jellyfish, and the latter, Lapps, the Dutch, and Argentines. Some prior cultural experience may be necessary if listeners are to respond fully to these allusions, but the greater challenge is posed by the highly ingenious rhymes with which Porter mixes the categories and expands his list. Thus, the word *Lithuanians* is connected alliteratively to *Letts* primarily so that the lyric can return to the title in the rhyme: "Let's do it." The Finns merely prepare the way for Siam and Siamese twins, just as shad enter the list of amorous fish mostly to enable the phrase *shad row*—a rhyme for the "shocks 'em I know" that accompanies the electric eels. The principal effect of these rhymes must be attracting the listener's attention to their author rather than to the romantic designs of the singer or even to the apparently universal force of sexual desire. Someone wrote this song in this way to distinguish it from other songs with similar subjects, we realize, and this recognition helps us to appreciate the more covert forms of lyric intertextuality.

As we have already seen, Porter's "You're the Top" is also distinguished by its ingenious rhyming of *Dante* and *Durante*, distinguished names from very different cultural realms. Elsewhere in the lyric, Porter makes equally incongruous linkages through clever rhyming, as when

Mahatma Gandhi is paired with Napoleon brandy, and a summer night in Spain with cellophane. These examples of what the rhetoricians call "zeugma"[6] attract our attention to the writer's daring as well as to his technical proficiency. Who would dare equate such cultural anomalies, even implicitly? Most likely this sort of daring is what Hischak had in mind when he wrote that "Porter taught the audience to listen for lyrics. Even more so than Wodehouse and Berlin before him, Porter made lyrics fun for the audience" (61). At the opposite extreme from the kind of lyric parodied in Gershwin's "Blah, Blah, Blah," Porter's rhyming of "the feet of Fred Astaire" with Camembert and Dutch master with Mrs. Astor in "You're the Top" shows zeugma to be a highly effective form of covert intertextuality.

Porter's cultural derivations—He was, after all, a Yale graduate!—are perhaps apparent in his song "Brush Up Your Shakespeare" from *Kiss Me Kate* (1948). Although not a boy-meets-girl song, this lyric belongs to the romantic tradition because the proposed result of brushing up one's knowledge of the Bard is that "the women you will wow" (Kimball 279-80). Of course, hoping to achieve success with the ladies is merely an excuse for Porter's outrageous rhymes, here often based on the titles of Shakespeare's plays. "[H]elluva fella" rhymes with *Othella*, *Troilus and Cressida* with "British embessida," and *Merchant of Venice* with "her sweet pound o' flesh you would menace." Especially in the first two cases, Porter's contrivances are the real subject of the song, as they are when he rhymes "flatter her" with "Cleopaterer" and "ravin'" with "The bard of Stratford-on-Avon." Listeners must of course contextualize this lyric intertextually in terms of their own knowledge of Shakespeare's works, but they must also must recognize on some level this lyric's relations with the songs that constitute the tradition's usual contours.

Porter acknowledges the tradition covertly in another fashion in "It's De-lovely." Because so many songs have used so many words to say pretty much the same things, "It's De-lovely" demonstrates that new songs must twist language as well as rhymes to make an original statement. There is, of course, no such word as *de-lovely*, but once this difficulty has been overcome—or at least ignored—the lyric is free to mix actual words including *delirious* and *delicious* with nonsense words like *delimit, diveen*, and *de vallop*. The result is still another song about how wonderful love can be that does not sound like just another song about how wonderful love can be. Like most of the songs discussed already, "It's De-lovely" was originally written for a Broadway show, Porter's *Red, Hot, and Blue* (1936), which also included "Ridin' High" and "Down in the Depths (On the Ninetieth Floor)." That these songs can be discussed individually, outside of their dramatic context, illustrates another point that Maher makes in his introduction to Wilder's *American Popular Song*: "[M]ost of the great innovators of American popular song have worked in the theater—have, in fact, made their careers in musical theater." Even so, Maher explains, "good musical theater songs . . . take on lives of their own, long outlasting their original shows" (xxx). "Thou Swell," a song written by Lorenz Hart for *A Connecticut Yankee* (1927), supports Maher's view and also resembles "It's De-lovely" in its free-handed approach to language. Although Hart invents no words for this song, his adoption of the antique *thou* and corresponding verb forms including *wouldst* and *couldst* (Hart 55) transforms this somewhat predictable love song into an original work distinguished by its intertextual clash with the conventional. The loved one—alternately the Yankee and his girl Sandy—is praised by the singer for her/his eyes, cheek, grace, and wit, as might be the case in most conventional love songs. Hart's use of the archaic *thou*, especially when coupled with the contemporary slang term *swell*, creates instead a sense of novelty. Frederick Nolan credits Hart's "dextrous marriage of medieval archaism and modern slang" with the song's achievement. "Thou Swell" was, according to Nolan, "daringly superior, both lyrically and musically, to even the best Broadway shows of the time" (108). Much of this superiority derives from Hart's intertextual exploitation of the tradition. Ira Gershwin's "'S Wonderful," written for *Funny Face* (1927), is another good example of this kind of covert intertextuality. Again, the sentiment is unexceptional: the singer claims that his lover makes his life wonderful, glamorous, "awful nice," just like Paradise, even as other swains have claimed for centuries. By beginning each statement with the elided word '*S*, however, Gershwin transforms these conventional sentiments into original lyrics. As we might perhaps expect by this point, he achieves this originality by invoking the tradition intertextually. The success of all three songs in later recordings by Ella Fitzgerald, Bobby Short, Carmen McRae, and others demonstrates the accuracy of Maher's insight that great theater songs take on an independent life long after the show has closed—or been forgotten.

"'S Wonderful" is worthy of discussion on another basis too. In expounding on the positive effects of love, the singer says that now his life is "glamorous" and that he is feeling "amorous." Clearly, Cole Porter is not the only classic popular lyricist capable of ingenious rhyming. Gershwin gives further evidence of this in "Embraceable You" (1930), when he rhymes the title phase with "irreplaceable you"; "arms about you" with "charms about you"; and "my heart grew tipsy in me" with "bring out the gypsy in me" (Kimball & Simon 125). As with some of

Porter's more noteworthy stretches, Gershwin's use of extended feminine rhymes attracts our attention more to the rhymes themselves than to their purported subjects.[7] We are reminded that we are listening to a song, not to an ecstatic lover. Frederick Nolan discusses Lorenz Hart's "Mountain Greenery" (1926) from this angle, claiming that the song "with its bright, insistent triplets, is pure Rodgers and Hart," and citing as evidence "the fresh uniqueness of the . . . rhymes" (80-81), especially the ones based on the title: *greenery/scenery/keener re-*(ception)*/beanery/cleaner-re*(treat). Without Rodgers' melody, it is probably impossible to recognize how naturally Hart absorbs these highly contrived feminine rhymes into his lyric. However, it is probably easier, without being captivated by the melody, to see how insistently Hart draws attention to his technique as a song writer.

As one might expect, Porter, Hart, and Gershwin were not the only artists producing intertextual song lyrics during this period. Other talented lyricists including Haven Gillespie, Oscar Hammerstein II, E. Y. Harburg, Johnny Mercer, and P. G. Wodehouse were also writing songs that were filled with cultural allusions and that deliberately displayed overt and covert textual testimony to the existence of the vital tradition of the classic American popular song.

Johnny Mercer's "Hooray for Hollywood" (1938), for example, written with Richard A. Whiting, is very well known. It is probably less well known that Mercer's lyric allusively establishes the milieu of Hollywood by citing celebrities like Shirley Temple, Aimee Semple, Donald Duck, Max Factor, and Tyrone Power and snobbishly excluding specific places like Chilicothe, Ohio, and Paducah, Kentucky. The artificiality associated with Hollywood is also conveyed allusively: the term *Coney* is an apt rhyme for *phony*, but it is also a reference to a famous amusement park (Bach & Mercer 61). The E. Y. Harburg/Harold Arlen song "It's Only a Paper Moon" (1932) makes a similar point in a similar way when Harburg's lyric explains the emptiness of life without love by asserting that "It's a Barnum and Bailey world" (Meyerson & Harburg 67). More extensive referencing—in the manner of Cole Porter's list songs—also had intertextual appeal to some of these other lyricists. One of Mercer's last songs, "My New Celebrity Is You" (1976), written with and for the jazz thrush Blossom Dearie, alludes to more than two dozen celebrities as well as to many specific places and art works. Since Mercer was known for writing the same sort of intricate Christmas rhymes that Frank Sullivan popularized in *The New Yorker* under the title, "Greetings, Friends," it is probably unsurprising that he might link the names *Ethel Merman* and *Woody Herman*. There would be no point to Mercer's doing so, however, if members of Blossom Dearie's audience lacked the prior cultural experience to make the necessary intertextual connections. This is even more true when Mercer rhymes Mia Farrow with Pierce Arrow, and then justifies the apparent anachronism by alluding to Farrow's role in the recent film, *The Great Gatsby* (Bach & Mercer 224-25). These examples suggest that, like Porter, Hart, and Gershwin, other tradition-conscious lyricists, including Mercer and Harburg, trusted their listeners to catch their allusions and contextualize new song lyrics within an already-existing cultural matrix, the "cultural encyclopedia" originally identified by Umberto Eco.

Other resemblances to Porter, Hart, and Gershwin are suggested by some of the overtly self-referential textual devices used by other lyricists of the time. The verse to Mercer's "You Were Never Lovelier" (1942), written with Jerome Kern, adopts a familiar device in asserting that the singer has never been able "to recite a fable" that might make him a success at parties (Bach & Mercer 108). As we have seen, Lorenz Hart's "But Not for Me" and Cole Porter's "You're the Top" begin with similar references to the literary tradition that constitutes the American popular song. As we have also seen, these writers then jump off from this premise to do what they have previously claimed to be impossible, that is, to write a love lyric of praise. Mercer does the same thing when he gets around to repeating the song's real message, contained in the title, "You Were Never Lovelier." Since this song was originally sung by Fred Astaire to Rita Hayworth in the film of the same title, the aptness of the song's sentiment should be apparent.[8]

Mercer's justly famous "Blues in the Night" (1941), with melody by Harold Arlen, calls on another familiar intertextual device. As in Ira Gershwin's lyric for "Sing Me Not a Ballad," Mercer asserts as part of his song about romantic sentiment that songs are the natural vehicle for romantic sentiment—in Mercer's case, for the sadder side. Even a mocking bird will "Sing the saddest song" when confronted with the sort of romantic heartbreak that has caused this singer to sing his own blues (Bach and Mercer 98). Duke Ellington's "I Let a Song Go Out of My Heart" (1938), written with Irving Mills, Henry Nemo, and John Redmond, also concentrates on the unsatisfactory side of love and also does so by asserting that a song is the most suitable vehicle for this sort of sentiment. In addition, this song's verse overtly invokes the popular song tradition by postulating that "Everyone has a favorite song" (*Great Music of Duke Ellington* 62). The twist in this case is that the lost loved one is the singer's favorite song, the "sweetest melody" that he or she has ever known. In another original touch, the lyric (perhaps predictably) begs, "Please come back sweet music," but then moves outside of romantic conventionality to add, "I know I was wrong" (63). An equation between the loved one and a song also underlies "The Song Is You" (1932) by Jerome Kern and Oscar Hammerstein II. Probably the most familiar part of Hammerstein's lyric is the opening claim, "I hear music when I look at you" (Hammerstein 134). The self-referential closing lines are, however, the most blatantly intertextual. "The music is sweet," the singer claims, and "The words are true." Is this about a loved one, the listener wonders, or is it about a song called "The Song Is You"? This question is tantalizingly left unanswered as the lyric concludes, "The song is you" (136). In each of these three songs, lyric attention slides back and forth from the loved one to the tradition of the popular song.

The Harburg/Arlen song "Down with Love" (1937) also requires divided, intertextual, attention from its listener. Simply giving the command contained in the title presupposes that "love" is conventionalized enough to be summed up in a single word. The lyric reinforces this supposition by listing properties conventionally associated with love, including, flowers, rice, shoes, and midnight blues. Since the last item at least suggests the popular song tradition, it is entirely plausible that the list goes on to include "moon" and "June," almost a short-hand version of the whole tradition. The decisive evidence arises when the lyric explicitly says, "Down with songs/That moan about night and day" (Meyerson & Harburg 114). If the lyric causes the listener to think about Cole Porter's "Night and Day" (1932), the intertextual gain is a bonus.

Overt intertextuality also reigns in the Harburg/Barton Lane song "If This Isn't Love" (1947), from the Broadway musical *Finian's Rainbow*. As Lorenz Hart develops his lyrics in "This Can't Be Love" and "It's Got to be Love" by directly calling on his listener's previous exposure to popular love songs, Harburg presupposes that we will assume the "moon" and "June" missing from his lyric merely on his assertion that "I'll eat my hat if this isn't love" (Meyerson & Harburg 247). Perhaps as an internal reference to this promise, the lyric also makes an external allusion to "Carmen Miranda" and a politically more adventurous reference to "red propaganda"—both references used to deny the opposite of what is being asserted. The "moon" and "June" tradition also functions overtly behind the Mercer/Whiting song "Too Marvelous for Words" (1937) and Hammerstein/Kern's "All the Things You Are" (1939). In the former lyric, the verse alludes to tradition by claiming, on behalf of the singer, "I search for phrases,/To sing your praises," and then concluding with the desperate praise contained in the title (Bach & Mercer 58). Along the way, Mercer cleverly rhymes "glamorous" with "amorous," but the lyric is impressive chiefly because of its effective invocation of the tradition. The same might be said of Hammerstein's effective exploitation of the hyperbolic element in this tradition. The loved one directly addressed in this lyric could only be flattered by being sincerely compared to the beauties of springtime, evening, and a star. Since the evening is connected to "a lovely song" (Hammerstein 3-6), it should perhaps be clear to her that these flattering comparisons are emerging from a long line of similar claims. It must certainly have been clear to Hammerstein, or he would not have adopted the generalizing title, "All the Things You Are." Though worlds away from Gershwin's "Blah, Blah, Blah" in sentiment, Hammerstein's lyric equally suggests the difficulties of writing originally with such a powerful tradition in the back of one's mind.

"Bill" (1927), another Kern/Hammerstein collaboration, this time with lyric assistance by P. G. Wodehouse, clearly connects their work with previously discussed songs like Hart's "My Funny Valentine." As in Hart's song, Bill is seemingly disqualified as a lover because of his departures from the conventional mold. Bill is not "one of those God-like kind of men." He lacks "a giant brain and a noble head," and so the singer can confidently say, "It's surely not his brain" that makes her love him so. Like Shakespeare's mistress, Bill is loved just for himself, "Because he's just my Bill" (Hammerstein 66-68). Through denial, then, the traditional kind of lover is intertextually invoked. Traditional language is similarly invoked in the Mercer/Harry Warren song, "Jeepers Creepers" (1938). In his commentary on this song, Bob Bach quotes Mercer's recollection that he heard Henry Fonda use this catchy phrase in a movie. "I thought it would be a cute idea for a song," Mercer explained (Bach & Mercer 63). While we might agree, we might also be inclined to assume by this point that the phrase's potential cuteness lies in its departure from the conventional language of praise adopted by poets from Shakespeare's time all through the twentieth century. Some advantages of this departure quickly appear as Mercer rhymes the words of the title with *peepers* and *weepers*, both far slangier terms than *eyes*, a word that appears only at the very end of the chorus. Equally adventurous is Mercer's rhyme of "heaters on" (for eyes) with "cheaters on" (for eyeglasses). After Shakespeare's ingenious strategy in "My Mistress' Eyes," one might have assumed that all the possible intertextual variations on this convention had been exhausted, but the puncturing of such assumptions is one of the principal advantages involved in the study of these song lyrics.

Mercer's skills as a rhymster are evident too in the jazz classic "Midnight Sun" (1954), written with Sonny Burke and Lionel Hampton. As Bach says in his commentary, this song is "[w]ithout question a Mercer tour de force." Bach then asks rhetorically, "[W]ho else could put together such rhymes without making it sound contrived?" (Bach and Mercer 173). Even without strongly disagreeing with the editor's highly partisan appraisal, we might be able to think by this point of some other lyricists who would be up to the task. Whether or not we would care to compile such a list, we would be forced to recognize the extraordinary achievement that Mercer's lyric represents. "[R]ed and ruby chalice" rhymes with "alabaster palace," and both phrases rhyme with "aurora borealis." Even more striking to my mind is the gorgeous phrase, "And we may see the meadow in December,/Icy white and crystalline." Exactly how contrived or uncontrived such language is probably must remain a matter of personal judgment, but it seems safe to assume that ingenuity of this sort inevitably must remind suitably experienced listeners of other lyrics less (or perhaps equally) ingenious.

Ingenuity of another kind is apparent in "You Go to My Head" (1938), by Haven Gillespie and J. Fred Coots. Gillespie's rhymes are good enough in their way, as in the triplets *refrain/my brain/champagne* and *brew/you/too*. More noteworthy in all probability is the elaborateness of the basic metaphor. As the title promises, the singer compares the effect of his loved one to the effects of strong drink. Thus, he conjures up "the bubbles in a glass of champagne," "a sip of sparkling burgundy brew," and "the kicker in a julep or two" (*Frank Sinatra's Songs of Romance* 20-21) as correlatives of her appeal. As in the case of the highly ingenious rhymes in many of Mercer's songs, we cannot lose sight of the writer of "You Go to My Head"—even in the presence of such an intoxicating loved one. We may thus grow aware of another instance of covert intertextuality.

As the coda to a discussion that could easily be extended, let us turn to one of Jerome Kern's early hits, "Who?" (1927), written with Otto Harbach and Oscar Hammerstein II (Hammerstein 54-57). Lacking the lush orchestral possibilities of songs like "Midnight Sun" and "You Go To My Head," this perky melody still provides intertextual possibilities in its lyric. In a less cynical variant on the device epitomized by "Blah, Blah, Blah," Harbach and Hammerstein begin their lines with the interrogative *who*. The following phrases *stole my heart away?, makes me dream all day?,* etc. perhaps merit little attention or comment, but the overall lyric formula constitutes another clever adaptation to the constraints and opportunities of a highly conventionalized musical genre.

Although some of these intertextual lyrics were written after 1950—and Mercer's "My New Celebrity Is You" as late as 1974—it is safe to say that the first half of the twentieth century constitutes the lifespan of the classic American popular song.[9] Just as there were probably many factors involved in the birth of this genre, many factors contributed to bring about its decline. In *The Oxford Companion to Popular*

Music Richard Gammond explains that "After Gershwin and the 1940s, popular music was to move away from craft to folk art, with the theatre proving to be the last bastion of the kind of music that Gershwin, Kern, Cole Porter, and Richard Rodgers created. A song of their period was something that could still be performed by anyone from the printed page; but concurrently the predominance of jazz was leading to popular music's being almost entirely what the performer made it and how it was interpreted on record" (222). An individual artist's "interpretation" of a song, rather than a composer or lyricist's ingenuity in finding a new way to write an old kind of song, became the principal gauge of musical value. The consequence of this shift in emphasis was, according to James T. Maher's introduction to Alec Wilder's *American Popular Song*, that "By 1950 the professional tradition in song writing was nearing its end. . . . Consumption patterns in popular music had changed rapidly in the post World War II years. Singers and singing groups enjoyed a new primacy in the ordering of economic priorities in the pop market. The big dance bands had priced themselves into oblivion" (xxxvi-xxvii). Even without succumbing to bleak nostalgia, we may lament the passing of such a tradition, all the while celebrating its many achievements, especially in regard to these artists' highly ingenious exploitation of the devices of intertextuality.

INTERTEXTUAL ANIMATION:
THE CLASSIC WARNER BROTHERS CARTOONS
AND *ROCKY AND BULLWINKLE*

In a 1995 essay about the classic *Looney Tunes* and *Merrie Melodies* cartoons made by the Warner Brothers studio, David Chute explains that "the one great advantage that movies made from drawings must have over movies made from photographs . . . [is] that absolutely anything is possible" (14). By this, Chute means that an anvil can be dropped from a great height onto the head of Wile E. Coyote in an animated cartoon and do no permanent damage to the character, whereas an anvil dropped on the head of a living actor—say, Harry Dean Stanton— would kill the man and, Chute says, outrage his union. However, movies made from drawings also share many properties with movies made from photographs. Previous chapters have revealed how frequently feature films create intertextual encounters to engage their audiences more fully. The same may be said of animated cartoons—and not only of those cartoons originally intended to be screened in motion picture theaters. Television animators raised on classic theatrical cartoons during childhood are just as inclined as their predecessors to turn to intertextual animation when they get to draw their own shows as adults.

In the cartoons produced by the Warner Brothers' studio from the 1930s through the 1960s,[1] for example, several forms of intertextuality can be easily identified. Sometimes individual cartoons call upon the viewers' extradiegetic cultural experience through brief or extended allusions to famous titles, events, and celebrities. Sometimes this allusive framework extends all the way to parody, either of a specific popular cultural text like Stanley Kramer's film *The Defiant Ones*, or more generally of a film genre like the Western or the swashbuckler. *The Rabbit of Seville* and *What's Opera, Doc?*, two justly famous cartoon parodies of classical music genres, clearly belong to this class of intertextuality also. Finally, these Warner Brothers cartoons sometimes allude directly to their own nature as cartoons, as when Daffy Duck gets into an argument with the artist who is drawing him in *Duck Amuck* or when he persuades Porky Pig to break his contract with Leon Schlesinger in *You Oughta Be in Pictures*. In all these cases, the primary animated text interacts fruitfully with one or more other texts with which members of the audience can be assumed to be already familiar. Intertextual encounters result.

Extradiegetic allusions come in all sizes in these cartoons. In *Eight Ball Bunny* (1950), for example, while Bugs Bunny is trying to get a baby penguin back to his home at the South Pole, they keep running into an animated Humphrey Bogart who asks Bugs each time, "Could you help out a fellow American who's down on his luck?" Bogey's face would probably be recognizable to most American movie-goers in 1950 under almost any circumstances. Since he is drawn here in his Fred C. Dobbs role from *The Treasure of Sierra Madre* (1948), his appearance and his pathetic request are inescapably intertextual. A similar air of the recently famous defines *Long Haired Hare*, a cartoon released the year before *Eight Ball Bunny*. The plot in this case involves a feud between a pop-music-loving Bugs Bunny and an obnoxious opera singer. After several minutes of low-comedy trickery, Bugs eventually assumes the role of a maniacal conductor when the tenor tries to give a performance. Significantly, the formally dressed Bugs now has Leopold Stokowski's trademark long curls and the maestro's furiously animated demeanor. Stokowski is a brilliant intertextual reference here since in 1949 he was the classical conductor most readily identifiable by most members of the cinema audience, perhaps because of his appearance in Walt Disney's *Fantasia* (1940). By the same token, nearly everyone was familiar with Alfred Hitchcock in 1961, and so his animated appearance in *The Last Hungry Cat* makes perfect intertextual sense. In an obvious allusion to the sort of macabre plotting favored on the then-enormously-popular television series, *Alfred Hitchcock Presents*, the plot of this cartoon requires Sylvester to experience excruciating pangs of conscience under the assumption that he has, at long last, actually devoured Tweety. By the end of the cartoon, Sylvester has become more than annoyed at the animated Hitchcock's pomposity, and so he lobs a brick at him. The closing shot shows a silhouette familiar from so many TV shows with a lump on its head.

In other cartoons, multiple celebrity references have a similar intertextual function—to elicit the audience's extradiegetic experience in a new context in order to afford a pleasing shock of recognition. The practice can perhaps best be understood as an animated form of the old vaudeville intertextual staple—doing impressions. The most obvious instance is probably *What's Cookin' Doc?*, released on the first day of 1944. In this cartoon, Bugs attends the Academy Awards ceremony and does impressions of such easily recognizable film personalities as Edward G. Robinson, Jerry Colonna, and Bing Crosby. *Hollywood*

Canine Canteen, released in 1946, alludes to these same familiar faces and voices as well as to the equally recognizable Jimmy Durante, Carmen Miranda, and Frank Sinatra. As in such live-action films as *Stage Door Canteen* (1943) and *Hollywood Canteen* (1944), simply recognizing celebrities affords one kind of pleasure. Animation adds a second level of aesthetic comparison and contrast. In an especially original twist, the celebrities in *Hollywood Canine Canteen* are drawn as dogs, an important element in the cartoon's punning references to some familiar bandleaders: "Hairy" James, Tommy "Dorgey," Lionel "Hambone," and "Boney" Goodman. Goodman, James, Dorsey, and Sinatra also appear—although not as dogs—in *Book Review*, a Daffy Duck cartoon released in the same year. Furthermore, in an intertextual device that I will speak more about later, Daffy enters this cartoon on the cover of an issue of *Looney Tunes Comics*.

The viewers' extradiegetic experience of American popular culture is also crucial to *The Ducksters* (1950), in which Daffy is the host of a radio program very much like *Truth or Consequences*, and Porky is his unfortunate contestant. Most of the humor turns on Daffy's abuse of Porky, but the usual comic violence—gongs, sledgehammers, explosions—is effectively contextualized here by the *Truth or Consequences* formula of question and answer, advice from the studio audience ("You'll be sorry!"), and Daffy's smarmy radio-MC's reluctance to invoke the promised punishment. There is enough familiar shtick here to entertain 'Nineties children who may be seeing this cartoon for the first time on television, but Chuck Jones obviously had in mind an original audience steeped in the conventions of old radio programs. In praise of another intertextual encounter, Will Friedwald and Jerry Beck say in *The Warner Brothers Cartoons* that *D'Fightin' Ones* (1961) is "One of [Friz] Freleng's greatest films of the entire sixties" (226). It is certainly one of the most clearly intertextual because it obviously parodies *The Defiant Ones*, Stanley Kramer's greatly celebrated 1958 film in which two escaped convicts, played by Tony Curtis and Sidney Poitier, are chained together against their wills and strong racial prejudices. In Freleng's version, the convicts—Sylvester and a mean bulldog—are divided by species rather than by race, and the thematic issues are much less serious. Even so—or perhaps for these very reasons—the intertextual influences are particularly strong.

Allusive intertextuality increases in the cartoons containing live-action cameos, as in *The Mouse That Jack Built*, directed by Bob McKimson and released in 1959. Here the premise is a *Jack Benny Program* featuring all the characters familiar to the audience from radio and—more recently—from television, except that they are here all drawn as mice. The intertextual resonances are especially clear because the voices are not supplied by Mel Blanc, as is usually the case, but by the *Benny* show's actual cast members. In an especially intertextual moment, a live-action Jack Benny comes onscreen to end *The Mouse That Jack Built.* Errol Flynn also guest-stars in one of these cartoons when his film *The Adventures of Robin Hood* (1938) is invoked as an intertext for *Rabbit Hood* (1949). In this film starring—as one might expect—Bugs Bunny, a live-action clip from Flynn's film concludes that cartoon. What, we might ask, is a viewer to do who hasn't seen Flynn's film? For anyone sitting in a movie theater in 1949, the question might seem disingenuous. By 2001, the number of viewers possessing the necessary intertextual background would be swelled enormously by those who had seen *The Adventures of Robin Hood* only on television. Perhaps some viewers today might be deprived of either experience. The intertext (or intertexts) is (or are) intended to be present in any case, whether any specific viewer "gets" them or not.

With *Duck Rogers in the Twenty Fourth and a Half Century* (1953), the referential dimension of the cartoon's intertextuality is at once specific and more general than the *Benny* program or Flynn's swashbuckler. The name *Buck Rogers* clearly resounds in the title, carrying with it a considerable stock of radio, comic book, and film serial allusions. In the second edition of their study of Warner Brothers cartoons—entitled *Looney Tunes and Merrie Melodies*—Friedwald and Beck suggest that we also contextualize this cartoon in the environment created by popular television space epics of the early 'Fifties, including *Captain Video* (251). The suggestion makes sense because Warner Brothers cartoons seem to have discovered space as a thematic topic around the same time that the rest of the culture did. This probably accounts for the first appearance in this film of the space creature who will later be identified in a series of Bugs Bunny cartoons as Marvin the Martian. In any event, *Duck Rogers* looks and sounds like many of the b-grade sci-fi movies of the day. The important intertextual point, of course, is that Chuck Jones was consciously creating a shlock space thriller for Daffy Duck, something he could do successfully only if he and the members of his audience were equally familiar with the unconscious shlock produced for live actors by other directors. Since we are just as familiar with movies of this sort today—if for no other reason than *Mystery Science Theater Three Thousand*—the beat goes on.

This kind of (perhaps) secondary cultural experience also seems to me to be at work in *The Rabbit of Seville* (1950) and *What's Opera, Doc?* (1957), the famous cartoons rooted in classical musical genres. While these are the only Warner Brothers cartoons ever recalled by a certain sort of academic—they don't even mention *One Froggy Evening* (1955) or *Raw! Raw! Rooster* (1956)—this seems to me the fault of the academics and not of the cartoons. Just as piano solos by Jose Iturbe and Oscar Levant could be called upon to interject some high-cultural seasoning into feature films of the time, so the score from Gioacchino Rossini's *The Barber of Seville* situates Bugs Bunny's feud with Elmer Fudd in a new cultural context—and temporarily legitimates animated cartoons for a certain sort of viewer. As *Long Haired Hare* suggests, there is probably some sort of high culture/low culture intertextual conflict involved whenever cartoon animals interact with figures from the world of classical music.[2] In *The Rabbit of Seville*, this clash is pushed all the way to parody as Rossini's music is used to closely underscore Bugs's maniacal activities of shaving, clipping, debagging, and generally abusing Elmer. The match of score to on-screen action is so close, in fact, and the new lyrics by Chuck Jones and Michael Maltese so apt, that there are surely thousands who associate this music *only* with Bugs Bunny and not with the celebrated opera stars who supposedly supply the cartoon with its intertext. For these viewers too, the fact that Bugs and Elmer enact a wedding scene in this cartoon probably establishes the kind of happy ending that "usually" occurs in operas. They might be quite surprised, therefore, when Bugs dies in the Wagnerian parody *What's Opera, Doc?* The object of parody in this case—Wagner's entire *Ring Cycle*—is less specific than the operatic intertext in *The Rabbit of Seville*, but the adaptation of music to action is equally brilliant. As Friedwald and Beck put it in *Looney Tunes and Merrie Melodies*, "There is matching and mis-matching of Wagner to Warners" (299). Though the action is somewhat less antic and more deliberately parodic than in the earlier classical music cartoon, Bugs still triumphs over Elmer through most of the picture. Even when Elmer slays Bugs and carries him toward the funeral pyre in the cartoon's conclusion, the rascally rabbit gets the last intertextual line: "Well, what did ya expect in an opera? A happy ending?" Surely there are just as many viewers who believe, on the basis of *What's Opera, Doc?*, that all operas end tragically as there are who believe, on the basis of *The Rabbit of Seville*, that all operas include a wedding scene.

For the intended audiences of some other cartoon parodies, the possession of cultural touchstones may be more confidently assumed. Taking into account that Warner Brothers intended these cartoons to be included on a bill with a feature film, the viewers' familiarity with the defining properties of popular film genres would be taken for granted. *Bugs Bunny Rides Again*, for example, was first released in 1948, the year in which *Fort Apache*, *Four Faces West*, *The Paleface*, *Red River*,

Yellow Sky, and numerous other Westerns also appeared. Possibly as a result, Bugs and Yosemite Sam are perfectly familiar with the conventions of gun fighting, calling each other out, challenging each other to get out of town, and poker playing. Bugs even says to Sam that they should play cards "like in the Western pictures." Friz Freleng confidently assumes that his viewers have seen as many Westerns as Bugs and Yosemite Sam. In 1963 Chuck Jones assumed similarly that his viewers would have enough background of horror movies to supply a rich intertext for his *Transylvania 6-5000*. Surely he was right in his assumptions. A spooky castle, bats, the magic name *Transylvania*, and a character drawn to resemble Bela Lugosi should be enough familiar elements to signal "vampire movie" to any viewer armed with the suitable cinematic experience. And what viewer might be assumed to lack such?

The final category of Warner Brothers cartoons requiring mention are those in which cartoons themselves are the intertexts. Daffy's entrance from the cover of an issue of *Looney Tunes Comics* in *Book Review* provides an example of this sort of overt intertextuality at the simplest level. *Stage Door Cartoon* (1944) is somewhat more complex. This cartoon first establishes a show-business intertext by alluding in its title to such popular celebrity-filled films of the time as *Stage Door Canteen*, just as *Hollywood Canine Canteen* does. *Stage Door Cartoon* introduces another kind of intertext, however, by having Bugs and Elmer briefly suspend their feud to watch a Bugs Bunny cartoon. When Elmer sees the on-screen Bugs pulling a trick on the on-screen Elmer by donning a sheriff's outfit, he concludes that the diegetic sheriff who has arrested him is also Bugs in disguise. This sheriff turns out to be real, however, and so Elmer is dragged off to jail. The diegetic Bugs is actually disguised as the orchestra conductor, Leopold Stokowski. We have seen Stokowski invoked as an intertext before, but we have not seen Bugs Bunny cartoons used in this way. Then again, why not? Aren't Warner Brothers cartoons part of American culture?

Rabbit Every Monday (1951) also refers directly to its nature as film, and it draws the viewer's attention even more directly to the medium itself. Early in the cartoon, Yosemite Sam turns to a member of an animated audience situated somewhere between the diegetic on-screen story and the actual audience and threatens to shoot a silhouetted man if he tries to leave the theater. The scene is not necessary to Sam's Elmer-Fudd-like pursuit of Bugs, but it does introduce another source of comedy into the cartoon by recognizing that the actual audience is in on the joke. This becomes even more important at the end of the cartoon. First, Sam forces Bugs into the belly of a wood-burning stove. Then, Bugs repeatedly comes out of the stove for ice, ash trays, and a bottle opener, while hot music plays within. Convinced by this evidence that a party is going on inside the stove, Sam jumps into the blaze, causing Bugs to feel sorry for "the little nimrod." When Bugs opens the oven, however, we see live-action, black-and-white film of a wild party, and the contrast inevitably draws our attention to the surrounding color animation. In recognition of this self-referential shock, Bugs says, "I don't ask questions, I just have fun." We need hardly add that it is intertextual fun.

You Oughta Be in Pictures (1940) surpasses the examples we have seen so far in exploiting the overtly intertextual possibilities inherent in mixing media. In pioneering anticipation of the techniques later used with such success in *Who Framed Roger Rabbit?* (1988), Friz Freleng cleverly combines footage of the animated Porky Pig and Daffy Duck with live-action film of Warner Brothers producer Leon Schlesinger (playing himself) and Michael Maltese (playing a movie studio security guard). At one point, Schlesinger even shakes hands with Porky. The reason for this technically sophisticated encounter is that Porky has been persuaded by Daffy to get out of his contract to appear in Schlesinger's Warner Brothers cartoons so that the pig can play romantic leading roles opposite Bette Davis and Greta Garbo. Of course, Daffy is only interested in taking over Porky's leading role in cartoons, but the gullible Porky believes him and ends up trying to sneak onto the live lot as countless aspiring actors have tried to do in countless other movies about the movies. In the sort of ploy familiar from such films, Porky eventually resorts to disguise—as Oliver Hardy. No one is fooled by Porky/ Ollie; he fails to break into live-action acting; and so he happily returns to a relieved Schlesinger's still-open arms. Along the way, Porky encounters intertextuality on the sets of Western and musical films as well as in his Hardy impression. Members of the audience also unavoidably encounter intertextuality when they are reminded that the cartoon they are watching right this minute is a film made by the same people who make Westerns, musicals, and romances. Another intertextual reminder is sent technically by this cartoon's clever mixing of live action and animation, a mix emphasized by the fact that this cartoon is made in black and white when the live audience in 1940 would naturally expect a color cartoon. What this all adds up to, according to *The Warner Brothers Cartoons*, is an "acknowledged classic cartoon" (73).

I would claim classic status also for *Duck Amuck* (1953) even though this cartoon is drawn in full color and lacks any live-action sequences. The premise of this plot (written by Michael Maltese) is that Daffy is feuding with his unseen animator. Every time the duck seems to be settling down in a typical cartoon situation at sea or at the North Pole, the animator changes the rules, and Daffy finds himself incorrectly dressed, suspended in mid-air, blown up, or otherwise frustrated. Because he is a cartoon character, no changes in his situation cause Daffy any lasting harm, even when the animator turns him into a half-duck-half-daisy. At the same time, because he is Daffy Duck, every change drives him ever closer to sputtering madness. When Daffy, drawn as a cowboy, tries to play his guitar, no music emerges from the sound track. When he asks for a close-up, the entire screen is filled with a microscopic view of a tiny portion of his face. When the ordeal finally seems over, the screen splits in half horizontally, and the bottom half of Daffy at the top of the screen begins a shouting match with the top half of Daffy at the bottom. In a final twist, it turns out that Bugs Bunny has been doing the frustrating animation all along. *Duck Amuck* thus provides us with the comic development expected in a Daffy Duck cartoon layered onto a highly acute form of overt intertextuality.

In an essay in *Film Comment*, John Robert Tebbel writes about these Warner Brothers cartoons: "Extraordinarily durable, these films would entrance each generation as soon as it was old enough to toddle in front of the television set. They sold billions of dollars' worth of toys and junk food to everyone born since World War II, and they're still going strong—the absolute gold standard of children's television programming, earning many times their purchase price for a succession of owners" (64). While I am certainly eager to join Tebbel in his high regard for these cartoons, the key item in his judgment to me is his very plausible assumption that most viewers today know these cartoons through television rather than through first-hand encounters in motion picture theaters.[4] Television is simply how contemporary Americans have encountered American culture—practically from birth. And this is true even of viewers who have gone on to produce their own animated cartoons. In an article in *Time*, for example, Richard Zoglin quotes Matt Groening, creator of the fabulously successful animated series *The Simpsons*: "I've always been inspired by old Jay Ward cartoons like Rocky and Bullwinkle, which was fairly primitive animation but had great writing, voices and music" (67). Rhetorically, Groening feels that he is on safe ground in explaining to his many fans that he has derived creative inspiration for his own animation from a source with which they may all be assumed to be familiar, an animated television show originally aired between 1959 and 1963. Most readers of this paragraph will probably agree that Groening is correct in his assumptions, because most adult Americans—and a substantial percentage of American children—have their own fond memories of the series that most people refer to as *Rocky and Bullwinkle*.[5] David Bianculli puts the case for these happy memories effectively: "How do you choose between a jewel-encrusted toy boat called 'The Ruby Yacht of Omar Khayyam' and an intelligence-increasing hat called the 'Kerwood Derby'?" (56). Bianculli's discussion of the show's appeal primarily focuses on its fondness for puns,[6] but his examples also link Jay Ward's cartoons with the Warner Brothers classics by coincidentally pointing to their intertextuality. That is to say that without extratextual knowledge of a Victorian poetic classic and of Garry Moore's TV announcer, viewers would be unable to appreciate the references in Ward's plots fully.

Since the earliest version of *Rocky and Bullwinkle* appeared on television in 1959, and the show is still appearing in re-runs on cable today, we can only conclude that Jay Ward must have been doing something right. At least part of what he was doing can be described in terms of the same sorts of intertextual encounters favored by the creators of Warner Brothers cartoons. At the simplest level, Ward's show referenced, alluded to, and punned upon a wide variety of high and low cultural phenomena. Since these cultural references appeared in the context of cliffhanging animated serials dramatizing the supposedly thrilling adventures of Rocky, Bullwinkle, and Duddley Do-right, we may amend the list of the show's intertextual encounters to include old film genres. Still other forms of intertextual dialogue were initiated by "Fractured Fairy Tales," Aesop and Son's updated fables, and episodes in "Peabody's Improbable History." Finally, Ward's show regularly engaged in the sort of self-referentiality that many take as a key signal of postmodernism. In all these ways, the program's sequences proleptically demonstrated the thoroughgoing intertextuality that has come to characterize TV animation in recent years with the emergence of *The Simpsons*, *Beavis and Butt-head*, and *The Animaniacs*. Like its descendants four decades later, Ward's show assumed the textuality of all mediated phenomena.

Perhaps the most significant form of intertextuality on *Rocky and Bullwinkle* is allusion—or what many today call "referencing." In the adventure entitled "The Treasure of Monte Zoom," for example, the allusively named villain, Boris Badenov, sings, "Mr. Wonderful, that's I," thereby alluding to the currently popular song, "Mr. Wonderful," and correcting the lyric's grammar at the same time. Later in the episode, Boris alludes to the popular television band-leader Lawrence Welk by intoning, "A-one and a-two," before blowing the magic horn that will supposedly put Bullwinkle to sleep. Later still, Boris poses as Spencer Traceback, the famous actor, causing Bullwinkle to say, "Yeah, I saw you in that picture about the old man fighting with the great big fish." Popular music, television, and motion pictures supply the antecedents for Ward's intertextual references in this adventure, but as subsequent developments in television history will demonstrate, these separate media will eventually come to constitute a single source of referencing called "American popular culture."

A more thoroughgoing form of allusion appears in "The Last Angry Moose," an adventure whose title alludes to Paul Muni's Oscar-nominated film, *The Last Angry Man* (1959). When Rocky and Bullwinkle go to the movies in their hometown of Frostbite Falls, Minnesota, at the beginning of this story, the featured film is *A Trolley Named Talullah*. This title clearly alludes to the highly acclaimed 1951 film, *A Streetcar Named Desire*, starring Marlon Brando, as well as to a well-known stage and screen actress, Tallulah Bankhead. The allusion to Marlon Brando is the more significant in terms of plotting since Bullwinkle is convinced by *A Trolley* that he too can have a career in the movies, a conviction that he demonstrates to Rocky by doing a pretty bad Brando impression. When Boris later poses as acting coach Alfred Hitchhike (read, Hitchcock) in order to bilk Bullwinkle of his savings, Hitchhike's tutoring involves classes in "slouching, advanced slouching, T-shirt ripping, contemporary beards and how they grew, and theoretical and applied mumbling." The acting "method" that Brando might be assumed to epitomize at that time is obviously the larger field of reference for this story's plot, in which the untalented Bullwinkle accidentally becomes a film star. However, Marlon Brando and "the method" are not the only sources of popular cultural references in this adventure. Bullwinkle's success is signaled by a newspaper headline that announces in true *Variety* fashion, "Antlers Antics Boffo at Box Office," and by a female radio correspondent who is always drawn wearing an outlandish hat, in the style of the influential gossip-columnist, Hedda Hopper.

Happily, Rocky and Bullwinkle's adventures are not the only opportunities for allusions and references on the show. As all fans of *Rocky and Bullwinkle* know, the show was actually an animated anthology in which the squirrel and moose were merely the most distinguished players. It is therefore appropriate that in a "Fractured Fairy Tale" segment about Little Red Riding Hood, the wolf has joined Ridinghoods Anonymous and draws inspiration from a book entitled *Words of Courage and Hope for Ridinghood Eaters*. In a "Mr. Know It All" segment about how to get into the movies for free, Bullwinkle advises going disguised as Flo Ziegfeld, and in an episode of Bullwinkle's "Poetry Corner," the moose's grandfather unexpectedly emerges from a Grandfather's clock only to ask allusively, "You were expecting maybe John Cameron Swayze?" A "Dudley Do-Right of the Mounties," episode has Little Nell appearing on Major Snidel's Amateur Hour and Dudley expressing his admiration for (once again!) Lawrence Welk. It is probable that most viewers, young and old, would have recognized TV newscaster Swayze and band-leader Welk at the time that these shows were first aired. Younger viewers would probably have been less likely to recognize Broadway mogul Florenz Ziegfeld (1867-1932), however, or *Major Bowes' Original Amateur Hour*, a show that flourished on radio from 1935-1946.[7]

And this is another significant factor about the allusive intertextuality of *Rocky and Bullwinkle*: original knowledge of a cultural phenomenon need not always precede experiencing the show's reference to it. In his *Dictionary of Teleliteracy*, David Bianculli says about Boris Badenov's name, "I was in my twenties before I got *that* pun" (56), an admission that many other viewers could probably endorse. Clearly, the audience for animated cartoons is far larger that the audience for operas like Modest Moussorgsky's *Boris Godunov* (1874). High cultural ignorance is not the only factor responsible for these sequential gaps, however. In "The Last Angry Moose" Bullwinkle hopes that he will become as big a star as Elmo Lincoln (the silent screen Tarzan). Then, after Bullwinkle becomes an accidental success, his movie debut is called the "biggest comedy hit since *Tillie's Punctured Romance*," a 1914 silent film. In the "Treasure of Monte Zoom," Bullwinkle gets sucked through the Frostbite Falls sewer system and emerges through the plumbing while a man is taking a shower. Significantly, the man is singing, "Nellie was a lady./Last night she died," as Bullwinkle pops through the shower head. Luckily, Bullwinkle knows the words to this song, and so he joins in, continuing tunefully, "Toll the bell for lovely Nell/My sweet Virginy bride." We should note that although Bullwinkle may know the words to this song, few members of the audience—irrespective of their ages—would. The lyrics thus signal "corny old song," instead of referring specifically to the viewer's prior experience.

Many—perhaps most—of the allusions in the "Dudley Do-Right" sequences operate in this way. Surely by 1960, most of the distinguishing properties of this animated story could function only as intentional anachronisms. Dudley's adventures as part of the North West Mounted Police belong to a period of the American cinema that flourished long before the births of most of the people watching them on television. The soundtrack music in the "Dudley Do-Right" episodes signals "silent film," as do the animated iris shots in which the principal players are introduced and the instructional title cards such as "Ladies. Please Remove Your Hats" and "Somebody's Baby Is Crying. Is It Yours?" In the same way, Dudley's naive heroism, Snidely Whiplash's villainy, and Little Nell's staunchly virginal status are intended to signal a comic antiquatedness rather than to trigger actual memories of stage or silent-film melodrama.[8]

One might wonder, then, how Ward's references might communicate with an audience probably unfamiliar with their original sources. One way, I suspect, is simply through tone. In the "Do-Right" sequences, especially, out-datedness is emphasized. Just as "Nellie was a Lady" can function as a representative "corny old song," so the conventions of silent-screen serials can be ironically italicized even for viewers who have never personally seen one of these serials. Just to be on the safe side, however, these intertextual anachronisms are usually grounded in some sort of obvious joke. Bullwinkle's emphasis on the name *Elmo Lincoln* turns it into a joke even for those who have never heard of the actor. Another obvious joke occurs when the title credits for one "Dudley Do-Right" episode say that Snidely Whiplash is "played by Sid Gould." This may seem at first a gratuitous reference to a convention of silent-screen credits, since Whiplash is an animated character. However, subsequent cards go on to say that Dudley is "played by Sid Gould, Jr."; Dudley's horse is "played by Sid Gould, Sr."; Nell is "played by Sid Gould's wife"; and Inspector Fenwick is "played by Sid Gould's Mother-in-Law." If repetition is the soul of comedy, as Henri Bergson claims,[9] then this episode of "Dudley Do-Right" can be understood to be comedically effective even apart from its possible intertextualities.

But, of course, I do not really wish to consider the show "apart from its possible intertextualities." Like the classic Warner Brothers cartoons of previous decades, *Rocky and Bullwinkle* also creates intertextuality through various forms of self-referentiality. One form derives from the show's basic nature as an anthology of discrete animated segments, each introduced with its own graphic and musical signatures. An episode of one of Rocky and Bullwinkle's adventures probably will begin with familiar circus-like theme music and a sequence in which Rocky dives from a high platform as Bullwinkle ineffectually maneuvers a tub of water down on the ground. As the flying squirrel swirls through the air, Bullwinkle fumbles around until he falls into the water. Then Rocky lands smoothly, and the two shake hands. A sign surrounded with blinking light bulbs says, "The Adventures of Rocky and Bullwinkle," and the current installment begins, as so many others have, with the ponderous voice of announcer William Conrad. Used over and over, in show after show, introductory sequences like this eventually end up referring to themselves as much as introducing another installment of a serial narrative.

The other introductory sequences operate similarly. A music-box-like theme always introduces the title, "Fractured Fairy Tales as Told by Edward Everett Horton," and an animated fairy always ends up being squished by the cover of the book containing this title. These sequences always end with the final notes of the airy theme music and a graphic scrolling of the words, "The End." "Dudley Do-Right," of course, has its own mock-thrilling theme music and its own standard introduction, in which Dudley rides in to save Nell from Snidely Whiplash, who has tied her to the railroad tracks. An episode of "Peabody's Improbable History" typically begins: "Hello again! Peabody here. Standing over by the WABAC [way back] machine is my pet boy, Sherman." Surely most viewers already know who Peabody and Sherman are, how they work together, and who is really the boss, but this introduction serves the intertextual function of reminding viewers of the many episodes of "Peabody's Improbable History" that they have already seen. Each time that Bullwinkle promises to pull a rabbit out of a hat in another oft-repeated sequence, Rocky says, "Again?" And that is the intertextual point of all of these animated modules: to remind us once again that we are seeing still another installment of a show that we have seen so many times before.

The viewer's consciousness of past viewing experiences is more than balanced by a profound self-consciousness on the part of Ward and his associates. The final group of intertextual encounters that we will examine, therefore, result from the show's acute use of what Linda Hutcheon calls overt self-referentiality. When Boris is endangered by a falling treasure chest in "The Treasure of Monte Zoom," for example, Natasha says reassuringly, "Don't worry, darling. Remember this is just cartoon." Boris replies, "I just found out what happens when a cartoon chest falls on a cartoon character. . . . It hurts!" At the end of this adventure, Boris falls off a cliff, and Rocky self-referentially exclaims, "Gee, an unhappy ending!" Boris says, "This must be one of those adult cartoons." Perhaps so![10] It is certainly one of those cartoons intended for viewers who have seen many others. This past experience is called upon again during the same adventure when William Conrad's voice-over says, "Boris has forgotten that our heroes always arrive in the ta-da nick of time." Aside from reminding us of the narrative's structural principles, this speech makes a joking reference to the conventions of serial drama by simulating a trumpet sound with the syllables *ta-da*. This turns out to be such a good joke that characters repeat it throughout the sequence. Every time our heroes' arrival is mentioned, someone adds "in the ta-da nick of time." Eventually, Rocky complains that Bullwinkle has said this enough times already. "I know," Bullwinkle admits, "but I love to say 'ta-da.' " As with the slightly varied references to Sid Gould in the "Dudley Do-Right" episode, repetition can carry the joke even to viewers with no personal memory of corny soundtrack music.

These viewers probably remember, however, that continuing episodes of Rocky and Bullwinkle's adventures always begin with

William Conrad's summary of the action to that point. To vary this pattern, Rocky mentions two spies in an episode of "The Treasure of Monte Zoom," and Bullwinkle responds by asking, "What two spies?" Rocky says in exasperation, "Oh boy, have you forgotten the plot again?" In a similar incident during "The Last Angry Moose," Rocky's conscience calls him to task for refusing to go with Bullwinkle to California. "Think of your friendship!" the tiny version of Rocky says. "Think of your years together! Think of the plot!" Viewers around 1960 might be reminded of the mocking way in which *Alfred Hitchcock Presents* treated television commercials. Viewers of any era can recognize the self-reference. These same viewers would probably appreciate the sequence in "The Treasure of Monte Zoom," in which Conrad's announcer voice laments that he has accidentally revealed our heroes' whereabouts to Boris. "What have I done?" he asks sorrowfully. Natasha answers, "Signed death warrant for moose, and spread the whole plot out for two more episodes." In fact, this episode is particularly rich in self-referential devices. Shortly before this exchange, Boris has heard Conrad whispering some plot summary and has asked him to repeat it. When Conrad refuses, Boris adopts a tone of voice familiar from many old movies. "We have ways of finding out," he says menacingly. Conrad wants to know how, and Boris says that he will merely rerun the tape. On the soundtrack, we the hear the familiar sound of a tape recorder running in reverse, and then the earlier sequence repeats, complete with Conrad's whispered summary. This is what causes Conrad to lament his complicity in Bullwinkle's possible demise. At least that is what he and Natasha think. We know better. We know that Bullwinkle will come through with flying colors and go on to other adventures like "The Guns of Abalone," "Louse on 92nd Street," and the college caper, "Wossamotta U."

We know that Bullwinkle will emerge unscathed from the most terrifying dangers because we know how to play our parts in the intertextual encounters featured in *Rocky and Bullwinkle*. For similar reasons, we know that Wile E. Coyote will not really be harmed by the falling anvil and that the ferret will not actually eat Foghorn Leghorn, no matter how hungry he claims to be. Hours, years—perhaps decades—of watching cartoons have habituated us to the conventions governing these animated narratives, just as years of total immersion in popular culture have helped us to recognize all or most of the references, puns, parodies, and allusions that constitute such a large portion of these cartoon texts. As consumers of American culture we are enrolled in a large community held together by our participation in such intertextual encounters in popular culture.

INTERTEXTUAL TV COMEDY:
JERRY SEINFELD AND DENNIS MILLER

In the discursive field surrounding the concept of *postmodernism*, debate has raged about many issues, including whether there even *is* such a phenomenon. It seems to me, however, that a recurrent element of arguments on all sides of these issues is an assumption that allusion, quotation, referencing, or what I have been calling "intertextual encounters" abound in the texts of various kinds on which some might be willing to bestow the title *postmodern* or that others might deny that classification to. Thus, Robert Morris asks in *Critical Inquiry* (1988): "To what other text can one assign that iconophilia, . . . that lust for the represented, and that appetite for the quotation than to the text of post-structuralism?" (346). The answer *no other sort of text* is clearly implied in Umberto Eco's "Innovation and Repetition: Between Modern and Post-Modern Aesthetics" (1985) when he writes that "It is typical of what is called post-modern literature and art . . . to quote by using (sometimes under various stylistic disguises) *quotation marks* so that the reader pays no attention to the content of the citation but instead to the way in which the excerpt from a first text is introduced into the fabric of a second one" (176). In this respect, if in no others, Eco is joined by Fredric Jameson, who notes, in *Postmodernism, or, The Cultural Logic of Late Capitalism* (1991), "the emergence of new kinds of texts infused with the forms, categories, and contents of that very culture industry so passionately denounced by all the ideologues of the modern, from Leavis and the American New Criticism all the way to Adorno and the Frankfurt School." And Jameson goes on to explain that "The postmodernisms have, in fact, been fascinated precisely by this whole 'degraded' landscape of schlock, kitsch, of TV series and *Reader's Digest* culture, of advertising and motels, of the late show and the grade-B Hollywood film, of so-called paraliterature, with its airport paperback categories of the gothic and the romance, the popular biography, the murder mystery, and the science fiction or fantasy novel; materials they no longer simply 'quote,' as a Joyce or a Mahler might have done, but incorporate into their very substance" (2-3). In other words, all these critics—and numerous others—see evidence of a postmodern sensibility at work when they recognize the presence of frequent and perhaps ironic intertextual encounters. Nowhere is this assumption more valid than in the more sophisticated comedy available on American television in the 1990s.

In a rerun of *The Simpsons* broadcast just before the close of the last millennium (16 Dec. 1999), for example, Homer and Marge sit at a piano during the show's opening and closings sequences singing, "Those Were the Days," like Archie and Edith Bunker on *All in the Family*. Homer even holds a cigar in his hand, as Archie always did. Significantly, the song's lyrics have been updated for this new setting. Gone are Herbert Hoover and the old LaSalle that functioned as symbols of the good old days from Archie's perspective in the 1970s. In their place are Fleetwood Mac and 8-track tapes, symbols of the 1970s that seem—despite the presence of the gender ambiguities and welfare state politics that troubled Archie back then—like the good old days to Homer in the 1990s. Surely there is a thematic lesson about historical relativism implicit in the way these lyrics are used in *The Simpsons*. But there is an even more striking intertextual lesson. Without some knowledge of 8-track tapes and Fleetwood Mac, the lyrics are senseless, as the entire sequence is without equal knowledge of *All in the Family*. This deliberate evocation of television knowledge is apparent, too, when the episode moves beyond the parodic introductory sequence into the diegetic narrative about how Lisa got her first saxophone. This story is generated when Bart accidentally tosses Lisa's instrument out the window, and it is run over by two huge semis. Once the saxophone is squashed enough for narrative purposes, a kid wearing a rain slicker rides up on a tricycle, squashes the sax some more, and then falls over sideways. The appropriate music from *Laugh-In* plays on the sound track, and audience members with sufficient intertextual memory of Artie Johnson doing the same thing on *Laugh-In* get the joke created by writers who obviously remember Rowan and Martin's show. We should observe further that the potential appreciative audience for these jokes is huge since the original viewers of *Laugh-In* have been substantially augmented by thousands of young people who have seen the show only in cable reruns. Thus a quintessential postmodern intertextual TV encounter takes place on an episode of *The Simpsons*.

While it would probably be productive to track the many intertextual encounters of this sort sprinkled throughout *The Simpsons*,[1] it seems to me even more productive to devote this attention to the successful television programs organized around comedians Jerry Seinfeld and Dennis Miller. While Miller's candidacy for such scrutiny seems apparent,[2] Seinfeld's inclusion may seem less plausible. After all, *Seinfeld* (1989-1998) was ostentatiously billed as "the show about nothing." Even so—or, perhaps, therefore—*Seinfeld* can easily be seen to share the "iconophilia," the "appetite for the quotation," the ironic use of "quotation marks," the creation of "texts infused with the forms, categories, and contents of [the popular] culture industry" that characterize Dennis Miller's monologues and the field of postmodern TV comedy more generally. Furthermore, we can see in the shows organized around both comedians the fondness for allusion and reference and the overt and covert textual self-consciousness that mark the classic popular songs and animation discussed earlier in this section.

Seinfeld is filled with all sorts of references and allusions to high and popular art, history, politics, and consumer culture. In the episode entitled "The Jacket,"[3] for example, George can't get the song "Master of the House," from *Les Miserables*, out of his head, to the annoyance of Elaine Benes's very scary father. From a simple narrative perspective, any song would probably fill the bill as an irritant here, but the bright catchiness of this particular tune contrasts effectively with Lawrence Tierney's intimidating performance as Mr. Benes, and the timeliness of the allusion to a current Broadway hit show contextualizes the joke in the discourse of contemporary New York popular culture. Timeliness is also a key factor in the episode called "The Checks" when Elaine hooks up with Bret, a potential new boyfriend who thinks of the Eagles hit, "Desperado," as "his" song. Because this song dates back to the mid-Seventies, this precise allusion effectively situates Bret as a classic-rock-listening Yuppie. When Elaine proposes another Eagles song, "Witchy Woman," as a candidate for "their" song, historical resonance continues to be a crucial component of the communication between *Seinfeld*'s writers (Steve O'Donnell, Tom Gammill, and Max Pross) and their audience. The same may be said for the theme song from the comic television show *The Greatest American Hero* (1981-1983), the tune from which George uses for his answering machine message in "The Susie." The original show, starring William Katt, never offered much in the way of plot, character, or even laughs, but David Mandel, author of "The Susie," must have watched the show nevertheless and had the theme song stuck in the back of his mind all those years, like "Master of the House." Clearly, Mandel assumed that many *Seinfeld* viewers would remember this airy pop tune also.

A more contemporary connection is established through another TV show, *Melrose Place*, in "The Beard." Not only is *Melrose Place* (1992-1999) closer in time to *Seinfeld* historically, it is also more significantly involved in the plot. In "The Beard" Jerry is interested in dating Sergeant Channing, a female police officer who is a fan of *Melrose Place*. Sergeant Channing's fondness for this show makes perfect sense in 1995, since *Melrose Place* consistently scored among the top ten TV ratings favorites at the time. When Jerry claims that he has never watched *Melrose Place*, the cop challenges him to take a lie detector test. Jerry successfully lies that he knows nothing about *Melrose Place* characters Sidney, Michael, Jane, Billy, Jake, and Allison, but he eventually breaks down under questioning, crying out, "Did Jane sleep with Michael again?" It turns out that Jerry has been secretly watching *Melrose Place* all along, a fact that destroys his chances with Sergeant Channing and annoys Elaine because it has deprived her of the chance to discuss with Jerry a show to which she is as devoted as Channing—and Jerry. The episode ends with Jerry, Elaine, George, and Kramer sitting on Jerry's couch in front of the TV as the theme from *Melrose Place* plays, a scene that the episode's writer, Carol Leifer, clearly must have assumed to be familiar in the same living rooms where people gathered to watch *Seinfeld*.

Popular films supply other easily accessible intertexts for *Seinfeld* episodes. Elaine blows her chance to get soup from the Soup Nazi in the episode of that title when she does an impression of Al Pacino in *Scent of a Woman* (1992). Jerry and Elaine blow their chances to become godparents in "The Bris" through their bad impressions of Marlon Brando in *The Godfather* (1972). When George sees his father without a shirt on in "The Doorman," he is offended at the sight of Frank's developing breasts. George tells Jerry that the experience was his "own personal *Crying Game*" (1992). At the grave of George's fiancee, Susan, Jerry offers a moving speech to her parents. Later Jerry admits to George that the words he spoke actually came from *Star Trek II: The Wrath of Khan* (1982) and that they actually applied to Mr. Spock's death not to Susan's. In all of these cases, writers and readers alike are assumed to have seen—or at least heard about—the same popular films, and so these films can serve effectively as intertexts for a wide variety of comic plots. Perhaps the high point in this sort of cinematic referencing occurs in "The Raincoats" when Jerry and his girlfriend Rachel are detected "making out" at *Schindler's List* (1993). The comic plot requires that Jerry and Rachel become sexually frustrated because Jerry's parents are staying in his apartment and because Rachel lives with her conservative Rabbi father. In one sense, any movie house could provide the fictional couple an opportunity for sexual privacy, but a crowded theater showing the Academy-Award-winning film about the Holocaust is the ideal choice diegetically because of Jerry and Rachel's Jewish backgrounds and intertextually because of the near worshipful adulation with which *Schindler's List* was publicly viewed at the time of this episode's original broadcast (1994).

Most fans of *Seinfeld* would anticipate, however, that the show's most comprehensive intertextual encounters involve Superman. As Mary Kaye Schilling and Mike Flaherty point out in the *Entertainment Weekly* special edition's Jerry Seinfeld glossary, "Though [Jerry] frequently references other superheroes, the Man of Steel is his undisputed fave and chief source of pop-cultural metaphors" (23). Thus, in "The Caddy" Jerry explains that Elaine's old high school nemesis, Sue Ellen Mischke, is her "Lex Luthor," Superman's arch rival. In "The Secret Code," we learn that Jerry's ATM password is "Jor-El," the name of Superman's father. In "The Face Painter" George describes his complicated emotional encounter with Siena, who just may be deaf in one ear, by saying that "It's like when Superman reversed the rotation of the earth to save Lois's life." Lois Lane also figures in "The Race," an episode with a particularly rich Superman intertext. Lois's name gets invoked in the script simply so that Jerry can say to his girlfriend of the week that he runs "faster than a speeding bullet, Lois." As the title of the episode implies, the plot involves a foot race between Jerry and an old high school acquaintance, Duncan. The climax occurs as Jerry out-races Duncan in the slow motion popular in *Superman* films while the soundtrack plays the familiar *Superman* theme.

As Umberto Eco's discussion of postmodernism leads us to expect, references and allusions in *Seinfeld* are drawn indiscriminately from all aspects of culture. Eco notes that "the media are relying on—and presupposing—the possession of pieces of information already conveyed by other media" (172), and *Seinfeld* responds by having Elaine characterize herself in "The Bookstore" as being like Tina Turner in her relations with Zach, a co-worker and unsatisfactory boyfriend. Elaine doesn't sing or dance well in high-heeled shoes, and so she is unlike Tina Turner in the most obvious ways, but Elaine is hoping that she can get other people in her office to view her as an emotionally abused woman, and so she may seem to resemble the Tina Turner familiar to viewers of 1998 TV talk shows. Similarly, when Kramer accidentally gets vanity license plates that spell "ASSMAN" in "The Fusilli Jerry," the characters speculate about whom the plates could actually be intended for. When George suggests Wilt Chamberlain, the reference has nothing to do with professional basketball but with *A View from Above*, the 1991 autobiography in which Chamberlain claimed to have had sex with 20,00 women. Higher up the cultural ladder, we learn in "The Scofflaw" that a traffic cop wearing an eye patch sees the multi-ticketed Newman as his Moby Dick and in "The Secret Code" that Maya Angelou volunteers at a charity soup kitchen. Although these references mostly involve simple name recognition, the intertextual encounters are at least partly literary. The same may be said of the intertextual encounter in which the old love letters saved from the wreckage of the Rosses' vacation cabin turn out to be letters from John Cheever to Susan's father ("The Cheever Letters"). While John Cheever was assuredly a widely recognized fiction writer, his appearance as a reference here is clearly attributable to the publication of *The Journals of John Cheever* (1991), in which the famous author wrote about his alcoholism and homosexual love affairs.

A similar referential mixture—this time, of celebrity with politics— is at work when Estelle Costanza compares her brassiere-clad husband to J. Edgar Hoover in "The Doorman" and when George describes an embarrassing encounter with a girl by telling Jerry in "The Phone Message," "So I just stand there like, remember how Quayle looked when Bentsen gave him that Kennedy line—that's what I looked like." Some political knowledge may be relevant in both cases, but an ear for the news of the day is probably all that is really required to participate in this rhetorical community. The same may be said when Elaine's boss, Mr. Pitt, ends the episode called "The Gymnast" looking like Adolph Hitler addressing a Nazi rally. Pitt is admittedly wearing Austrian-looking riding clothes (because he had earlier hoped to go horseback riding in the park), and he has a thick, black mustache on his upper lip (because he accidentally touched himself with ink-stained fingers), but Mr. Pitt is nothing like Hitler in any significant way. The intertextual joke is purely visual, and it requires little knowledge of history or politics. In fact, the less one knows about the Second World War, the funnier the joke is. Funny or not, however, it is apparent that the writers, Alec Berg and Jeff Schaffer, intended to communicate with their audience intertextually through this image.

Other allusions and references are more diegetically functional. In "The English Patient" Elaine is one of the few Americans who will admit in 1997 that she finds the 1996 Academy-Award smash *The English Patient* boring. In this respect *The English Patient* serves as *Schindler's List* does in "The Raincoats," as the movie that everyone is supposed to admire. "The English Patient" surpasses "The Raincoats" in terms of intertextual organicism, however, since the comic plot of the former also requires a character named Neil to be so badly burned by a crepe that his gorgeous girlfriend will take him to England for burn treatment. All parallels to the plot of *The English Patient* are surely deliberate. In "The Boyfriend" Kramer and Newman act as conspiracy nuts caught up in a bizarre tale about how baseball star Keith Hernandez spat on them following a 1987 Mets game at Shea Stadium. Using a golf club as a pointer, Jerry enacts the role of a Zapruder film analyst to demonstrate that Hernandez could not have been solely responsible and that there must have been a "second spitter" on the grassy knoll outside the stadium. As it turns out, there was a "second spitter"—Roger McDowell, whom Newman had taunted throughout the game. Many assassination buffs would love to have such a clear answer to all their questions about what "actually" happened when John Kennedy was killed in Dallas. Since—like Larry David and Larry Levin—we have all heard these questions asked and probably seen the Zapruder film analyzed, our shared intertextual encyclopedia permits the writers to make a new joke out of old material.

Another tragedy—the 1994 O. J. Simpson murder case—provides the intertext for several episodes of *Seinfeld*. In "The Big Salad" Kramer fears that he has inadvertently incited former baseball player Steve Genderson to murder. In a direct parallel to the O. J. case, Kramer and Genderson are seen on television fleeing from the police in a white Bronco just as Al Cowlings and O. J. did. In "The Maestro" Jackie Chiles, a recurring character based on O. J.'s flamboyant attorney, Johnnie Cochran, represents Kramer in a lawsuit based on Kramer's having been burned by a cup of too-hot caffe latte sold to him by Java World. In addition to the Cochran parallels, this episode alludes to the controversial 1994 law suit in which Stella Liebeck was awarded $2.9 million in compensation for the too-hot cup of McDonald's coffee that spilled in her lap. Jackie Chiles/Johnnie Cochran also appears in "The Caddy" in a case based on Sue Ellen Mischke's having caused a traffic accident by wearing a brassiere on the outside of her sweater. In an obvious reference to the gloves that didn't quite fit O. J. Simpson in his trial, Jackie asks Sue Ellen to try on a bra in court. As in the O. J. case, the garment does not fit, and so the defendant wins the case.

Other sustained references include the film *Midnight Cowboy* (1969) in "The Mom and Pop Store" and *The Merv Griffin Show* (1962-86) on the episode of the same name. However, the point should be clear without further discussion that *Seinfeld* often engaged in both localized and extended cultural references of the sort popular in Warner Brothers cartoons. "The Merv Griffin Show" episode points to still another way in which *Seinfeld* resembles those cartoons and the other forms of textually self-conscious intertextual encounters we have been examining. In this episode Kramer transforms his apartment into the set of *The Merv Griffin Show* and interacts with his friends as if he were a talk-show host and they were his guests. The writer of this episode, Bruce Eric Kaplan, even works Jim Fowler of *Wild Kingdom* into the script because Fowler is such a regular guest on actual shows of this kind that his presence establishes an especially convincing intertext. In this way Kaplan reminds viewers that *Seinfeld* is also a TV show, a part of what Mimi White calls the "all-encompassing present text" of television. Kramer helps writers give similar reminders in several episodes. In "The Keys" Kramer moves to California and gets a small part on *Murphy Brown* (1988-1998). In "The Opposite" Kramer appears on *Live with Regis & Kathy Lee* (1989-2000) to promote his new coffee table book. In both episodes stars easily recognizable from their own hit television shows help to remind viewers that *Seinfeld* is also a television show. Although less obviously identified with television, Kramer's possible appearance in a Woody Allen film in "The Alternate Side" and his accidental Tony Award in "The Summer of George" signal "show business" even so, and thus indicate textual self-consciousness rather than referential opacity. As Eco claims, when a spectator is "aware of the quotation, the spectator is brought to elaborate ironically on the nature of such a device and to acknowledge the fact that he has been invited to play upon his encyclopedic competence" (171).

Other intertextual invitations of this sort are issued when episodes refer to the diegetic Jerry's career as a comedian. This happens when Jerry appears on *The Tonight Show* in "The Trip, Part I" along with George Wendt and Corbin Bernsen, who play themselves. When Jerry appears on *Tonight* again in "The Showerhead," host Jay Leno also appears in a cameo role. In a variation on this theme, Bryant Gumble interviews Jerry on the *Today* show in "The Puffy Shirt." When Jerry is booked to appear on Charles Grodin's talk show in "The Doll," he hopes to get comic mileage out of a barbecue sauce bottle that looks like Grodin. Beyond television appearances, Jerry claims to be substituting for Carrot Top at Bally's in Atlantic City in "The Money," an episode in which his parents reiterate their advice that he give up comedy and enter the management training program at Bloomingdale's. In "The Little Jerry," the previous but related episode, Jerry's parents encourage him to get out of comedy and into advertising. The cumulative effect of these incidents is to remind viewers that a comedian named Jerry Seinfeld is playing a character named Jerry Seinfeld on a television show of that name. In intertextual terms, this self-consciousness is very acute.

Seinfeld also signals its nature as a TV sitcom in various covert ways. "The Bizarro Jerry" episode creates a competing group of three male friends for Elaine, each more decent and normal than Jerry, George, or Kramer. On the allusive level, some viewers are probably reminded of Superman's bizarro opposite. On the level of the comic plot, viewers are entertained to see Elaine struggling to choose between the two trios of totally opposite friends. But the most compelling effect of the episode is to remind viewers of what Jerry, George, and Kramer are really like week after week and thus to remind viewers of why we are attracted to this particular sitcom rather than to its dozens of competitors. When Elaine and George temporarily switch personalities in "The Abstinence," there is considerable comic delight in seeing George as bright and efficient, but this delight results primarily from knowing how ineptly he usually acts, from comparing the usual and the unusual intertextually. Through a similar switch in the previous episode, "The Chicken Roaster," sleep deprivation and switched apartments turn Jerry temporarily into Kramer. It is surely fun to watch a manic Jerry and a composed Kramer, but it is fun mostly for those who are used to the opposite, status quo.

The most overtly self-conscious episodes of *Seinfeld* are those focused on George and Jerry's efforts to develop their own sitcom, just as the most overtly self-conscious song lyrics are the ones about writing songs. In "The Pitch" Jerry and George try to interest NBC network executives in putting on a TV show "about nothing." The difficulties that Jerry and George encounter in this episode seem comic rather than tragic or dramatic because viewers know that the two friends—or their real life counterparts, Jerry Seinfeld and Larry David—will triumph in the end. Otherwise, we would not be watching all of this action on *Seinfeld* right now. This recognition intertextually points the audience toward comedy in "The Checks" also, even though Jerry and George seem to have tremendous difficulties trying to interest Japanese TV executives in their unproduced show. The apex of overt textual self-consciousness, however, must be "The Pilot." In this episode the network has finally given Jerry and George a chance to make an episode of their sitcom. As actors read for the parts of George, Elaine, and Kramer, viewers are reminded of these diegetic characters' distinguishing, humorous qualities. At the same time, the episode suggests that Jason Alexander, Julia Louis-Dreyfus, and Michael Richards must also have read for their parts once upon a time.[4] That Jerry will play Jerry on the pilot episode just as Jerry Seinfeld plays Jerry on *Seinfeld* merely confirms this conjunction between the highly successful "show about nothing" and its intertextual matrix, especially the "all-encompassing present text" of television..

In her essay "Crossing Wavelengths: The Diegetic and Referential Imaginary of American Commercial Television," from which this phrase is derived, Mimi White conjectures that "[R]egular television viewers are the 'best' viewers, capable of deriving the greatest potential satisfaction from any single show because they are in the advantageous position of understanding the rules of the game" (61). These are the viewers best equipped to connect "The Pilot" intertextually to the ongoing *Seinfeld* series, to appreciate it when Jerry gets a shot on the *Tonight* show, complete with a guest appearance by Jay Leno, and to learn that Jerry watches *Melrose Place* just as they do. These are also the viewers ideally situated to appreciate highly self-conscious TV comedy shows like *The Simpsons* (1989-) and *The Larry Sanders Show* (1992-1998) starring Garry Shandling. These same viewers are the primary and ideal audience for Dennis Miller.

Dennis Miller first came to national prominence as a regular cast member of *Saturday Night Live* from 1985-1991, and although he has appeared in motion pictures including *The Net* (1995), *Bordello of Blood* (1996), and *Murder at 1600* (1997), his celebrity status has continued to derive from television—from a series of HBO comedy specials, including *Mr. Miller Goes to Washington* (1988), *Dennis Miller: Black and White* (1990), *They Shoot HBO Specials, Don't They?* (1993), *Citizen Arcane* (1996), and *The Millennium Special—1,000 Years, 100 Laughs, 10 Really Good Ones* (1999), and from his appearances as a talk-show host, first in a daily late-night slot on ABC for a few months in 1992, and then weekly on HBO with the Emmy-Award-winning *Dennis Miller Live*. If we add to these credentials, *Rants* (1996) and *Ranting Again* (1998), Miller's two book-length collections of monologues from his *Live Show*, Dennis Miller's contributions to postmodern comedy are accounted for. Since Miller and the members of his audience both participate in the hypermediated culture of contemporary America, this comedy may be assumed to consist of a highly self-referential form of rhetoric and incessant references to American popular culture.[5]

Specifically, we should assume that viewers of *Dennis Miller Live* cannot help but be aware of the conventions of presentational television in general, as well as of the conventionalized way in which earlier stand-up comedians like Bob Hope would sometimes "break-up" while performing on television, and of the conventionalized references to comedy writers and failed jokes in monologues delivered by Johnny Carson and his many imitators. Thus, at the beginning of the *Dennis Miller Live* show featuring Paul Sorvino, Miller acknowledges the audience's initial applause by saying, "Thank you for reacting so well to the coaching." In case there is any doubt that such applause is elicited through electronic means, Miller says at the same point on the show with Melissa Etheridge, "A little slow on the applause up front. Whatta ya got Monty Clift working the applause sign?" Since the applause has been perfectly satisfactory—and almost identical in volume—in both cases, the purpose of these remarks can only be to direct the audience's attention directly to the convention of having a lighted applause sign in a television studio. Since audiences—especially those sitting in the studio—know already that these signs exist, a potentially limiting convention is thereby intertextually redefined as a comic opportunity.

The familiar convention by which Johnny Carson and Ed McMahon would dissect a failed joke in order to engage the audience in efforts to reinvigorate or "save" the written material, also functions in a postmodern form in Miller's performances. When the audience groans at Miller's joke, "Gingrich has more chins than an 'Impeach Al D'Amato' rally," Dennis says, "You gotta quit moaning or I am going to turn on you viciously. Either laugh or don't, but don't give me that whiny moan shit all night" (*Rants* 183). Despite their apparent discomfort with the possible slight to Asian Americans in the Gingrich joke, the audience laughs appreciatively at the rejoinder. The joke is thus saved, but a significant light has been thrown on the rhetorical compact between Miller and his audience, especially on those elements of the compact dealing with politically sensitive issues. This is also the point on the show with Larry King when Miller identifies a dwarf in a news photo as "America's Olympic gold medal hopeful in the dwarf toss," and the audience gasps in shock. "OK," Miller sneers, "so my joke made him a dwarf!" The laugh is recovered, Miller satirizes political correctness, and he self-referentially identifies what he has just said as a "joke."

In another example, drawn from *Rants*, Miller says about public funding for the arts, "Face it, most of those politicos think PBS is what makes their wives so cranky each month. Oh, I'm sorry, I shouldn't have said that. I meant to say, what makes their mistresses so cranky each month" (44). Seeing this in print makes us suspect that many of the other apparently impromptu rejoinders may also have been planned to create the kind of commentary on convention so central to other forms of postmodern art. As Silvio Gaggi has observed about hieratic art in his *Modern/Postmodern: A Study in Twentieth-Century Arts and Ideas*, with the advent of postmodernism, "art images began to be used as a means of examining the nature of images themselves. And stories and novels began to be concerned with the processes and problems of writing" (20). In the popular art of stand-up comedy, Dennis Miller shows the same to be true. When Miller gets a big laugh on the show with Paul Sorvino after a joke about the Pope, he comments, "It's all in the delivery, that joke. Absolutely nothing there when you peel back its thin outer shell." In a similar vein, when Miller seemingly digresses on the show with Sheriff Joe Arpaio to tell a joke he has often told before about a smelly French cabdriver, the audience dissolves in laughter. Dennis smirkingly observes, "Joke has become my 'Freebird,'" simultaneously commenting self-referentially on his own work, making a popular cultural allusion, and even dropping the definite article in a brilliant gesture of insider hipness.

Miller assumes—and probably assumes correctly—that members of his audience know that there is a Lynyrd Skynyrd song called

"Freebird" and know further the way in which the song has come to represent the band synecdochally. Probably the allusion establishes an illusion of inner-circle exclusivity also—in contrast to the people whose song of reference might be "Blue Suede Shoes" or "The Way We Were." As John J. O'Connor observes in a review of Miller's *They Shoot HBO Specials, Don't They?* references of this sort "become a handy mechanism for generational identity" (C20).

These are most probably the same rhetorical forces at work when Miller observes in a monologue reprinted in *Rants* that "people have this innate ability to switch from one form of entertainment to another. Just ask the guys who banked on vaudeville or bought stock in Betamax, or better yet, ask Gary Burghoff and McLean Stevenson . . . they're sharing a pad, aren't they?" (188). The historical progression in these allusions from vaudeville to sitcoms might elsewhere attract comment. In the current context, however, the most significant element is Miller's confidence that he does not need to identify the TV show *M*A*S*H* to help his audience catch the principal part of the joke. During another one of the reprinted *Rants*, Miller responds to a young person who asks him to interpret a dream during an airplane flight, "What am I, Queequeg?" (172). Perhaps Allan Bloom and William Bennett might be encouraged to perceive a cultural paradigm shift by this apparent literary allusion.[6] Perhaps they would be right, but I don't think so. M. Thomas Inge argues in his essay "Melville as Popular Culture" that "[m]illions of Americans who have never read a word by Melville know the names [of his characters]" (67). As Inge explains, their information comes through popular culture osmosis—in the case of Miller's reference to Queequeg, probably from the John Huston film of *Moby Dick* (1956) starring Gregory Peck. This seems probable to me because Miller writes in another "Rant" that he objects politically only to the religious right, not to "good simple religious folk." To the latter group, Dennis says, "Well, anyway, you're good people and I got no quarrel with you, Atticus" (7). Although it is probable that thousands of Miller's listeners have read Harper Lee's novel, *To Kill a Mockingbird* (1960), it is certain—Bloom and Bennett's wishes notwithstanding—that many thousands more have seen the film (1962) based on the book, once again starring Gregory Peck.

This kind of highly mediated textual common ground is where, as a true postmodernist, Miller meets his audience. In a published *Rant*, Miller ridicules Dan Quayle's political ambitions as follows: "I am appalled that this Chuzzlewit can actually aspire to the presidency outside the walls of a mental institution and people don't tie him down and scrape his frontal lobes with a trowel like some demented *Clockwork Orange* Droogie who's due to be rewired" (149). Again, Charles Dickens's 1844 novel notwithstanding, the primary reference *may* be to Anthony Burgess's 1962 novel, *Clockwork Orange*, but I suspect that the reference draws on a different sort of experience for most of Miller's American audience—Stanley Kubrick's 1971 film based on the novel. This also seems probable when Miller writes in another *Rant*: "What sort of perfect, *Harrad Experiment* society are we striving for, folks? One where you will be forced by the rigid puritanical mentality of your pin-head, Gladys Kravitz neighbors into a tightly constricted, overly regimented existence?" (36). Gladys Kravitz is the key. Miller's primary audience is an American TV generation for whom *Bewitched* (1964-72) is an even more recognizable cultural reference than the 1973 movie, directed by Ted Post and starring Don Johnson—or the best-selling work of popular fiction on which it was based, Robert H. Rimmer's *The Harrad Experiment* (1966). Significantly, when Miller lambastes Quayle again on the ground that he lacks political *gravitas*, Miller says that the former vice-president "shouldn't have been second in command of the Hekawi Indians from 'F Troop' [1965-67], much less the third most powerful nation on the face of this planet. Always had that freshly tasered Norma Desmond look on his face" (179). The sequence of allusions is typical, as is the undifferentiating equivalency among television shows, beauty fads, classic films, and international geopolitics.

Simple recognition is all that is required to grasp the vehicles in most of Miller's literary metaphors also. In satirizing personally-designed wedding ceremonies, Miller objects to "wedding vows written by the bride and groom that are so sickeningly schmaltzy they make *The Bridges of Madison County* look like Milton's *Paradise Lost*" (163). Having to identify the author of *Paradise Lost* shows that Miller is operating rhetorically outside the domain guarded by Bloom and Bennett. Therefore, I am fairly sure that the audience's "legitimate theater" experiences are not the grounding for another literary reference: "Now I know a lot of us are the product of a union so Gothic in its dysfunction it makes the couples in *Who's Afraid of Virginia Woolf* look like Steve and Eydie" (165). The names of the second couple suggest that the first couple should be identified as Dick and Liz up on the screen, rather than George and Martha on stage. In the same way, we may assume, as in the case of Miller's reference to Atticus Finch, that the filmed version of *To Kill a Mockingbird* is the source of this metaphor: "Came into Phoenix the other day, the woman working the X-ray machine had the attention span of Boo Radley" (172-73). There is no need to make assumptions about the reference's literary origins when Miller says, "I'm telling you it's a madhouse out there. I feel like Heston waking up in the field and seeing the chimp on top of the pony" (48). *Planet of the Apes* (1968), starring Charlton Heston, may be assumed to be part of Dennis Miller's, Miller's writers', and everyone in the audience's intertextual encyclopedia.

Covert textual self-consciousness also confirms Miller's postmodern rhetorical bonding with his audience when he uses elaborate, perhaps overly elaborate, metaphors to make jokes. As Aristotle explains about such metaphorical practice in Chapter 22 of *The Poetics*: "To employ such license at all obtrusively is, no doubt, grotesque. . . . Even metaphors, strange (or rare) words, or any similar forms of speech, would produce the like effect if used without propriety, and with the express purpose of being ludicrous" (Bate 34). In postmodern usage, we might anticipate a deliberate flouting of Aristotle's warning, and that is what we get in some of Miller's more outrageous metaphors. It requires an extravagant mental leap to say, as Miller said on the show with Larry King, that Strom Thurmond's "birthday cake has more candles than a Sting video," or to claim that, when proponents of a humane criminal justice system are faced with an actual robbery, "you're changing your tune faster than Elvis Costello on *Saturday Night Live*," as Miller claims on the show with Sheriff Joe Arpaio. In both cases, the resemblance between tenor and vehicle[7] seems so slight and so "obtrusive" that the issue of rhetorical "moderation" hardly enters the picture. We can only agree with Aristotle that such metaphors are created by Miller with "the express purpose of being ludicrous," or of attracting the audience's attention to the comedian's means of communication.

The humor in such cases largely derives from the fact that the metaphors are based on a purely verbal analogy between tenor and vehicle. The candles on Thurmond's cake signify age; those in Sting's music video, arty atmosphere. The "tune" sung by political liberals is figurative, while Elvis Costello's is literal. Two other striking metaphors of this sort are devoted to environmental issues in Miller's *Rants*: "We need the ozone, and currently, it has more holes in it than the plot of a Steve Allen murder mystery" (129); "If Exxon dragged its feet any more on that [Alaskan oil spill] cleanup they'd look like Richard the Third" (130). Here, the issues are serious, but the metaphoric technique is the use of deliberately exaggerated antanaclases[8] based on the terms *holes* and *foot-dragging*. Members of Miller's audience are, of course, unlikely to name or recognize sophisticated rhetorical devices, but they are very likely to recognize both the ingenious vehicles and the postmodern, self-advertising technique that Miller uses. In consequence, they experience Dennis Miller's jokes by means of an intertextual encounter.

In his 1997 essay, "History and Humor," Joseph Boskin expends considerable energy to explain why we find things funny. Along the way, he writes that "Sigmund Freud, in his pathbreaking work *Wit and Its Relation to the Unconscious* (1905), posited that humor is wholly a social process wherein the shared actions of the participants allow them to agress and/or regress together. Similarly, ethologist Konrad Lorenz in his study *On Aggression* (1963) offered that "'laughter forms a bond' but simultaneously 'draws a line.' In this way, laughter produces a 'strong fellow feeling among the participants and joint aggressiveness against outsiders'" (18). Putting aside the issue of possible aggression, which seems to trouble critics of humor so deeply, we may glimpse in these references to "bonds" and "fellow feeling" analogies to the "interpretive communities" and "generational identity" elsewhere postulated by Stanley Fish and John J. O'Connor as definitions of rhetorical communities. We laugh at Dennis Miller and Jerry Seinfeld, in other words, because we feel ourselves part of a community composed of those who recognize what's going on or, to put it another way, because our intertextual encyclopedias are suitably stocked to appreciate the allusions and the self-referential textuality of these postmodern comic texts, to enable us to have intertextual encounters with them.

CONCLUSION

Toward the close of the previous chapter, some theoretical insights of Sigmund Freud and Konrad Lorenz were quoted by Joseph Boskin to explain the ways in which humor can create rhetorical communities. Boskin goes on to report in his essay, "History and Humor," on "Henri Bergson's observation in *Laughter* (1900) that complicity is inextricably involved in humor." According to Bergson, "Our laughter is always the laughter of a group. You would hardly appreciate the comic if you felt yourself isolated from others. Laughter appears in need of an echo" (qtd. in Boskin 18). In this respect, humor can be seen to resemble irony, at least as irony is understood by Wayne C. Booth in *A Rhetoric of Fiction* (1983): "Irony is always thus in part a device for excluding as well as including, and those who are included, those who happen to have the necessary information to grasp the irony, cannot but derive at least part of their pleasure from a sense that others are excluded" (304). In light of these remarks, we can see that possessing the appropriate clues to humor or irony can connect one to others similarly endowed, just as it can serve to separate one from those lacking the "right stuff." As I hope I have illustrated in my previous chapters, communities defined by shared inter-texts clearly belong in this same classification. And, as I hope I have also demonstrated, these communities can embrace film and popular culture as well as traditional literature.

Historically, the isolated encounters of individuals with texts of various sorts have usually attracted the attention of literary critics and writers of memoirs. How a now-mature reader or viewer came to be the sensitive receiver of textual signals that he or she now is is a story that has often been told, usually by beginning with an account of a little girl or boy alone in a darkened movie theater or a well-lighted place eagerly devouring films and books and developing the imaginative skills that would stand the grown woman or man in good stead years later. Especially when these rich imaginative encounters occurred in otherwise unpromising environments—the English midlands, rural Nebraska, the mean streets of a modern megapolis—the individual formation of a mature aesthetic sensibility seems to be a never-ending source of interest.

Writers who try to explain how we read or how we understand what is up on the screen also tend to stress the individual encounter of human subject and aesthetic object. Thus, when Sue Halpern reviews two semi-autobiographical books by the Texas writer Larry McMurtry in 1999, she insists that "The novelist . . . begins and ends in solitude, and offers his work to readers one at a time" (30). Michael Meyer writes similarly about reading literature in *The Bedford Introduction to Literature* (1993): "Careful, deliberate reading—the kind that engages a reader's imagination as it calls forth the writer's—is a means of exploration that can take a reader outside whatever circumstance or experience previously defined his or her world" (11). Concluding a list of illustrations that could easily be extended, Richard M. Gollin claims about the isolated experience of film viewing in *A Viewer's Guide to Film: Arts, Artifices, and Issues* (1992): "A common reason people go to the movies is that in fantasy, movies extend our personal experience into places most of us never travel, dramatizing events or ordeals most of us never confront or would wish to confront as ourselves, in worlds inhabited by people more fascinating or amusing than their counterparts in our own lives" (20-21). Common to all these helpful explanations, and to the numerous aesthetic biographies and autobiographies that could be invoked, is the assumption that each of us encounters every text in isolation, or at best in temporary conjunction with the artist responsible for the text.

This one-on-one sort of encounter is what Holden Caulfield assumes when he says in J. D. Salinger's *The Catcher in the Rye*, "What really knocks me out is a book that, when you're all done reading it, you wish that the author that wrote it was a terrific friend of yours and you could call him up on the phone whenever you felt like it" (18). A similar kind of assumption about artists and the individual members of their potential audience lies behind Gerald Prince's explanation of the technical rhetorical entity that he calls the "narrattee": "This 'you' with the white hands, accused by the author [of *Le Pere Goriot*] of being egotistical and callous, is the narratee. It's obvious that the latter does not resemble most readers of *Le Pere Goriot* and that consequently the narratee of a novel cannot be automatically identified with the reader: the reader's hands might be black or red not white; he might read the novel in bed instead of in an armchair; he might lose his appetite upon learning about the old merchant's unhappiness" (228). Prince's argument is theoretically sophisticated in a way that Salinger's fictional teenager—and perhaps Salinger himself—could only vainly strive to imitate, and yet both novelist and critic assume that reading primarily involves the individual subject's isolated encounter with the text. On the other hand, my focus in this book has been on the knowledge and experience that the subject shares not only with the artist responsible for the text but also with the other members of the text's potential audience, the shared experience that constitutes intertextual encounters.

In previous chapters we have seen how references and allusions to characters and stories in the Bible can help to create intertextual encounters for some readers, as the narrative tradition of the American Dream can for others. In much the same way that the Roman audience for Virgil's *Aeneid* could be assumed to be familiar with ancient Greek literature and especially with the Homeric epics, so readers during the English neoclassical period could be assumed to recognize contemporary "imitations" of classical texts. Other forms of intertexts might be counted upon to create rhetorical communities for artists addressing later audiences, such as those familiar with the historical events and socioeconomic environment of cultural phenomena like the "matter" of the Rosenbergs. Furthermore, because there is considerable interest in the proposition that all signifying objects may be regarded as texts, we should expect that other intertextual communities would develop outside of the realm of literature proper. Thus, the rich tradition of American popular music resonates with intertextual encounters between songs, between composers, and between individual performances and the popular music tradition—all available to suitably informed or suitably alert listeners. The tradition of popular films offers other intertextual encounters to suitably equipped viewers—encounters between films and print texts such as *The Scarlet Letter*, between films and film genres such as the road picture, and between films and their conventional contents such as the story of Hollywood. In Hollywood pictures, as in some forms of print narrative, moreover, encounters between a central, diegetic text and a represented, metadiegetic print or film narrative can provide readers and viewers with additional intertextual encounters. The broad field of popular culture offers audiences still other intertextual encounters by means of popular allusions, stylistic imitation, self-referentiality, and overt and covert textual self-consciousness. To latch on to all these possibilities obviously calls for considerable experience and alertness, especially in the case of a comedian like Dennis Miller whose postmodern comedy assumes that all of American culture is a synchronous text. Just how responsive any individual member of a potential audience can be expected to be is, of course, a challenging question for critics as well as for artists hoping to create intertextual fiction, film, or popular culture.

Although I cannot answer the question of just how responsive any individual member of a potential audience can be expected to be, I can provide anecdotal testimony. When I was a child during the early 1950s, I used to see Sophie Tucker on TV variety shows. She looked to me mostly like an old, overweight, over-made-up woman who sang corny songs, usually "Some of these Days." I could tell from the way Sophie Tucker was introduced, however, that her appearance was a big deal of some sort to other (probably older) people. Seeing Jimmy Durante's former partner, Eddie Jackson, was a similar experience for me. On television, I saw an old man with a pot belly wearing evening clothes and a top hat who sang and perhaps danced a little. This was probably on some show hosted by Jimmy Durante, because the most salient fact about Eddie Jackson to me in the early 1950s was that at some time in the distant past he had been Durante's performing partner, along with a deceased performer named Clayton, the "Mrs. Calabash" that Durante always said good night to. Jackson's performance on television wasn't all that impressive—I seem to recall an over-the-top rendition of "Bye Bye Blackbird"—but it was clear that his appearance—like Tucker's—was intended to be accepted as significant nevertheless. It was apparently up to me and other young viewers to figure out for ourselves, or to accept on faith, the cultural value of these experiences. I suppose in our own ways we did so. Something similar can be said about Ted Lewis. I knew that there was or had been someone with that name since so many of the impressionists I saw on *The Ed Sullivan Show* imitated what I assumed to be Lewis's voice, usually by asking, "Is everybody happy?" It is important to note that I had probably never heard the original Ted Lewis, but I easily assumed that he must have sounded like the voice common among these impressionists. When I finally saw Ted Lewis singing "Me and my Shadow" on TV—if in fact I ever did see him—I must have connected the man with the clarinet and battered top hat on the TV screen to the simulated voice that I had been carrying around in my head for months or years. The result was my intertextual encounter with Ted Lewis. My understanding of Ted Lewis today is not much different.

In retrospect it seems likely that the primary point of these much-trumpeted celebrity appearances was to recall vaudeville, a phenomenon long dead by the time I was watching television but still alive in the minds of those who had actually seen vaudeville performances—especially those by the legendary stars I have been recalling. If so, this intention was fulfilled. The effect of these otherwise unaccountable performances on me was to create a strong sense of what vaudeville was—singing, dancing, and snappy patter, assuredly, but also juggling, unicycle-riding, and animal acts. This sense came not only from *The Ed Sullivan Show* and similar performance venues like *The Colgate Comedy Hour*, but also from the many films in which vaudeville and vaudevillians played a significant role in the plot. The *locus classicus* for these films was the death of vaudeville that occurred around 1930. In these films, talented vaudeville performers were sometimes shunted aside by show-biz progress, perhaps to see their children succeed in the new media, as in *Ziegfeld Girl* (1941), or it turned out that well-executed vaudeville performances were exactly what the public still hungered for, despite dire predictions to the contrary, as in *Babes in Arms* (1939). In either case, performances within the film as well as diegetic discussions of the economic and aesthetic nature of the business gave cinema audiences a distinct sense—true or mistaken—of what vaudeville was like. Surely this can be said for audience members who had never seen a vaudeville show as well as for those who had, and this is the point I want to make by calling up those dear dead days.

As I sat on the couch in my parents' living room in Philadelphia watching TV during the early 1950s, I did not have a notebook in my lap to jot down phrases like "Is everybody happy?" and "Good night, Mrs. Calabash, wherever you are." Nor did I keep a list of the celebrated names invoked by comedians like Bob Hope. (It was, in fact, many years before I learned that the often-mentioned James Petrillo was president of the musicians' union during a very acrimonious strike in the late 1940s.) Even so, all of these details became faint entries in my cultural encyclopedia waiting until further information filled them in and activated them as useful popular culture references. The same thing is happening, it seems to me, to kids watching *The Simpsons* or *Mystery Science Theater 3000* in the late 1990s and early 2000s. These youngsters may not know yet who James Dean was, or Yul Brenner, or Jackie Robinson, but they have heard the names on one of these shows. They may not have heard of the Cowsills before or the Ink Spots either. Nor have they had to "duck and cover" during an a-bomb drill, and perhaps they have never eaten Pez candy. But eventually these references will take up suitable spaces in their fields of reference, just as the icons and totems of vaudeville did in mine. This is how popular cultural literacy develops.

It seems to me that this is also how hieratic cultural literacy develops. Everyone has to run into John Donne's "A Valediction: Forbidding Mourning" and William Faulkner's *The Sound and the Fury* for the first time at a point in life when the person is incapable of fully apprehending the difficult master work. Many years later, after reading the work repeatedly, thinking about it, probably reading commentaries, and participating in discussions, this person has acquired considerable reading mastery and can stand in front of a class of undergraduates and dazzle them with his or her mastery of these thorny texts. At this point, the professor can speak for a cultural community even while helping to enroll others in the community. This is how intertextual communities are formed.

Before one is fully enrolled in a hieratic or popular cultural community, however, other forms of intertextual encounters are still possible.

Because of Leslie Fiedler's article "Come Back to the Raft Ag'n, Huck Honey" (1948), for example, thousands of readers have been forced to read Mark Twain's novel *Adventures of Huckleberry Finn* differently than they would have done if Fiedler had never written his controversial essay. In his article Feidler proposes a gay/racial subtext beneath "the infantile, the homoerotic aspects" of Twain's narrative.[1] This was a shocking suggestion at the time—and is perhaps shocking to many still today. Because of, or in spite of, this air of controversy, readers who adopted Fiedler's perspective would naturally see incidents and characters in Twain's novel differently than they would have otherwise. Students who encountered Twain's novel in a class taught by teacher "A," who accepted Fiedler's premise, would therefore read a very different novel than the students in the classroom next door where teacher "B" was indifferent to what Fiedler had said. And this difference would develop because of the intertext supplied by Fiedler's interpretation. Let us say, to continue this hypothetical experiment, that another teacher, "C," rejected Fiedler's reading outright. Even so, the Fiedlerian reading would continue to function as an intertext in this classroom, lurking deconstructively in the shadows behind this offended teacher's reading, leading teacher "C" to changes of emphasis and over-compensations in the resulting interpretation. It is clear, then, that intertexts like Fiedler's essay can interact with primary texts in a variety of ways and thus provide readers with quite varied intertextual encounters.

But, let's say that a group of readers encounter *Adventures of Huckleberry Finn* in some cultural backwater in which students and their teacher, "D," alike know nothing of Fiedler or gay studies, and further that no one creates this Fiedlerian intertext even accidentally. These people still read the book, don't they, even though this supposedly valuable intertext is absent? They do, and they probably still encounter Twain's book in a very rich context because "Come Back to the Raft" is not the only possible intertext. There are also the intertexts of southwest humor, and later, historical, developments of the "bad boy" image, and the parodies of Shakespeare and genteel verse—to name just a few. Surely all of these intertexts enrich the hypothetical readings that we are discussing. In fact, the possibility of so many intertexts for *Adventures of Huckleberry Finn* may explain why Twain's book is so regularly accepted as a literary classic.

In this respect we may wish to import an analogy in which *Adventures of Huckleberry Finn* is compared to a fruitcake. A truly rich fruitcake, like the ones baked by Buddy and his dotty cousin in Truman Capote's "A Christmas Memory,"[2] contains walnuts, and cherries, and citron, and raisins, and canned pineapple. A true connoisseur of fruitcakes would be shocked to hear someone say that a very rich cake could be made without the walnuts or without the citron. To a certain sort of palate, it just wouldn't be fruitcake without these ingredients.[3] To other palates less familiar with fruitcakes brimming with nuts and citron, the resulting cake would be rich and satisfying indeed, as rich perhaps as *Adventures of Huckleberry Finn* might be without the intertext of Fiedler's theory. This seems to me an adequate response to the frequent concern, stated in representative form by Thaïs Morgan in my first chapter: "We are left with the uncomfortable implication that any set of intertexts will always be only those intertexts noticed by the individual analyst" (19). To reservations of this sort about intertextuality, we may respond with the questions, What's so bad about that? And, can't we learn progressively to notice more intertexts?

To answer my own questions, I will say that there is nothing especially wrong with this—probably inevitable—situation and that noticing more and more intertexts is pretty much what acculturation is all about. Throughout life we read new and old books, see new and old films, encounter new and old products, styles, and recipes. Each of these experiences increases our capacity for intertextual encounters. As Jonathan Culler explains in *The Pursuit of Signs: Semiotics, Literature, Deconstruction* (1981), intertextuality is "less a name for a work's relation to prior texts than a designation of its participation in the discursive space of a culture" (103). In other words, any time we experience any kind of text we are contributing to our intertextual encyclopedias, and these contributions will be drawn upon when the opportunity for an intertextual encounter appears. Often we are prevented by inattention, carelessness, or sloth from experiencing this encounter fully. Occasionally, though, we get all of our intertextual ducks in a row and end up seeing Jay Gatsby or Bugs Bunny in a new light. This is what I have been trying to do in this book. This is what I hope my readers will continue to do.

Notes

Introduction

1. See 2 Samuel 13-19. In his masterful two-volume work, *Faulkner: A Biography*, Joseph Blotner shows that Faulkner originally intended to use the title *Dark House* (891) for this highly intertextual novel.

2. "Word, Dialogue, and Novel," in *Desire in Language: A Semiotic Approach to Literature and Art* (66).

3. See, for example, Jay Clayton, and Eric Rothstein, *Influence and Intertextuality in Literary History* (18-21).

4. See Linda Hutcheon's observation in *A Poetics of Postmodernism*: "As later defined by Barthes . . . and Riffaterre . . . intertextuality replaces the challenged author-text relationship with one between reader and text, one that situates the locus of textual meaning within the history of discourse" (126).

5. In the Introduction to *Intertextuality in Faulkner*, Michel Gresset writes about "this relatively new and extremely stimulating concept of intertextuality," that "its theoretical extension is almost infinite" (15).

6. "The Irish Ballad," *Songs and More Songs by Tom Lehrer* (1997).

7. Reprinted in *Is There a Text in This Class?: The Authority of Interpretive Communities* (Cambridge: Harvard UP, 1980), 147-73.

8. Fish's article originally appeared in *Critical Inquiry*, 2.3 (1976). In the next volume Douglas Bush and Steven Mailloux both called Fish to task for thinking incorrectly about interpretation, especially the interpretation of John Milton's works. See "Professor Fish on the Milton *Variorum*," by Douglas Bush, *Critical Inquiry*, 3.1 (1976): 179-82, and "Stanley Fish's 'Interpreting the *Variorum*,'" by Steven Mailloux (183-90). Fish replied immediately to these criticisms in "Interpreting the *Variorum*" (191-96), reprinted in *Is There a Text in this Class?* (174-80).

9. See Bakhtin's typical remark in *Problems of Dostoevsky's Poetics*: "The idea begins to live, that is, to take shape, to develop, to find and renew its verbal expression, to give birth to new ideas, only when it enters into genuine dialogic relationships with other ideas, with the ideas of *others*. Human thought becomes genuine thought, that is, an idea, only under conditions of living contact with another and alien thought, a thought embodied in someone else's voice, that is, in someone else's consciousness expressed in discourse" (88; Bakhtin's emphasis).

10. See John Fiske's explanation in *Television Culture* (1989): "The theory of intertextuality proposes that any one text is necessarily read in relationship to others and that a range of textual knowledges is brought to bear upon it. These

relationships do not take the form of specific allusions from one text to another and there is no reason for readers to be familiar with specific or the same texts to read intertextually. Intertextuality exists rather in the space *between* texts" (108; Fiske's emphasis).

11. *Television: Technology and Cultural Form* (78-118).

Chapter 1

1. Although his political opponents applied the sobriquet "Ragged Dick" mockingly to Richard Nixon, Tom Wicker's *One of Us: Richard Nixon and the American Dream* suggests that the ironies involved may be quite complex.

2. In his exhaustive "Explanatory Notes" to the *Cambridge Edition* of *The Great Gatsby*, Matthew J. Bruccoli explains: "This cowboy character was created by Clarence E. Mulford in 1907, but *Hopalong Cassidy* was not published until 1910 (Chicago: McClurg). Therefore the 1906 date on Gatsby's copy is anachronistic" (204).

3. Frederick J. Hoffman, for example, writes: "[Fitzgerald's] judgment of Daisy was severe; as the final, particular embodiment of Gatsby's purpose, she was unequal to the task, first of understanding his love, then of realizing the effort he had made to recover the one moment in the past that seemed worth while to him" (142). Nearly a quarter-century later, Brian Way concludes, "Daisy is a trivial, callous, cowardly woman who may dream a little herself but who will not let her dreams, or such unpleasant realities as running over Myrtle Wilson, disturb her comfort. That Gatsby should have dreamt of her, given his marvelous parties for her, is his special fate" (99).

4. Perhaps the motivation for these romantic/ironic allusions lies in Frye's observation, "In every age the ruling social or intellectual class tends to project its ideals in some form of romance, where the virtuous heroes and beautiful heroines represent the ideals and the villains the threats to their ascendancy" (*Anatomy* 186). If so, the narrative functions of Gatsby as hero, Daisy as love object, and Tom as villain take on increased intertextual clarity.

5. "If inferior in power or intelligence to ourselves, so that we have the sense of looking down on a scene of bondage, frustration, or absurdity, the hero belongs to the *ironic* mode" (Northrop Frye, *Anatomy of Criticism*, 34; Frye's emphasis).

6. "The Dead Center: An Introduction to Nathanael West," *The Complete Works of Nathanael West*, vii-xxii. On West's politics, see Jay Martin, *Nathanael West: The Art of His Life*, esp. 219ff.

7. Madonna Marsden typifies Alger's formula in this way: "For Alger . . . success was definitely a combination of Puritan luck and Ben Franklin's pluck. The repetition of this unvarying literary formula through at least seventy books raised the 'luck plus pluck' hypothesis almost to the validity of a scientific law" (140).

8. But see Tom Buchanan's dinner table conversation in *The Great Gatsby*: "Civilization's going to pieces. . . . Have you read 'The Rise of the Colored Empires' by this man Goddard? . . . The idea is if we don't look out the white race will be—will be utterly submerged. It's all scientific stuff; it's been proved" (14).

9. On the proletarian novel, see Walter B. Rideout, *The Radical Novel in the United States, 1900-1954: Some Interrelations of Literature and Society* (1992); Daniel Aaron, *Writers on the Left: Episodes in American Literary Communism* (1961); Barbara Foley, *Radical Representations: Politics and Form in U. S. Proletarian Fiction, 1929-1941* (1993).

10. In the *Autobiography* Franklin writes: "Perhaps the most important Part of that Journal is the *Plan* to be found in it which I formed at Sea, for regulating my future Conduct in Life. It is the more remarkable, as being form'd when I was so young, and yet being fairly faithfully adhered to quite thro' to old Age." This pattern of moral goal-setting consists first of all of a list of thirteen virtues that Franklin sought to acquire: Temperance, Silence, Order, Resolution, Frugality, Industry, Sincerity, Justice, Moderation, Cleanliness, Tranquility, Chastity, and Humility. Though greatly ridiculed by D. H. Lawrence in *Studies in Classic American Literature* (1923), this list directly influences the behavior of fictional characters created by Alger, Fitzgerald and West. The second part of Franklin's plan of moral improvement—mandated by his pursuit of Order— consists of a daily schedule accounting for all the time between his rising at 5:00 a.m. and his midnight bedtime. Traces of this schedule can be glimpsed in the lives of real and fictional American Dreamers, ranging from the electronic pocket schedules carried by so many up-and-coming corporate workers today, to the tips provided in business magazines by "highly organized persons," to— most pertinently—the daily schedule worked out in the back of his Hopalong Cassidy book by the young James Gatz.

Chapter 2

1. Connections between the texts discussed in this chapter and those discussed in Chapter 1 may be glimpsed in Patricia Ann Carlson's remark in *Hawthorne's Functional Settings: A Study of Artistic Method* (1977): Robin "is a country boy, but he is also vain and ambitious. He has come to the city in the hope of making his fortune—not through the Alger formula of hard work and heartiness but by ensconcing himself in the good graces of a wealthy foster father" (134). Along the same line, Lea B. Newman says that "[s]ome of the details of Robin's arrival parallel Franklin's account of his first encounters in Philadelphia recorded in his *Autobiography*" (222).

2. The tale is filled with passages like the following: "Robin . . . hastened away, pursued by an ill-mannered roar of laughter from the barber's shop" (211); "[N]o sooner was he beyond the door, than he heard a general laugh"

(214); "Robin seemed to hear the sound of drowsy laughter stealing along the solitary street" (218). Like Jonathan, Robin "has a most prodigious effect upon [the] risibility" of these characters.

3. In light of all these critical disputes, Newman writes, "Is 'My Kinsman' worth it? Quite simply, yes. Superlatives are applied routinely to this story. [Marius] Bewley calls it 'one of the masterpieces in American literature.' . . . [Hyatt] Waggoner says it achieves a 'perfection of embodiment'" (229).

4. Cf. Newman: "The twenty or so sources and influences that are reviewed above contribute to this disparity because each suggests a corresponding interpretation—some historical, some mythic, some psychological, and each with a different moral slant" (225).

5. Introduction, *Intertextuality in Faulkner* (8).

6. George Marion O'Donnell, "Faulkner's Mythology," *Kenyon Review,* 1 (1939): 285-99; Malcolm Cowley, Introduction, *The Portable Faulkner,* 1946 (New York: Viking, 1964), 14-16; Hyatt H. Waggoner, *William Faulkner: From Jefferson to the World* (Lexington: U of Kentucky P, 1959), 89-100; Gregory Fortner, "Faulkner's Black Holes: Vision and Vomit in Sanctuary," *Mississippi Quarterly,* 49.3 (1996): 537-62.

7. Gerald Langford shows in *Faulkner's Revision of* Sanctuary: *A Collation of the Unrevised Galleys and the Published Book* that the Virgil and Fonzo episode was originally Chapter 16 (7).

8. Edmond Volpe writes in *A Reader's Guide to William Faulkner* (1964) that "The entire episode of young Snopes and his friend living at Miss Reba's without knowing it is a house of prostitution has little thematic or tonal relationship to the rest of the novel" (143). More recently (1990), in "Pop Goes the Faulkner: In Quest of *Sanctuary*," Leslie Fiedler criticizes "the rather hackneyed, but much admired (overadmired, I am convinced) 'Stupid Rube in the Big City' anecdote, in which a pair of Snopses take a brothel for a hotel" (89).

9. See Vladimir Propp, *Morphology of the Folktale,* trans. Laurence Scott, 2nd ed. (Austin: U of Texas P, 1968), 79-91.

10. In a letter to Cecil Dawkins (10/5/58), O'Connor wrote, "I have always listened with profit to what [John Crowe Ransom] has had to say about my stories—except when he wanted me to change the title of 'The Artificial Nigger'" (*Habit of Being* 297).

11. For a good presentation of this view, see Lucinda MacKethan, "Redeeming Blackness: Urban Allegories of O'Connor, Percy, and Toole," *Studies in the Literary Imagination,* 27.2 (Fall 1994): 29-39.

12. See also Rodney Allen, "Mr. Head and Hawthorne: Allusion and Conversion in Flannery O'Connor's 'The Artificial Nigger,'" *Studies in Short Fiction,* 21 (1984): 20.

13. Ronald Schliefer writes, "Head, hick that he is, believes that an inferno underlies Atlanta and fears to be sucked down the sewer" (165).

14. Frederick Asals, *Flannery O'Connor: The Imagination of Extremity* (81, 88); Louis D. Rubin, Jr., "Flannery O'Connor's Company of Southerners or 'The Artificial Nigger' Read as Fiction Rather Than Theology," *A Gallery of Southerners* (115-234).

15. According to Lyday, in *"Sanctuary:* Faulkner's *Inferno,"* Faulkner "absorbed the quintessence of Dante's vision of evil, made it part of his own, and successfully incorporated that vision into a plausible modern context" (253).

16. In addition to his smart-alecky come-backs, Nelson's general behavior signals "shrewdness." Thus, even before their journey begins, Mr. Head "fell asleep thinking how the boy would at last find out that he was not as smart as he thought he was" (251).

17. See Daniel G. Hoffman's observation: "It is characteristic of Robin that he always accepts the most simplistic rationalizations of the most baffling and ominous experiences" (120).

18. Convinced that "it is sometimes necessary to teach a child a lesson he won't forget, particularly when the child is always reasserting his position with some new impudence" (208), Mr. Head intends Nelson's current trip to Atlanta to teach him more valuable lessons than the ones he may have learned by living in the city as a small baby because "A six-month-old child don't know a nigger from anybody else" (252).

19. The issues remain unresolved in 1995, as this assessment by Peter J. Bellis attests: "What Hawthorne's story ['My Kinsman, Major Molineux'] does, I would suggest, is to challenge this notion of revolution as continuity or inheritance by deliberately reinscribing discontinuities—class conflict and racial violence—into its narrative of revolutionary change" (103).

20. Joseph R. Urgo surveys this highly ingenious criticism on *Sanctuary* helpfully in "Temple Drake's Truthful Perjury: Rethinking Faulkner's *Sanctuary," American Literature,* 55.3 (1983): 97-119.

21. A. R. Courtland advances a related thesis in "From Sermon to Parable: Four Conversion Stories by Flannery O'Connor": "Another letter written the same year [1955] suggests that 'The Artificial Nigger' began as a simple account of the adventures of two country bumpkins out of their element in the big city but during the course of composition grew into something more" (59).

22. *Sewanee Review,* 70 (1962): 395-407.

23. According to Blotner, when Major Oldham challenged Faulkner about the Hawthornean title of his book of poems, *The Marble Faun* (1924), Faulkner replied, "Who's Hawthorne? The title is original with me" (379).

Chapter 3

1. *Criticism: The Major Texts,* ed Walter Jackson Bate (25). Contrast Aristotle's view with the contemporary view of the historian's role articulated by Linda Hutcheon: "Historians are now being urged to take the contexts of their own inevitably interpretive act into account: the writing, reception, and 'critical reading' of narratives about the past are not unrelated to issues of power, both intellectual and institutional" (*A Poetics of Postmodernism* 97).

2. *E. L. Doctorow: Essays and Conversations,* ed. Richard Trenner, 31-47.

3. See Alice Jardine's judgment in "Flash Back, Flash Forward: The Fifties, The Nineties, and the Transformed Politics of Remote Control": "In fact, our historical, cultural, and political memory leaves little doubt that the Rosenberg Event was in many ways the central event of the American 1950s, even perhaps of the American twentieth century," *Secret Agents: The Rosenberg Case, McCarthyism, and Fifties America* (113).

4. To illustrate Dobbs's claim, we may cite David Thorburn, as the representative of many others on the pro-Rosenberg side: "I take it as beyond argument that whether or not the Rosenbergs were guilty of anything, they were certainly railroaded," "The Rosenberg Letters," in *Secret Agents* (171). Pearl K. Bell can speak for the anti-Rosenberg faction in her scathing review of *The Public Burning*: "The historical evidence is plain enough to anyone who has not been cowed by the nimble reshufflings of revisionist piety, and it cannot be misused by a novelist for his self-defined purposes as though what he chooses to tell us is all that we can know" (3).

5. See, for example, Norris J. Lacy's entry on *Matiere de Bretagne* in *The Arthurian Encyclopedia*, which classifies "acceptable literary material" for the medieval writer into "The Matter of France . . . of Rome . . . and of Britain" (377-78).

6. Cf. "The Secret about Secrets," by Stanley Goldberg, in *Secret Agents* (48).

7. On the style of the Rosenbergs' prison letters, see David Thorburn, "The Rosenberg Letters," in *Secret Agents* (171-82).

8. In an interview with Paul Levine, Doctrow says, "Once I got going [on *Daniel*], I found myself looking things up, but not in any systematic way" (62), "The Writer as Independent Witness," *E. L. Doctorow: Essays and Conversations* (57-69).

9. Cf. Doctorow's essay, "False Documents": "I am thus led to the proposition that there is no fiction or nonfiction as we commonly understand the distinction: there is only narrative," *E. L. Doctorow: Essays and Conversations* (26).

10. In an interview with Larry McCaffery, Coover explains, "Life's too complicated, we just can't handle all the input, we have to isolate little bits and

make reasonable stories out of them. . . . All of them, though, are merely arti-fices—that is, they are always in some ways false, or at best incomplete. There are always other plots, other settings, other interpretations" (50), "Robert Coover on His Own and Other Fictions; An Interview," *Novel Vs. Fiction: The Contemporary Reformation* (45-63).

11. Note Nixon's closeness here to Linda Hutcheon's theory in *A Poetics of Postmodernism*: "Historiographic metafiction self-consciously reminds us that, while events did occur in the real empirical past, we name and constitute those events as historical facts by selection and narrative positioning. And, even more basically, we only know of those past events through their discursive inscription, through their traces in the present" (97).

12. See Robert Towers' judgment in his review of *The Public Burning*: "Though one is aware that a show of erudition about a recent decade can be rather easily worked up by reading back issues of *Time* and the *Times*, the inclu-siveness of Coover's re-creation is astonishing," "Nixon's Seventh Crisis," *The New York Review of Books,* 29 Sept. 1977: 8.

13. "Robert Coover, *The Public Burning*, and the Art of Excess," *Critique: Studies in Modern Fiction,* 23.3 (1982): 5-28.

14. On the correspondence that Zinnemann creates between his diegetic narrative and the film's running time, see *Kiss Kiss Bang Bang*, by Pauline Kael (184). On the historical parallel, note the analysis by Ronald Radosh and Joyce Milton in *The Rosenberg File: A Search for theTruth*: "[T]he Supreme Court succumbed to the illusion that the Rosenberg issue could and would be resolved only by their speedy execution" (411).

15. Philip W. Leininger and James D. Hart, eds., *The Oxford Companion to American Literature*, 6th ed. (432).

16. See Doctorow's claim in his essay, "False Documents," "we have it in us to compose false documents more valid, more real, more truthful than the 'true' documents of the politicians or the journalists or the psychologists," in *E. L. Doctorow: Essays and Conversations* (26).

17. While keeping up with action in the Korean War, Coover's narrator recounts, "The hardnosed 187th Airborne Regimental Combat Team, com-manded by an up-and-coming tough-as-nails brigadier general named West-moreland, is flown in from Japan to round up Rhee's rampaging prisoners, put them back in the barbed-wire stockades, and quell the riots" (70), a totally irrel-evant detail without the reader's familiarity with Westmoreland's subsequent connection with the war in Vietnam.

18. See Norman Mailer, *The Armies of the Night: History as a Novel/The Novel as History* (1968).

19. The complexity of the "matter" of the Rosenbergs is made especially clear by the discovery in 1995 that Julius Rosenberg probably *was* a Soviet spy, even though Ethel probably was not. See "Decoded Soviet Messages Affirm

Rosenberg Spy Case," *Los Angeles Times,* 12 July 1995, LEXIS-NEXIS Academic Universe.

20. Supporting opinion abounds. See John Ramage's view in "Myth and Monomyth in Coover's *The Public Burning*": "Coover's Nixon is simply a caricature of the historical one of *Six Crises* who converts his life into a series of carefully staged 'crises,' featuring himself as the embattled but detached hero alert to turn every historical gap into personal gain" (61). See also Geoffrey Woolf's review in *New Times*: "What we have here is the manipulation of a received mythology, whose tablets are *Six Crises* and the prison letters of the Rosenbergs, to create a rival mythology" (53).

21. See *Public Papers of the Presidents of the United States, Dwight D. Eisenhower, 1953* (306-16, 1-8).

22. Coover's decision should perhaps be read in light of his negative review of Louis Nizer's *The Implosion Controversy* in *The New York Times Book Review* (11 Feb. 1973): "Throughout the book Nizer stretches and contracts time according to dramatic whim, invents whole scenes and fictionalizes freely (especially when those involved are conveniently dead), avoids all controversy and sensationalizes wherever possible . . ." (5).

Chapter 4

1. Bruce Daniels observes in *Journal of Popular Culture*, "Perhaps no movie was ever more widely and negatively reviewed" (3).

2. See Cowley's "Five Acts of *The Scarlet Letter*," *College English,* 19 (1957): 11-16.

3. See "Hester, Sweet Hester Prynne—*The Scarlet Letter* in the Movie Market Place," *Literature/Film Quarterly,* 2 (1974): 100-09. See also Peter Morris, ed., *Dictionary of Films* (328), in which the earliest cinematic version of *The Scarlet Letter* is dated 1908.

4. Before coming to America, the director spelled his name Sjostrom.

5. Julian Smith reports that Walthall played opposite Gish in *The Birth of a Nation* in 1915 and that his reduced status in the 1926 version "is a moving experience for the student of film" (104). Walthall's reappearance in the 1934 version probably provides another occasion for reflection—perhaps on the order of one's response to Robert Duvall's Chillingworth in the Demi Moore film.

6. The comic relations between the two actors are illustrated in the film's adaptation of elements from the earlier film. Smith writes about the 1926 version: "Giles [the barber] is seen being rapped on the head for sneezing during religious service, seen courting the Beadle's daughter, Patience, through a speaking tube . . . and being denounced for stealing a kiss from Patience" (104). In 1934, Bartholomew, as Church warden, raps Samson on the head for sleeping during one of Dimmesdale's sermons, Bartholomew courts the widow Crak-

stone through a speaking tube, and Samson is put in the stocks for laughing on the Sabbath.

7. In *The Scarlet Mob of Scribblers: Rereading Hester Prynne* (2000), Jamie Barlowe sees the contemporary updating evident in Colleen Moore's Hester as evidence of the cultural activity that she calls "Hester-Prynne-ism": "the continuously and relentlessly functioning cultural dichotomy of the good-woman vs. the bad-(but desirable)-woman-who-needs-instruction-or-punishment" (12).

8. As Welsh writes, "In the novel, Hawthorne advances her years, whereas in the film Wenders makes her younger and more comely" (2660).

9. Perhaps Sarah's presence in these shots explains the presence of Demi Moore's female slave, Mituba, in the 1995 version.

10. This character, played by Rafael Albaicin, was preceded by in 1934 by a similarly atmospheric Indian, to whom Walthall's Chillingworth spoke in a patois supposed—according to 1930s standards—to be a native American language. Significantly, the role was uncredited. These characters were succeeded in the 1995 version by great crowds of Indians supposed—according to 1990s standards—to be authentic native Americans. However, many reviewers traced their ancestry not to early American history but to *The Last of the Mohicans* and *Dances with Wolves*. See, for example, Todd McCarthy's review in *Variety,* 16-22 Oct. 1995: 94.

11. See Matthiessen's *American Renaissance: Art and Expression in the Age of Emerson and Whitman* (1941) and Winters's "Maule's Curse, or Hawthorne and the Problem of Allegory" (1938).

12. For a fuller discussion of the causes and effects of Hawthorne's stylistic indirection, see my *Hawthorne's Narrative Strategies*, esp. 22-46.

13. While the *Times* found Walthall's role a definite plus, the reviewer in *Variety* wrote that Walthall "plays the husband with a make-up suggestive of Shylock and mannerism much the same, though the reason for this is far from explained."

14. The opportunity for a leading actress to take a stand on contemporary social issues by acting in an historical narrative is evident, perhaps, in Judy Brennan's revelation in *Entertainment Weekly* (4 Feb. 1994) that "Meg Ryan reportedly lobbied hard for the part."

15. But see Richard Corliss's comment in *Time*: "Among the top 20 paperbacks in *USA Today*'s best-seller list is *The Scarlet Letter*—the Cliffs Notes version. Bibliophiles who purchase that slim volume in lieu of dozing over the original will get a much clearer view of Nathaniel Hawthorne's 1850 tale of heroism and hypocrisy than those visiting the new movie adaptation" (94).

Chapter 5

1. See Leo Braudy's claim in *The World in a Frame: What We See in Films*: "Instead of dismissing genre films from the realm of art, we should . . . examine what they accomplish. Genre in films can be the equivalent of conscious reference to tradition in the other arts—the invocation of past works that has been so important a part of the history of literature, drama, and painting" (108).

2. In *Rabelais and His World*, Bakhtin writes: "The grotesque body, as we have often stressed, is a body in the act of becoming. . . . This is why the essential role belongs to those parts of the grotesque body in which it outgrows its own self, transgressing its own body, in which it conceives a new, second body: the bowels and the phallus. These two areas play the leading role in the grotesque image, and it is precisely for this reason that they are predominantly subject to positive exaggeration, to hyperbolization; they can even detach themselves from the body, as something secondary. (The nose can also in a way detach itself from the body.) Next to the bowels and the genital organs is the mouth, through which enters the world to be swallowed up. And next is the anus. All these convexities and orifices have a common characteristic; it is within them that the confines between bodies and between the body and the world are overcome: there is an exchange and an interorientation. This is why the main events in the life of the grotesque body, the acts of bodily drama, take place in this sphere. Eating, drinking, defecation and other elimination (sweating, blowing the nose, sneezing), as well as copulation, pregnancy, dismemberment, swallowing up by another body—all these acts are performed on the confines of the body and the outer world, or on the confines of the old and new body" (317).

3. See Michael Holquist's explanation in *Dialogism: Bakhtin and His World*: "Dialogism argues that all meaning is relative in the sense that it comes about only as the result of the relation between two bodies occupying *simultaneous but different space*, where bodies may be thought of as ranging from the immediacy of our physical bodies, to political bodies and to bodies of ideas in general (ideologies)" (20-21; Holquist's italics).

4. See *The Birdcage* (1996), directed by Mike Nichols.

5. See, for example, Aileen S. Kraditor's Introduction to *Up from the Pedestal: Selected Writings in the History of American Feminism* (3-24).

Chapter 6

1. The claustrophobic setting of the Earle surely would suggest Sartre's hell to some viewers. Jami Bernard, for one, says in summary: "Things go wrong quickly for Barton as he sinks deeper and deeper into the hell that is normal human existence, magnified and refracted through the heaving, sobbing

walls and toilets and stressed seams of the sweltering Hotel Earle" (85). David Ansen agrees by stressing the spiritual compromise that brought Fink to Hollywood: "'Barton Fink' is a postmodern Faustian comedy whose ultimate destination is hell itself" (57). In Jack Mathews' view, the film "is a Faustian tale about a self-important 1940s New York playwright who sells his soul for a job in Hollywood and discovers when he gets there that he is already in hell." Although Mathews adds, "I don't know that that's what the eccentric Coen brothers actually had in mind" (85), his interpretation makes good sense, as do the other readings based on hell and damnation.

2. Cf. Arthur Miller's opinion, recorded in a review of *Barton Fink* in the Nov. 1991 issue of *Premiere*: "The only thing about Hollywood that I am sure of is that its mastication of writers can never be too wildly exaggerated" (108).

3. We might wish to connect the Coen brothers' intertextual use of The Book of Daniel to its use by E. A. Doctorow in his novel of that title.

4. Altman's film was also widely perceived as satiric. As Leonard Feinberg explains in his classic study *The Satirist: His Temperament, Motivation, and Influence*, "Like other arts and philosophy, satire is primarily concerned with the nature of reality. Unlike other arts and philosophy, which emphasize what is real, satire emphasizes what *seems* to be real but isn't. . . . the essence of satire is persistent revelation and exaggeration of the contrast between reality and pretense" (7). Thus, in *Newsweek* David Ansen called *The Player* a "dead-on satire of everything shallow, venal and hypocritical in the movie business" (61). Terrence Rafferty says in *The New Yorker* that "the movie veers from psychological-thriller suspense to goofball comedy to icy satire: it's Patricia Highsmith meets Monty Python meets Nathanael West" (82). Altman comments in *One on One with Robert Altman*: "Most people in Hollywood have taken the attitude that this is all some big thing about them and all this, and that it's a big satire on them." However, he adds: "It isn't! It's using Hollywood as a metaphor."

5. In *The New Yorker* a disapproving Terrence Rafferty says that the Coens "started out . . . as genre-movie parodists and cynical wits—smary-alecky conoisseurs of trash" (76). The more favorably disposed Richard Schickel agrees in *Time* that "The Coens' earlier films, like those of many young filmmakers, worked out of, and off of, the American genre tradition" (58). In his *Rolling Stone* review, Peter Travers sees this knowledge as the point of origin not only for *Barton Fink* but for all the Coens' films (74). David Ansen adds in *Newsweek* that "the Coens explode convention with a shocking violent twist, at which point all the familiar genre signposts are abandoned and the audience enters terra incognita" (57). It is intertextually significant that the way to this uncharted land winds through very familiar cinematic territory.

6. In *A Dictionary of Narratology*, Gerald Prince defines *metadiegetic* as "pertaining to or part of a diegesis . . . that is embedded in another one and,

more particularly, in that of the primary narrative" (50). Or, we might say, a narrative within another narrative, a film within a film.

7. Edmond Grant concludes in *Films in Review* that the film's "technical bravura dazzles while you watch it" (79); in *New York*, David Denby concedes that the Coens' cinematic technique "has its fascinations," but concludes that "the Coens haven't yet learned how to bring them out into the light of drama" (84); Terrence Rafferty is even more critical in *The New Yorker*: "At times, Joel Coen's baroque technique . . . achieves the insufferable elegance of Alain Resnais" (77); however, J. Hoberman wins the negativity prize by writing, "In its sour formalism, bleak humor, and empty world stylistics, *Barton Fink* is reminiscent of Roman Polanski's *The Tenant* (which, given Polanski's power as chair of the Cannes jury, may account for the film's unprecedented three awards)" (90).

8. Terrence Rafferty speaks for many other reviewers in *The New Yorker* (20 Apr. 1992) by identifying "the opening sequence of 'The Player' . . . [as] an insolently elaborate eight-minute tracking shot" (81); see also Mary E. Belles in *Magill's Cinema Annual 1993*, 303-06.

9. This suggestion develops when Levy proposes that movie executives should take their basic story ideas from current newspaper headlines. Although the suggestion may remind us more of made-for-television films than of Hollywood productions, a similar merchandising mentality operates in both environments. The headline "Mudslide kills 60 in Slums of Chile," for example, is translated by Levy as: "Triumph over tragedy. Sounds like a John Boorman picture. You slap a happy ending on it, and the script'll write itself." Boorman's films suddenly rise up to interact with Levy's fictional suggestions. Simultaneously, television films about the social problem of the week rise up to interact with both. Whether conceived for the large or the small screen, the voices of Levy's unproduced story lines enter the viewer's consciousness and so cannot be ignored.

10. Early in the meeting in which he proposes taking all future movie scripts from the daily headlines, Levy asks, "Who wrote the new ending to *Fatal Attraction*?" and provides his own answer: "The audience." Like earlier references to corporate shakeups at real-life studios, Paramount and Columbia, this passage both increases the mimetic illusion of Altman's film and calls up a significant intertext for his audience.

Chapter 7

1. According to Peter Gammond's *The Oxford Companion to Popular Music*, the term *tin pan alley* was probably coined by Monroe H. Rosenfeld "who, in his newspaper column, likened the noise going on there to the clashing of tin pots" (573).

2. Cf. "The shepherds' swains shall dance and sing/For thy delight each May morning:/If these delights thy mind may move,/Come live with me and

be my love," Christopher Marlowe, "The Passionate Shepherd to His Love" (ll. 21-24), *The Norton Anthology of Poetry* (185-86).

3. See Sonnet 18, "Nor shall death brag thou wander'st in his shade,/ When in eternal lines to time thou grow'st: /So long as men can breathe, or eyes can see,/So long lives this, and this gives life to thee" (11.11-14); and Sonnet 65, "where, alack,/Shall Time's best jewel from Time's chest lie hid?/Or what strong hand can hold his swift foot back?/ . . . /O, none, unless this miracle have might,/That in black ink my love may still shine bright" (11.9-14), *The Norton Anthology of Poetry* (187-88).

4. In her liner notes to Ella Fitzgerald's *The Rodgers and Hart Songbook*, Deena Rosenberg writes, "Given the value Rodgers and Hart placed on originality and individuality, their work would be incomplete without a song that directly attacked the use of clichés. The Gershwins, Yip Harburg, and Harold Arlen addressed themselves to the task in songs like 'Blah Blah Blah' (1930) and 'What Can You Say in a Love Song? (That Hasn't Been Said Before)' (1934)." According to Rosenberg, "My Romance" is Rodgers and Hart's effort in this direction.

5. Thomas Hischak argues that "It was [P. G.] Wodehouse who opened up the comic and dramatic possibilities of rhyme" (29). This, of course, does not detract from later achievements in rhyme such as Porter's.

6. For an ample illustrated discussion of zeugma, see *Princeton Encyclopedia of Poetry and Poetics* (905-06).

7. Hischak notes a different approach to this lyric element when he reports that "[Oscar] Hammerstein was very particular about his use of rhyme. He felt that rhymes that grab attention usually distract from the meaning of the lyric" (40).

8. See Alec Wilder's opinion in *American Popular Song*: "[E]very song written for Fred Astaire seems to bear his mark. Every writer, in my opinion, was vitalized by Astaire and wrote in a manner they had never quite written in before: he brought out in them something a little better than their best—a little more subtlety, flair, sophistication, wit, style, qualities he himself possesses in generous measure" (109).

9. In her liner notes to *The Very Thought of You: Jeri Southern, The Decca Years, 1951-1957*, Kathryn King incisively refers to such songs as "that superb classic repertoire that grew up in the United States between roughly 1920 and the 1950s."

Chapter 8

1. In their book, *Looney Tunes and Merrie Melodies*, Jerry Beck and Will Friedwald supply the following background for this discussion: "Warner Bros., having made sound movies popular with *The Jazz Singer*, saw a good thing when producer Leon Schlesinger brought the first all 'talk-ink' cartoon charac-

ter to them. Ex-Disney animators Hugh Harman and Rudolph Ising had created a pilot film featuring their speaking character, a black boy named Bosko. The test film was just that, all talk. Warner Bros. suggested they make the character less ethnic, more like Mickey Mouse, and more musical, incorporating popular songs from the studio's new feature musicals. With that, Looney Tunes and Merrie Melodies were born. And though the road was a bit bumpy in the 1930s, the films eventually settled into a style which nurtured many top animation talents (Friz Freleng, Chuck Jones, Tex Avery, Bob Clampett, Frank Tahslin, Bob McKimson, etc.) and created many superstars (including Bugs Bunny, Daffy Duck, Porky Pig, and the Road Runner) and hundreds of lesser lights (Egghead, Charlie Dog, Marvin Martian, et al), Intro. n.p.

2. See Jane Feuer's discussion, "Opera vs Jazz: The Theme of Popular vs Elite Art," in *The Hollywood Musical* (54-57).

3. Faint echoes of Glenn Miller's celebrated recording, "Pennsylvania 6-5000," are merely an intertextual bonus in this cartoon.

4. See David Chute's judgment in 1995: "There are now very few people under 35 who have seen a short cartoon on a big screen" (15).

5. As David Bianculli explains in his *Dictionary of Teleliteracy*, *Rocky and His Friends* aired on ABC 1959-1961; *The Bullwinkle Show* aired on NBC 1961-1963. However, "Today, the two shows . . . are lumped together in memory, referred to under the generic term 'Rocky and Bullwinkle'" (54).

6. Keith Scott explains in *The Moose That Roared* that co-creator Bill Scott's "love of puns, and his sheer mastery of when to let one fly, is evident in place names like the mountain called Whyntchataka Peak, and Boris's many aliases, such as the removalist Van N. Storridge," and he adds that "[w]ordplay was always lurking . . ." in the *Rocky and Bullwinkle* scripts (113).

7. On the *Original Amateur Hour*, see *Tune in Yesterday: The Ultimate Encyclopedia of Old-Time Radio, 1925-1976*, by John Dunning (387-89).

8. According to Keith Scott, writer Chris Hayward was responsible for most of the "affectionate put-downs of the filmmaking conventions of a bygone time" in the *Dudley Do-Right* scripts (168-69).

9. See "Laughter: Essay on the Meaning of the Comic," trans. by Maurice Charney (560, 558).

10. In *Understanding Movies*, 8th ed., Louis Gianetti observes, "A popular misconception about animated movies is that they are intended primarily for the entertainment of children—perhaps because the field was dominated for so many years by Disney. In actuality, the gamut of sophistication in this genre is as broad as in live-action films" (121).

Chapter 9

1. For a good example of what might be done along these lines, see Matthew Henry, "The Triumph of Popular Culture: Situation Comedy, Post-

modernism and *The Simpsons,*" *Studies in Popular Culture,* 17.1 (1994): 85-99.

2. Richard Zoglin writes in *Time* (30 May 1994) that "Miller's monologues teem with outré literary and pop-culture references" (67).

3. In anticipation of the final, hour-long *Seinfeld* show, *Entertainment Weekly* published an entire issue (4 May 1998) devoted to the series. Included was a complete listing, summary, and critique of the previous 168 episodes. This has been my primary resource for identifying individual episodes, but similar listings can be found on various web pages.

4. Cf. John Fiske's observation in *Television Culture* (1989): "Vertical intertextuality is that between a primary text, such as a television program or series, and other texts of a different type that refer explicitly to it. These may be secondary texts such as studio publicity, journalistic features, or criticism, or tertiary texts produced by the viewers themselves in the form of letters to the press or, more importantly, of gossip and conversation" (108).

5. When Miller became a color commentator on ABC *Monday Night Football,* explanations of these references began to appear on the broadcasts and on a website called "The Annotated Dennis Miller."

6. Cf. Allan Bloom, *The Closing of the American Mind* (1987) and William J. Bennett, ed., *The Book of Virtues: A Treasury of Great Moral Stories* (1993).

7. According to William Harmon and Hugh C. Holman's *A Handbook to Literature,* 7th ed., *tenor* and *vehicle* are "Terms used by I. A. Richards for the two elements of a METAPHOR. The *tenor* is the discourse or subject that the *vehicle* illustrates; the *vehicle* is the FIGURE that carries the weight of the comparison. According to Richards's definition, a METAPHOR always involves these two ideas" (514).

8. In *A Handlist of Rhetorical Terms* (1968), Richard A. Lanham defines this ostentatious metaphorical technique—"homonymic pun"—as "antanaclasis" (123).

Conclusion

1. Leslie Fiedler, "Come Back to the Raft Ag'n, Huck Honey," *Partisan Review,* 15 (1948): 664-71.

2. Truman Capote, "A Christmas Memory," Brooks and Warren, ed., *Understanding Fiction* (436-45).

3. See John T. Edge's commentary on Capote's fruitcakes in "The Fruitcake Defense," *Gourmet,* Dec. 2000: 60.

WORKS CITED

Aaron, Daniel. *Writers on the Left: Episodes in American Literary Communism.* New York: Harcourt, 1961.

Alger, Horatio, Jr. *Silas Snobden's Office Boy.* Foreword by Ralph D. Gardner. Garden City, NY: Doubleday, 1973.

Allen, Rodney. "Mr. Head and Hawthorne: Allusion and Conversion in Flannery O'Connor's 'The Artificial Nigger.'" *Studies in Short Fiction* 21.1 (1984): 17-23.

Altman, Rick. *The American Film Musical.* Bloomington: Indiana UP, 1987.

——. "A Semantic/Syntactic Approach to Film Genre." *Film Genre Reader II.* Ed. Barry Keith Grant. Austin: U of Texas P, 1995. 26-40.

Altman, Robert. *One on One with Robert Altman. The Player.* Dir. Robert Altman. New Line Home Video, 1993.

——. "Robert Altman on *The Player.*" Interview with Richard T. Jameson. *Film Comment* May-June 1992: 20-30.

Ames, Christopher. *Movies about the Movies: Hollywood Reflected.* Lexington: UP of Kentucky, 1997.

The Annotated Dennis Miller. http://www.britannica.com/bcon/original/article/0,5744,12332,00.html

Ansen, David. "Abandon Hope, All Ye Who Enter Here." Rev. of *Barton Fink.* Dir. Joel Coen. *Newsweek* 26 Aug. 1991: 57.

——. "Hester Prynne's Hot Tub." *Newsweek* 16 Oct. 1995: 87.

Aristotle. *Poetics.* Bate, ed. 19-39.

Arlen, Michael. "The Tyranny of the Visual." *The New Yorker* 23 April 1979: 125-32.

Arpad, Joseph. Introduction. *A Narrative of the Life of David Crockett of the State of Tennessee Written by Himself.* Ed. Arpad. New Haven, CT: College & University P, 1972. 7-37.

Asals, Frederick. *Flannery O'Connor: The Imagination of Extremity.* Athens: U of Georgia P, 1982.

Axelrod, Mark. "Once Upon a Time in Hollywood; or, The Commodification of Form in the Adaptation of Fictional Texts to the Hollywood Cinema." *Literature/Film Quarterly* 24.2 (1996): 201-08.

Bach, Bob, and Ginger Mercer. *Our Huckleberry Friend: The Life, Times and Lyrics of Johnny Mercer.* Secaucus, NJ: Lyle Stuart, 1982.

Baker, Larry. "The PBS *Scarlet Letter:* Showing Versus Telling." *The Nathaniel Hawthorne Journal, 1978.* Ed. C. E. Frazer Clark, Jr. Detroit: Gale, 1984. 219-29.

Bakhtin, Mikhail. *The Dialogic Imagination: Four Essays.* Trans. Caryl Emerson and Michael Holquist. Austin: U of Texas P, 1981.

——. *Problems of Dostoevsky's Poetics.* Ed. and trans. Caryl Emerson. Minneapolis: U of Minnesota P, 1984.

——. *Rabelais and His World.* Trans. Helene Iswolsky. Bloomington: Indiana U P, 1984.

——. *Speech Genres and Other Late Essays.* Trans. Vern W. McGee. Ed. Caryl Emerson and Michael Holquist. Austin: U of Texas P, 1986.

Barlowe, Jamie. *The Scarlet Mob of Scribblers: Rereading Hester Prynne.* Carbondale: Southern Illinois UP, 2000.

Barth, John, "Lost in the Funhouse." *Lost in the Funhouse: Fiction for Print, Tape, Live Voice.* 1968. New York: Grosset, 1969. 72-97.

Barthes, Roland. "The Death of the Author." *Image—Music—Text.* Trans. Stephen Heath. New York: Hill and Wang, 1977. 142-48.

Bate, Walter Jackson, ed. *Criticism: The Major Texts.* Enlarged ed. New York: Harcourt, 1970.

Bauer, Dale M., and Susan Jaret McKinstry. Introduction. *Feminism, Bakhtin, and the Dialogic.* Ed. Bauer and McKinstry. Albany: State U of New York: 1991. 1-6.

Beck, Jerry, and Will Friedwald. *Looney Tunes and Merrie Melodies: A Complete Illustrated Guide to the Warner Bros. Cartoons.* New York: Holt, 1989.

Behrman, S. N. "Two Algers." Introduction to *Strive and Succeed: Two Novels by Horatio Alger.* New York: Holt, 1967. v-xii.

Bell, Pearl K. "Coover's Revisionist Fantasy." *Commentary* Oct. 1977: 67-69.

Belles, Mary E. Rev. of *The Player.* Dir. Robert Altman. *Magill's Cinema Annual 1993.* Ed. Frank N. Magill. Pasadena, CA: Salem P, 1993. 303-06.

Bellis, Peter J. "Representing Dissent: Hawthorne and the Drama of Revolt." *ESQ* 41.2 (1995): 97-119.

Bennett, William J., ed., *The Book of Virtues: A Treasury of Great Moral Stories.* New York: Simon & Schuster, 1993.

Bercovitch, Sacvan. *The Office of The Scarlet Letter.* Baltimore: Johns Hopkins UP, 1991.

Bergson, Henri. "Laughter: Essay on the Meaning of the Comic." Trans. Maurice Charney. *Classic Comedies.* Ed. Charney. New York: Meridian, 1994. 557-64.

Bernard, Jami. Rev. of *Barton Fink.* Dir. Joel Coen. *New York Post* 21 Aug. 1991: 23. Rpt. in *Film Review Annual 1992.* 84-85.

——. Rev. of *Thelma & Louise.* Dir. Ridley Scott. *New York Post* 24 May 1991: 27. Rpt. In *Film Review Annual, 1992.* 1466.

Bewley, Marius. *The Eccentric Design: Form in the Classic American Novel.* New York: Columbia UP, 1963.

Bianculli, David. *Dictionary of Teleliteracy: Television's 500 Biggest Hits, Misses, and Events*. New York: Continuum, 1996.

Billson, Anne. Rev. of *Barton Fink*. Dir. Joel Coen. *New Statesman & Society* 14 Feb. 1992: 36. Rpt. in *Film Review Annual 1992*. 81-82.

——. Rev. of *Thelma & Louise*. Dir. Ridley Scott. *New Statesman & Society* 12 July 1991: 33. Rpt. In *Film Review Annual, 1992*. 1463-64.

Bloom, Allan. *The Closing of the American Mind*. New York: Simon & Schuster, 1987.

Blotner, Joseph. *Faulkner: A Biography*. New York: Random, 1974.

Booth, Wayne C. *The Rhetoric of Fiction*. 2nd ed. Chicago: U of Chicago P, 1983.

Boozer, Jack. "Seduction and Betrayal in the Heartland: *Thelma and Louise*." *Literature/Film Quarterly* 23.3 (1995): 188-96.

Boskin, Joseph. "History and Humor." *The Humor Prism in 20th-Century America*. Ed Boskin. Detroit: Wayne State UP, 1997. 17-27.

Braudy, Leo. *The World in a Frame: What We See in Films*. Garden City, NY: Anchor/Doubleday, 1976.

Brennan, Judy, and Jess Cagle. "News & Notes." *Entertainment Weekly* 4 Feb. 1994: 8+.

Brooks, Cleanth. *William Faulkner: The Yoknapatawpha Country*. New Haven: Yale UP, 1963.

——, and Robert Penn Warren. *Understanding Fiction*. 2nd ed. New York: Appleton-Century Crofts, 1959.

Brooks, Peter. *Reading for the Plot: Design and Intention in Narrative*. New York: Knopf, 1984.

Bush, Douglas. "Professor Fish on the Milton *Variorum*." *Critical Inquiry* 3.1 (1976): 179-82.

Carlson, Margaret. Rev. of *Thelma & Louise*. Dir. Ridley Scott. *Time* 24 June 1991: 57. Rpt. In *Film Review Annual 1992*. 1470-71.

Carlson, Patricia Ann. *Hawthorne's Functional Settings: A Study of Artistic Method*. Amsterdam: Editions Rodopi, 1977.

Cawelti, John G. "The Question of Popular Genres Revisited." *In the Eye of the Beholder: Critical Perspectives in Popular Film and Television*. Ed. Gary E. Edgerton, Michael T. Marsden, and Jack Nachbar. Bowling Green, OH: Bowling Green State U Popular P, 1997. 67-84.

Chavez, Linda. "An Immorality Tale for our Time." *USA TODAY* 19 Oct. 1995: 13A.

Christensen, Thor. "You've Heard That Song Before." *(Nashville) Tennessean* 25 Apr. 1998: 3D.

Chute, David. "Keeping Up with the Jones." *Film Comment* Dec. 1995: 14-15.

Clayton, Jay, and Eric Rothstein. *Influence and Intertextuality in Literary History*. Madison: U of Wisconsin P, 1991.

Clements, Marcelle. "Altman's 'The Player': More Than Just Smug Revenge." *Premiere* June 1992: 128.

Cobley, Evelyn. "Mikhail Bakhtin's Place in Genre Theory." *Genre* 21 (1988): 321-38.

"Coming Soon: *The Scarlet Letter*." Advertisement. *Entertainment Weekly* 4 Feb. 1994: n.p.

Conroy, Jack. *The Disinherited*. New York: Covici, Friede, 1933.

Cooper, James Fenimore. *The Pioneers*. 1823. New York: Washington Square, 1962.

Coover, Robert. *The Public Burning*. New York: Viking/Richard Seaver, 1977.

——. Rev. of *The Implosion Controversy*. By Louis Nizer. *New York Times Book Review* 11 Feb. 1973: 4-5.

Corliss, Richard. Rev. of *The Scarlet Letter*. Dir. Roland Joffé. *Time* 23 Oct. 1995: 94.

Courtland, A. R. "From Sermon to Parable: Four Conversion Stories by Flannery O'Connor." *American Literature* 55 (1983): 55-71.

Cowley, Malcolm. "Five Acts of *The Scarlet Letter*." *College English* 19 (1957): 11-16.

——. Introduction. *The Portable Faulkner*. 1946. New York: Viking, 1964. 1-24.

Coyle, William. Introduction. *Adrift in New York and the World Before Him*. By Horatio Alger, Jr. New York: Odyssey, 1966. v-xvii.

Culler, Jonathan. *The Pursuit of Signs: Semiotics, Literature, Deconstruction*. Ithaca, NY: Cornell UP, 1981.

Daniels, Bruce. "Bad Movie/Worse History: The 1995 Unmaking of *The Scarlet Letter*." *Journal of Popular Culture* 32.4 (Spring 1999):1-11.

Dardis, Tom. *Some Time in the Sun*. New York: Scribner's, 1976.

"Decoded Soviet Messages Affirm Rosenberg Spy Case." *Los Angeles Times* 12 July 1995. LEXIS-NEXIS Academic Universe.

Denby, David. "Barton Stinks." Rev. of *Barton Fink*. Dir. Joel Coen. *New York* 26 Aug. 1991: 128-29.

——. Rev. of *The Scarlet Letter*. Dir. Roland Joffé. *New York* 23 Oct. 1995: 57.

——. Rev. of *Thelma & Louise*. Dir. Ridley Scott. *New York* 10 June 1991: 55. Rpt. In *Film Review Annual 1992*. 1464-65.

Dobbs, Michael. "Were They Really Guilty? Julius Rosenberg's Handler Offers New Evidence." *The Jerusalem Post* 10 Apr. 1997. LEXIS-NEXIS Academic Universe

Doctorow, E. L. *The Book of Daniel*. 1971. New York: Bantam, 1983.

——. "False Documents." Trenner, ed. 16-27.

Donohue, Denis. *Walter Pater: Lover of Strange Souls*. New York: Knopf, 1995.

Dryden, John. "An Essay of Dramatic Poesy." Bate, ed. 129-60.

——. "Preface to Fables, Ancient and Modern." Bate, ed. 160-71.

Dunne, Michael. *Hawthorne's Narrative Strategies*. Jackson: UP of Mississippi, 1995.

——. *Metapop: Self-referentiality in Contemporary American Popular Culture*. Jackson: UP of Mississippi, 1992.

Dunning, John. *Tune in Yesterday: The Ultimate Encyclopedia of Old-Time Radio, 1925-1976*. Englewood Cliffs, NJ: Prentice-Hall, 1976.

Eco, Umberto. "Innovation and Repetition: Between Modern and Post-Modern Aesthetics." *Daedalus: Journal of the American Academy of Arts and Sciences* 114.4 (Fall 1985): 161-84.

Edge, John T. "The Fruitcake Defense." *Gourmet* Dec. 2000: 60.

Eisenhower, Dwight D. *Public Papers of the Presidents of the United States, Dwight D. Eisenhower, 1953*. Washington: United States Printing Office, 1958-1961.

Estrin, Mark W. "'Triumphant Ignominy' on the Screen." *The Classic American Novel and the Movies*. Ed. Gerald Peary and Roger Shatzkin. New York: Ungar, 1977. 20-29.

Faulkner, William. *Absalom, Absalom!* 1936. New York: Vintage, 1987.

——. *As I Lay Dying*. 1930. New York: Vintage, 1985.

——. *Sanctuary*. 1931. New York: Random, 1958.

Feinberg, Leonard. *The Satirist: His Temperament, Motivation, and Influence*. Ames: Iowa State UP, 1963.

Feuer, Jane. *The Hollywood Musical*. 2nd ed. Bloomington: Indiana UP, 1993.

Fiedler, Leslie. "Come Back to the Raft Ag'n, Huck Honey." *Partisan Review* 15 (1948): 664-71.

——. "Pop Goes the Faulkner: In Quest of *Sanctuary*." *Faulkner and Popular Culture*. Ed. Doreen Fowler and Ann J. Abadie. Jackson: UP of Mississippi, 1990. 75-92.

Film Review Annual 1992. Ed. Jerome Ozer. Englewood, NJ: Film Review Pubs., 1992.

Fish, Stanley. "Interpreting the *Variorum*." *Is There a Text in This Class?: The Authority of Interpretive Communities*. Cambridge: Harvard UP, 1980. 147-73.

Fiske, John. *Television Culture*. London and New York: Routledge, 1989.

Fitzgerald, F. Scott. *The Great Gatsby. The Cambridge Edition of the Works of F. Scott Fitzgerald*. Ed. Matthew J. Bruccoli. New York: Cambridge UP, 1991.

Fodor, Sarah J. "Marketing Flannery O'Connor: Institutional Politics and Literary Evaluation." *Flannery O'Connor: New Perpectives*. Ed. Sura P. Rath and Mary Neff Shaw. Athens: U of Georgia P, 1996. 12-37.

Foley, Barbara. *Radical Representations: Politics and Form in U.S. Proletarian Fiction, 1929-1941*. Durham, NC: Duke UP, 1993.

Fortner, Gregory. "Faulkner's Black Holes: Vision and Vomit in *Sanctuary*." *Mississippi Quarterly* 49.3 (1996): 537-62.

Frank Sinatra's Songs of Romance. New York: Remick Music, 1954.

Franklin, Benjamin. *The Autobiography*. *Writings*. New York: Library of America, 1987. 1305-1469.

Friedwald, Will, and Jerry Beck. *The Warner Brothers Cartoons*. Metuchen, NJ: Scarecrow, 1981.

Frye, Northrop. *Anatomy of Criticism: Four Essays*. 1957. Princeton, NJ: Princeton UP, 1971.

——. "The Archetypes of Literature." *Fables of Identity: Studies in Poetic Mythology*. New York: Harcourt, 1963. 7-20.

——. "Myth, Fiction, and Displacement." *Fables of Identity: Studies in Poetic Mythology*. New York: Harcourt, 1963. 21-38.

——. *The Secular Scripture: A Study of the Structure of Romance*. Cambridge, MA: Harvard UP, 1976.

Furia, Philip. *Ira Gershwin: The Art of the Lyricist*. New York: Oxford UP, 1996.

Gaggi, Silvio. *Modern/Postmodern: A Study in Twentieth-Century Arts and Ideas*. Philadelphia: U of Pennsylvania P, 1989.

Gammond, Richard. *The Oxford Companion to Popular Music*. New York: Oxford UP, 1993.

Garber, Marjorie, and Rebecca L. Walkowitz. *Secret Agents: The Rosenberg Case, McCarthyism, and Fifties America*. New York: Routledge, 1995.

Gardner, Ralph D. Foreword. *Silas Snobden's Office Boy*. By Horatio Alger, Jr. Garden City, NY: Doubleday, 1973. 5-26.

Gelman, David, and Cynthia H. Wilson. "Masterpiece of Our Own." *Newsweek* 2 April 1979: 94.

George Segal, A Retrospective. Exhibition at the Jewish Museum. New York City, Summer 1998.

Gianetti, Louis. *Understanding Movies*. 8th ed. Upper Saddle River, NJ: Prentice-Hall, 1999.

Gleiberman, Owen. "Red Letter Daze." *Entertainment Weekly* 20 Oct. 1995: 43-44.

Gollin, Richard M. *A Viewer's Guide to Film: Arts, Artifices, and Issues*. New York: McGraw-Hill, 1992.

Grant, Edmond. Rev. of *Barton Fink*. Dir. Joel Coen. *Films in Review* Dec. 1991: 406. Rpt. in *Film Review Annual 1992*. 78-80

——. Rev. of *Thelma & Louise*. Dir. Ridley Scott. *Films in Review* Aug. 1991: 256. Rpt. in *Film Review Annual 1992*. 1461-62.

Green Acres Website. http://www.maggiore.net/greenacres/

The Great Music of Duke Ellington. Melville, NY: Belwin Mills, 1973.

Gresset, Michel. Introduction. *Intertextuality in Faulkner*. Ed. Gresset and Noel Polk. Jackson: UP of Mississippi, 1985. 3-15

——. "Of Sailboats and Kites: The 'Dying Fall' in Faulkner's *Sanctuary* and Beckett's *Murphy*." *Intertextuality in Faulkner*. Ed. Gresset and Noel Polk, Jackson: UP of Mississippi, 1985. 57-72.

Hall, Mordaunt. Rev. of *The Scarlet Letter*. Dir. Victor Seastrom. *New York Times* 10 Aug. 1926: 19:2.

Halpern, Sue. "Back to Life in Texas." Rev. of *Walter Benjamin at the Dairy Queen: Reflections at Sixty and Beyond* and *Duane's Depressed*. By Larry McMurtry. *New York Review of Books* 2 Dec. 1999: 30-32.

Hamilton, Ian. *Writers in Hollywood, 1915-1951*. New York: Harper, 1990.

Hammerstein, Oscar, II, ed. *The Jerome Kern Songbook: The Words and Music of 50 of His Best-Loved Songs*. New York: Simon & Schuster, 1955.

H[ardie], C[olin] G[raham]. "Virgil." *The Oxford Classical Dictionary*. Ed. N. G. L. Hammond and H. H. Scullard. 2nd ed. Oxford: Clarendon P, 1970. 1123-28.

Harmon, William, and C. Hugh Holman. *A Handbook to Literature*. 7th ed. Upper Saddle River, NJ: Prentice-Hall, 1996.

Harrison, Antony H. *Victorian Poets and Romantic Poems: Intertextuality and Ideology*. Charlottesville: UP of Virginia, 1990.

Hart, Dorothy, ed. *Thou Swell: The Life and Lyrics of Lorenz Hart*. New York: Harper & Row, 1976.

Hawkes, John. "Flannery O'Connor's Devil." *Sewanee Review* 70 (1962): 395-407.

Hawthorne, Nathaniel. "My Kinsman, Major Molineux." *The Snow-Image and Uncollected Tales*. Ed. J. Donald Crowley. Columbus: Ohio State UP, 1974. 208-31. Vol. 9 of *The Centenary Edition of the Works of Nathaniel Hawthorne*. 22 vols.

——. *The Scarlet Letter*. Columbus, OH: Ohio State UP, 1962. Vol. 1 of *The Centenary Edition of the Works of Nathaniel Hawthorne*. 22 vols.

Henry, Matthew. "The Triumph of Popular Culture: Situation Comedy, Postmodernism and *The Simpsons*." *Studies in Popular Culture* 17.1 (1994): 85-99.

Hischak, Thomas. *Word Crazy: Broadway Lyricists from Cohan to Sondheim*. New York: Praeger, 1991.

Hoberman, J. Rev. of *Barton Fink*. Dir. Joel Coen. *Village Voice* 27 Aug. 1991: 70. Rpt. in *Film Review Annual 1992*. 89-90.

Hoffman, Daniel G. "Yankee Bumpkin and Scapegoat King." *Form and Fable in American Fiction*. New York: Oxford, 1961. 113-25.

Hoffman, Frederick J. *The Twenties: American Writing in the Postwar Decade*. New York: Collier, 1962.

Holquist, Michael. *Dialogism: Bakhtin and His World.* New York and London: Routledge, 1990.

"A Home on the Range." *American Poetry: The Nineteenth Century.* Ed. John Hollander. New York: Library of America, 1993. 831-32.

Hutcheon, Linda. *Narcissistic Narrative: The Metafictional Paradox.* Waterloo, ONT: Wilfred Laurier UP, 1980.

——. *A Poetics of Postmodernism: History, Theory, Fiction.* New York: Routledge, 1988.

Inge, M. Thomas. "Melville as Popular Culture." *Perspectives on American Culture: Essays on Humor, Literature, and the Popular Arts.* West Cornwall, CT: Locust Hill P, 1994. 67-114.

Iser, Wolfgang. *The Implied Reader: Patterns of Communication in Prose Fiction from Bunyan to Beckett.* Baltimore: Johns Hopkins UP, 1974.

James, Henry. "The Art of Fiction." Kaplan & Anderson, ed. 387-404.

Jameson, Fredric. *Postmodernism, Or, The Cultural Logic of Late Capitalism.* Durham, NC: Duke UP, 1991.

Jameson, Richard T. Introduction. "Robert Altman on *The Player.*" *Film Comment* May-June 1992: 20-21.

Jardine, Alice. "Flash Back, Flash Forward: The Fifties, the Nineties, and the Transformed Politics of Remote Control." Garber and Walkowitz 107-23.

Jarrell, Randall. "Five Poets." *Yale Review* Autumn 1956. *Kipling, Auden & Co.: Essays and Reviews, 1935-1964.* New York: Farrar, Straus and Giroux, 1980. 262-72.

Jefferson, Thomas. *Notes on the State of Virginia.* 1787. Ed. Thomas Peden. Chapel Hill: U of North Carolina P, 1955.

Johnson, Brian. "Feminist Fast Lane." Rev. of *Thelma & Louise.* Dir. Ridley Scott. *Maclean's* 27 May 1991: 64-65.

Johnson, Samuel. *Johnson's Lives of the Poets: A Selection.* Ed. J. P. Hardy. Oxford: Clarendon P, 1971.

——. "Preface to Shakespeare." Kaplan & Anderson, ed. 201-31.

Kael, Pauline. *Kiss Kiss Bang Bang.* Boston: Little, Brown, 1968.

Kaplan, Charles, and William Anderson, eds. *Criticism: Major Statements.* 4th ed. New York: Bedford/St. Martin's, 2000.

Kenner, Hugh. *The Pound Era.* Berkeley: U of California P, 1971.

Kimball, Robert, ed. *The Complete Lyrics of Cole Porter.* New York: Knopf, 1983.

——, and Alfred Simon. *The Gershwins.* New York: Atheneum, 1973.

King, Kathryn. Liner Notes. *The Very Thought of You: Jeri Southern, The Decca Years, 1951-1957.* Decca GRD-671, 1999.

Klare, Karl E. "Arbitrary Convictions? The Rosenberg Case, the Death Penalty, and Democratic Culture." Garber and Walkowitz 275-89.

Kowal, Patricia. "Thelma and Louise." *Magill's Cinema Annual 1992*. Ed. Frank N. Magill. Pasadena, CA: Salem P, 1992. 399-402.

Kraditor, Aileen S. Introduction. *Up From the Pedestal: Selected Writings in the History of American Feminism*. Chicago: Quadrangle, 1968. 3-24.

Kristeva, Julia. "Word, Dialogue, and Novel." *Desire in Language: A Semiotic Approach to Literature and Art*. Ed. Leon S. Roudiez. Trans. Thomas Gora, Alice Jardine, and Leon S. Roudiez. New York: Columbia UP, 1980. 64-91.

Kuhn, Thomas S. "Logic of Discovery or Psychology of Research?" *Criticism and the Growth of Knowledge*. Ed. Imre Lakatos and Alan Musgrave. Cambridge: Cambridge UP, 1970. 1-23.

Lacy, Norris J. "*Matiere de Bretagne*." *The Arthurian Encyclopedia*. Ed Lacy. New York: Garland, 1986: 377-78.

Lane, Anthony. "Picture Books." *The New Yorker* 9 Feb. 1998: 76-79.

——. "Scarlet Women." *The New Yorker* 30 Oct. 1995: 112-14.

Langford, Gerald. *Faulkner's Revision of* Sanctuary*: A Collation of the Unrevised Galleys and the Published Book*. Austin: U of Texas P, 1972.

Lanham, Richard A. *A Handlist of Rhetorical Terms*. Berkeley and Los Angeles: U of California P, 1968.

Lawrence, D. H. *Studies in Classic American Literature*. 1923. New York: Viking, 1964.

LeClair, Thomas. "Robert Coover, *The Public Burning*, and the Art of Excess." *Critique: Studies in Modern Fiction* 23.3 (1982): 5-28.

Lehan, Richard. The Great Gatsby*: The Limits of Wonder*. Twayne's Masterwork Studies. Boston: Hall, 1990.

Lehrer, Tom. "The Irish Ballad." *Songs and More Songs By Tom Lehrer*. Rhino CD 72776, 1997.

Leininger, Philip W., and James D. Hart. *The Oxford Companion to American Literature*. 6th ed. New York: Oxford UP, 1995.

Levine, Paul. "The Writer as Independent Witness." Interview with E. L. Doctorow. Trenner, ed. 57-69.

Lewis, Roger. "Money, Love, and Aspiration in *The Great Gatsby*." *New Essays on the Great Gatsby*. Ed. Matthew J. Bruccoli. New York: Cambridge UP, 1985. 41-57.

Lyday, Lance. "*Sanctuary*: Faulkner's *Inferno*." *Mississippi Quarterly* 35.3 (1982): 242-53.

MacKethan, Lucinda. "Redeeming Blackness: Urban Allegories of O'Connor, Percy, and Toole." *Studies in the Literary Imagination* 27.2 (Fall 1994): 29-39.

Maher, James T. Introduction. *American Popular Song: The Great Innovators, 1900-1950*. By Alec Wilder. xxiii-xxxix.

Mailer, Norman. *The Armies of the Night: History as a Novel/The Novel as History*. New York: New American Library, 1968.

Mailloux, Steven. "Stanley Fish's 'Interpreting the *Variorum*.'" *Critical Inquiry* 3.1 (1976): 183-90.

Marsden, Madonna. "The American Myth of Success." *Popular Culture: An Introductory Text*. Ed. Jack Nachbar and Kevin Lause. Bowling Green, OH: Bowling Green State U Popular P, 1992. 134-48.

Martin, Jay. *Nathanael West: The Art of His Life*. New York: Farrar, Straus and Giroux, 1970.

Martin, Wallace. *Recent Theories of Narrative*. Ithaca: Cornell UP, 1986.

Mason, M. S. Rev. of *Thelma & Louise*. Dir. Ridley Scott. *Christian Science Monitor* 1 July 1991: 11. Rpt. In *Film Review Annual 1992*. 1459-60.

Mathews, Jack. Rev. of *Barton Fink*. Dir. Joel Coen. *Newsday* 21 Aug. 1991: II.44. Rpt. in *Film Review Annual 1992*. 85-86.

Matthiessen, F. O. *American Renaissance: Art and Expression in the Age of Emerson and Whitman*. New York: Oxford UP, 1941.

Mazurek, Raymond A. "Metafiction, the Historical Novel, and Coover's *The Public Burning*." *Critique: Studies in Modern Fiction* 23.3 (1982): 29-42.

McCaffery, Larry. "Robert Coover on His Own and Other Fictions: An Interview." *Novel Vs. Fiction: The Contemporary Reformation*. Ed. Jackson I. Cope and Geoffrey Green. Norman, OK: Pilgrim, 1981. 45-63.

——. "A Spirit of Transgression." Interview with E. L. Doctorow. Trenner, ed. 31-47.

McCarthy, Todd. Rev. of *The Scarlet Letter*. Dir. Roland Joffé. *Variety* 16-22 Oct. 1995: 94.

McFarlane, Brian. *Novel to Film: An Introduction to the Theory of Adaptation*. Oxford: Clarendon P, 1996.

Meeter, Glenn A. "Beyond Lexicon: Biblical 'Allusion' in Faulkner." *Mississippi Quarterly* 49 (1996): 595-602.

Metz, Walter. "Toward a Post-structural Influence in Film Study: Intertextuality and *The Shining*." *Film Criticism* 22.1 (1997): 38-61.

Meyerson, Harold, and Ernie Harburg. *Who Put the Rainbow in* The Wizard of Oz*?* Ann Arbor: U of Michigan P, 1993.

Michael Meyer, ed. *The Bedford Introduction to Literature*. 3rd ed. Boston: St. Martin's, 1993.

Miller, Arthur. Rev. of *Barton Fink*. Dir. by Joel Coen. *Premiere* Oct. 1991: 108.

Miller, Dennis. *The Rants*. New York: Doubleday, 1996.

Morgan, Thaïs E. "Is There an Intertext in This Text?: Literary and Interdisciplinary Approaches to Intertextuality." *American Journal of Semiotics* 3.4 (1985): 1-40.

Morris, Peter, ed. *Dictionary of Films*. Berkeley and Los Angeles: U of California P, 1972.

Morris, Robert. "Words and Images in Modernism and Postmodernism." *Critical Inquiry* 15.2 (1988): 337-47.

Muller, Gilbert H. "The City of Woe: Flannery O'Connor's Dantean Vision." *Georgia Review* 23.2 (1969): 206-13.

Murphy, Kathleen. "Only Angels Have Wings." *Film Comment* July/Aug. 1991: 26-29.

Neale, Steve. "Questions of Genre." *Film Genre Reader II*. Ed. Barry Keith Grant. Austin: U of Texas P, 1995. 159-83.

Newman, Lea Bertani Vozar. *A Reader's Guide to the Short Stories of Nathaniel Hawthorne*. Boston: Hall, 1979.

Nixon, Richard M. *Six Crises*. New York: Doubleday, 1962.

Nolan, Frederick. *Lorenz Hart: A Poet on Broadway*. New York: Oxford UP, 1994.

Normand, Jean. *Nathaniel Hawthorne: An Approach to an Analysis of Artistic Creation*. Trans. Derek Cotman. Cleveland: Case Western Reserve U, 1970.

The Norton Anthology of Poetry. 3rd ed. Ed. Alexander Allison, et al. New York: Norton, 1983.

O'Brien, Geoffrey. "Recapturing the American Sound." *New York Review of Books* 9 Apr. 1998: 45-51.

O'Connor, Flannery. "The Artificial Nigger." 1955. *The Complete Stories of Flannery O'Connor*. New York: Farrar, Straus and Giroux, 1971. 249-70.

——. *The Habit of Being*. Ed. Sally Fitzgerald. New York: Farrar, Straus and Giroux, 1979.

O'Connor, John J. "How the Smile of Comedy Has Turned Wolfish." *New York Times* 15 April 1993: C20.

O'Donnell, George Marion. "Faulkner's Mythology." *Kenyon Review* 1 (1939): 285-99.

Prince, Gerald. "Introduction to the Study of the Narratee." 1973. *Narrative/ Theory*. Ed. David H. Richter. White Plains, NY: Longman, 1996. 226-41.

Princeton Encyclopedia of Poetry and Poetics. Enlarged ed. Ed. Alex Preminger, et al. Princeton, NJ: Princeton UP, 1974.

Propp, Vladimir. *Morphology of the Folktale*. Trans. Laurence Scott. 2nd ed. Austin: U of Texas P, 1968.

Radosh, Ronald, and Joyce Milton. *The Rosenberg File: A Search for the Truth*. New York: Holt, Rinehart and Winston, 1983.

Rafferty, Terrence. "Killer." Rev. of *The Player*. Dir. Robert Altman. *The New Yorker* 20 Apr. 1992: 81-82.

Ramage, John. "Myth and Monomyth in Coover's *The Public Burning*." *Critique: Essays in Modern Fiction* 23.3 (1982): 52-68.

Reed, Joseph W. *American Scenarios: The Uses of Film Genre*. Middleton CT: Wesleyan UP, 1989.

Rev. of *High Noon*. Dir. Fred Zinnemann. *Time* 14 Jul. 1952: 20, 22.

Rev. of *The Scarlet Letter*. Dir. Carl Harbaugh. *Variety* 16 Feb. 1917.

Rev. of *The Scarlet Letter*. Dir. Victor Seastrom. *Variety* 11 Aug. 1926.

Rev. of *The Scarlet Letter*. Dir. Richard G. Vignola. *Variety* 25 Sept. 1934.

Reynolds, David S. *Beneath the American Renaissance: The Subversive Imagination in the Age of Emerson and Melville*. New York: Knopf, 1988.

Rideout, Walter B. *The Radical Novel in the United States, 1900-1954: Some Interrelations of Literature and Society*. New York: Columbia UP, 1992.

Riffaterre, Michael. "Intertextual Representation: On Mimesis as Interpretive Discourse." *Critical Inquiry* 11.1 (1984): 141-62.

The Rocky & Bullwinkle Episode Guide. http://web.cc.stevens-tech.edu/~dbelson/bullwinkle.html

Rosenberg, Deena. Liner Notes. Ella Fitzgerald. *The Rodgers and Hart Songbook*. Verve 821 693-1 Y-1, 1956.

Ross, Alan. "The Dead Center: An Introduction to Nathanael West." *The Complete Works of Nathanael West*. New York: Farrar, Straus and Cudahy, 1957. vii-xxii.

Rourke, Constance. *American Humor: A Study of the National Character*. New York: Harcourt, 1931.

Rubin, Louis D., Jr. "Flannery O'Connor's Company of Southerners or 'The Artificial Nigger' Read as Fiction Rather Than Theology." *A Gallery of Southerners*. Baton Rouge: Louisiana State UP, 1982. 115-34.

Salinger, J. D. *The Catcher in the Rye*. 1951. New York: Bantam, 1979.

Saperstein, Jeffrey. "Irony and Cliché: Malamud's *The Natural* in the 1980s." *Literature/Film Quarterly* 24.1 (1996): 84-87.

Scharnhorst, Gary, and Jack Bales. *The Lost Life of Horatio Alger, Jr.* Bloomington: Indiana UP, 1985.

Schickel, Richard. Rev. of *Thelma & Louise*. Dir. Ridley Scott. *Time* 24 June 1991: 52. Rpt. in *Film Review Annual 1992*. 1471-75.

——. "A Three-Espresso Hallucination." Rev. of *Barton Fink*. Dir. Joel Coen. *Time* 26 Aug. 1991: 58-59.

Schilling, Mary Kaye, and Mike Flaherty. "The Seinfeld Chronicles." *Entertainment Weekly* 4 May 1998: 18-90.

Schleifer, Ronald. "Rural Gothic: The Stories of Flannery O'Connor." *Critical Essays on Flannery O'Connor*. Ed. Melvin J. Friedman and Beverly Lyon Clark. Boston: Hall, 1985. 158-68.

Scott, Keith. *The Moose That Roared: The Story of Jay Ward, Bill Scott, a Flying Squirrel, and a Talking Moose*. New York: St. Martin's, 2000.

Shaw, Mary Neff. "'The Artificial Nigger': A Dialogical Narrative." *Flannery O'Connor: New Perspectives*. Ed. Sura P. Rath and Mary Neff Shaw. Athens: U of Georgia P, 1996. 139-51.

Sitwell, Robynn J. "In the Air Tonight: Text, Intertextuality, and the Construction of Meaning." *Popular Music and Society* 19.4 (Winter 1995): 67-103.

Smith, Julian. "Hester, Sweet Hester Prynne—*The Scarlet Letter* in the Movie Market Place." *Literature/Film Quarterly* 2 (1974): 100-09.

Sobchack, Thomas. "Genre Film: A Classical Experience." *Film Genre Reader II*. Ed. Barry Keith Grant. Austin: U of Texas P, 1995. 102-13.

Spatz, Joseph. *Hollywood in Fiction: Some Versions of the American Myth*. The Hague: Mouton, 1969.

Spivey, Ted. R. "Flannery O'Connor, James Joyce, and the City." *Studies in the Literary Imagination* 20.2 (1987): 87-95.

Stack, Frank. *Pope and Horace: Studies in Imitation*. New York: Cambridge U P, 1985.

Stam, Robert. *Subversive Pleasures: Bakhtin, Cultural Criticism, and Film*. Baltimore: Johns Hopkins UP, 1989.

Steinbeck, John. *In Dubious Battle*. New York: Covici, Friede, 1936.

Steiner, T. R. "West's Lemuel and the American Dream." *Southern Review* 4.7 (1971). Rpt. in *Modern Critical Views: Nathanael West*. Ed. Harold Bloom. New York: Chelsea, 1986. 99-109.

Taylor, Gary. Introduction. *Henry V. The Oxford Shakespeare*. Ed. Taylor. New York: Oxford UP, 1984. 1-74.

Tebbel, John Robert. "Looney Tunester." *Film Comment* Sept.-Oct. 1992: 64-66.

Thomson, Clive. "Bakhtin's 'Theory' of Genre." *Studies in Twentieth Century Literature* 9.1 (1984): 29-40.

Thorburn, David. "The Rosenberg Letters." Garber and Walkowitz. 171-82.

Tompkins, Jane. *West of Everything: The Inner Lives of Westerns*. New York: Oxford UP, 1992.

Towers, Robert. "Nixon's Seventh Crisis." Rev. of *The Public Burning*. By Robert Coover. *New York Review of Books* 29 Sept. 1977: 8-10.

Travers, Peter. "What's in the Box?" Rev. of *Barton Fink*. Dir. Joel Coen. *Rolling Stone* 22 Aug. 1991: 71+.

Trenner, Richard, ed. *E. L. Doctorow: Essays and Conversations*. Princeton: Ontario Review P, 1983.

Tudor, Andrew. "Genre and Critical Methodology." *Movies and Methods: An Anthology*. Ed. Bill Nichols. Berkeley: U of California P, 1976. 118-26.

Turan, Kenneth. Rev. of *Barton Fink*. Dir. Joel Coen. *Los Angeles Times* 21 Aug. 1991: 1. Rpt. in *Film Review Annual 1992*. 80-81.

——. Rev. of *Thelma & Louise*. Dir. Ridley Scott. *Los Angeles Times* 24 May 1991: Calendar 1. Rpt. in *Film Review Annual 1992*. 1462-63.

Tyler, Royall. *The Contrast. The American Tradition in Literature*. 9th ed. Ed. George Perkins and Barbara Perkins. Boston: McGraw-Hill, 1994. 1: 461-97.

Urgo, Joseph R. "*Sanctuary* and the Pornographic Nexus." *Novel Frames: Literature as Guide to Race, Sex, and History in American Culture*. Jackson: UP of Mississippi, 1991. 77-112.

——. "Temple Drake's Truthful Perjury: Rethinking Faulkner's *Sanctuary*." *American Literature* 55.3 (1983): 435-44.

Variety's Film Reviews 1907-1988. 20 vols. New York: Bowker, 1983-88.

Variety Television Reviews, 1923-1988. Ed. Howard H. Prouty. 15 vols. New York: Garland, 1988.

Verevis, Constantine. "Re-Viewing Remakes." *Film Criticism* 21.3 (1997): 1-19.

Volpe, Edmond. *A Reader's Guide to William Faulkner*. New York: Farrar, Straus, 1964.

Waggoner, Hyatt H. *William Faulkner: From Jefferson to the World*. Lexington: U of Kentucky P, 1959.

Way, Brian. "The Great Gatsby." *F. Scott Fitzgerald's* The Great Gatsby. Ed. Harold Bloom. New York: Chelsea, 1986. 87-108.

Welsh, James M. "Classic Folly: *The Scarlet Letter*." Rev. of *The Scarlet Letter*. Dir. Roland Joffé. *Literature/Film Quarterly* 23.4 (1995): 299-300.

——. "*The Scarlet Letter (Der Scharlachrote Buchstabe)*." *Magill's Survey of Cinema: Foreign Language Films*. Ed. Frank N. Magill. Englewood Cliffs: Salem P, 1985. 6: 2658-61.

West, Nathanael. *A Cool Million, or, the Dismantling of Lemuel Pitkin*. 1934. *The Complete Works of Nathanael West*. New York: Farrar, Straus and Cudahy, 1957. 141-255.

White, Mimi. "Crossing Wavelengths: The Diegetic and Referential Imaginary of American Commercial Television." *Cinema Journal* 25.2 (Winter 1986): 51-64.

Wicker, Tom. *One of Us: Richard Nixon and the American Dream*. New York: Random, 1991.

Wilder, Alec. *American Popular Song: The Great Innovators, 1900-1950*. Ed. with an intro. by James T. Maher. New York: Oxford UP, 1972.

Williams, Raymond. *Television: Technology and Cultural Form*. New York: Schocken, 1975.

Williamson, George. *A Reader's Guide to T. S. Eliot: A Poem-By-Poem Analysis*. 2nd ed. New York: Farrar, Straus & Giroux, 1966.

Willis, Susan. "Aesthetics of the Rural Slum: Contradictions and Dependency in 'The Bear.'" *Social Texts* 2 (Summer 1979): 82-103. Rpt. in *Faulkner: A Collection of Critical Essays*. Ed. Richard H. Brodhead. Englewood Cliffs: Prentice-Hall, 1983. 179-94.

Winters, Yvor. "Maule's Curse, or Hawthorne and the Problem of Allegory." 1938. In *In Defense of Reason*. 3rd ed. Chicago: Swallow, 1947. 157-75.

Wloszczyna, Susan. "Is the 'A' for Adaptation or Abomination?" *USA TODAY* 13 Oct. 1995: 1D-2D.

Woolf, Geoffrey. "An American Epic." *New Times* 19 Aug. 1977: 48-57.

Zoglin, Richard. "Comedically Incorrect." *Time* 30 May 1994: 67.

——. "What's Up, Doc? Animation! The Cartoon Boom in TV and Movies Is Reviving a Neglected Craft." *Time* 6 Aug. 1990: 66-67.

INDEX